THE USA PATRIOT ACT OF 2001: Balancing Civil Liberties and National Security

A Reference Handbook

Other Titles in ABC-CLIO's
CONTEMPORARY
WORLD ISSUES
Series

Books in the Contemporary World Issues series address vital issues in today's society such as genetic engineering, pollution, and biodiversity. Written by professional writers, scholars, and nonacademic experts, these books are authoritative, clearly written, up-to-date, and objective. They provide a good starting point for research by high school and college students, scholars, and general readers as well as by legislators, businesspeople, activists, and others.

Each book, carefully organized and easy to use, contains an overview of the subject, a detailed chronology, biographical sketches, facts and data and/or documents and other primary-source material, a directory of organizations and agencies, annotated lists of print and nonprint resources, and an index.

Readers of books in the Contemporary World Issues series will find the information they need in order to have a better understanding of the social, political, environmental, and economic issues facing the world today.

THE USA PATRIOT ACT OF 2001: Balancing Civil Liberties and National Security

A Reference Handbook

Howard Ball

CONTEMPORARY WORLD ISSUES

A B C ☰ C L I O

Santa Barbara, California
Denver, Colorado
Oxford, England

Library of Congress Cataloging-in-Publication Data
Ball, Howard, 1937–
    The U.S.A. Patriot Act of 2001 : balancing civil liberties and national security : a reference handbook / Howard Ball.
        p.   cm.— (ABC-CLIO's contemporary world issues series)
    Includes bibliographical references and index.
    ISBN 1-85109-722-8 (hardcover : alk. paper)
    ISBN 1-85109-727-9 (e-book)
1. United States. Uniting and Strengthening America by Providing Appropriate Tools Required to Intercept and Obstruct Terrorism (USA PATRIOT ACT) Act of 2001.   2. Civil rights—United States.   3. Internal security—United States.   4. National security—Law and legislation—United States.   5. Terrorism—United States—Prevention.   I. Title: USA Patriot Act of 2001.   II. Title.   III. Series: Contemporary world issues.
    KF4850.B35 2004
    345.73'02—dc22

                                                                2004005430

08 07 06 05 04   10 9 8 7 6 5 4 3 2 1

This book is also available on the World Wide Web as an eBook. Visit abc-clio.com for details.

ABC-CLIO, Inc.
130 Cremona Drive, P.O. Box 1911
Santa Barbara, California 93116-1911

This book is printed on acid-free paper ∞.
Manufactured in the United States of America

For all those dedicated men and women serving to protect the people in America's war against terror, with special thanks to my friends in the Richmond, Vermont, Rescue squad— it's been my pleasure to "run" with you.

Contents

Introduction

Thomas L. Friedman, the Pulitzer Prize–winning journalist for the *New York Times,* recently wrote: "September 11, 2001, amounts to WW III—the third great totalitarian challenge to open societies in the last 100 years." He went on with a quote:

> World War II was the Nazis, using the engine of Germany to try to impose the reign of the perfect race, the Aryan race. The Cold War was the Marxists, using the engine of the Soviet Union to try to impose the reign of the perfect class, the working class.

And 9/11 was the religious totalitarians, Islamists, using suicide bombing to try to impose the reign of the perfect faith, political Islam. (Abdullah Schlieffer, quoted in Friedman 2004, 26)

This new asymmetrical war, a "holy war," according to the enemy leaders, is the most dangerous one, for it threatens the very essence of a free society. Unlike the Nazis and the Communists, today the United States and other Western societies "face people who hate us more than they love life." The Islamic militants are too willing to commit suicide "by making themselves into human bombs, using the most normal instruments of daily life—an airplane, a car, a garage door opener, a cellphone, fertilizer, a tennis shoe—you create a weapon that is undeterrable, undetectable, and inexhaustible."

These human bombs attack the most essential element of an open society: trust.... Islamic militants have the potential to erode our lifestyle. Because the only way to deter a suicidal enemy ready to use the instruments of daily life to kill us is by gradually taking away trust. We start by stripping airline passengers, then we go to fingerprinting all visitors, and we will end up removing cherished civil liberties. (Friedman 2004, 26)

This book examines the actions of presidential administrations—especially the administration of Republican president George W. Bush (2001–)—as they slowly assessed the *unique* threat that radical, suicidal Islamic fundamentalists pose to a free and open democratic society. Reassessment led, immediately after 9/11, to the development of a national security policy in order to prevent another day of infamy.

The government's daunting task of trying to generate and implement policy after 9/11 (the USA Patriot Act of 2001 and the creation of the Department of Homeland Security are the major policy outcomes) to contain and capture and punish these suicide bombers has led to a serious clash between cherished civil liberties and national security. Such clashes are not new in U.S. history. As the first chapter illustrates, whenever the nation is threatened or goes to war, some groups in the society see their liberty eroded by governmental actions to protect national sovereignty and win the war.

However, as the Friedman essay acknowledges, the new war being fought against the United States is unlike all others. The enemy is within, the enemy is not in uniform, there are no clear and defined battle lines, and civilians are the primary target. The enemy is using the daily instruments of commerce and communication in a free society to prepare for the next 9/11.

Fear, more and more, is replacing trust in the United States. For example, a citizen looks carefully and cautiously at the person sitting next to her on a flight from Burlington, Vermont, to New York City. The wary passenger notes skin color, sees the turban as a cause of concern, and quickly looks at her fellow passenger's shoes to determine whether a bomb of some kind is implanted in them. The Department of Homeland Security has created a national alert system and people are aware of the warning colors flashed across television screens. In the past decade, governmental law enforcement agencies (FBI) and information-gathering organizations (CIA) have been given extremely broad—and secretive—powers to oversee the actions of all persons residing in the United States.

Civil liberties groups, from the mid-1990s on, have loudly protested the loss of basic civil liberties protections found in the Bill of Rights and in the Fourteenth Amendment's due process clause. Trust in the decency of government operatives has been replaced with suspicion and skepticism about the zeal and lack of restraint on law enforcement officers in the post-9/11 laws passed and executive orders issued. Equally troubling is the great distrust of some American publics regarding the motives of the leaders of the government, from President George W. Bush down to the FBI special agents in the field who conduct sneak-and-peek searches.

At bottom, as this book lays out for the reader, the United States is confronted with an invisible enemy who must be rooted out using techniques that weaken the core principle of trust. All the participants in this tragic drama — the police officer; the judge who issues a search warrant; the Bush administration's attorney general, John Ashcroft; the president of the United States, George W. Bush; and the strident critics of the administration's national security policies and procedures—cherish the bedrock principles of free government and civil liberties found in the Constitution.

All, however, have different views about how far a society can balance civil liberties with national security. Those differences lie at the heart of this war against terror. In days past when a war ended, trust was slowly restored along with the civil liberties that had been taken away during the conflagration. However, in this war against terrorism, there is no perceived, reasonable end to the battles given the fanaticism and hatred of the terrorist. We do not know whether, in the long run, our free society will not be significantly—radically—changed as government does all it can do to deter the terrorists. My task is to lay out, in a straightforward manner, the events and the challenges created by the Islamic terrorists who have declared "jihad" against the United States. Clearly, the twenty-first century is fraught with dangers unlike those faced in all earlier millennia—and we have barely entered it.

Howard Ball
Richmond, Vermont
January 2004

Abbreviations

ABAJ	American Bar Association Journal
ABCC	Alien Border Control Committee
ACLU	American Civil Liberties Union
ACU	American Conservative Union
ATA	Anti-Terrorism Act
ATF	Alcohol, Tobacco, Firearms
CCR	Center for Constitutional Rights
CDT	Center for Democracy and Technology
CIA	Central Intelligence Agency
CNSS	Council for National Security Studies
COINTELPRO	Counterintelligence Program (FBI)
CPI	Center for Public Integrity
CRS	Congressional Research Service
CSG	Counter-Terrorism and Security Group
CSIS	Center for Strategic and International Studies
CTC	Counter-Terrorism Center
DHS	Department of Homeland Security
DOD	Department of Defense
DOJ	Department of Justice
FAA	Federal Aviation Administration
FALN	Puerto Rican Nationalist Movement
FBI	Federal Bureau of Investigation, DOJ
FCNL	Friends Committee on National Legislation
FEMA	Federal Emergency Management Agency
FISA	Foreign Intelligence Surveillance Act
FISC	Foreign Intelligence Security Court
FOIA	Freedom of Information Act
FTO	foreign terrorist organization
GAO	General Accounting Office
IEEPA	International Emergency Economic Powers Act
IG	Inspector General
INA	Immigration and Naturalization Agency
INS	Immigration and Naturalization Service

MAD	Mutually Assured Destruction
MDC	Metropolitan Detention Center
NAACP	National Association for the Advancement of Colored People
NHSA	National Homeland Security Agency
NSA	National Security Act
NSC	National Security Council
NSDD	National Security Decision Directive
NSEERS	National Security Entry-Exit Registration System
OHS	Office of Homeland Security
OSHA	Occupational Safety and Health Administration
PDD	Presidential Decision Directive
TIPS	Terrorism Information and Prevention System
TSC	Terrorist Screening Center
TTIC	Terrorist Threat Integration Center
USA PATRIOT Act	United and Strengthening America by Providing Appropriate Tools Required to Intercept and Obstruct Terrorism Act
WMD	weapons of mass destruction
WTC	World Trade Center (Twin Towers), New York City

1

Terrorist Actions against Americans and Governmental Efforts to Protect National Security Before September 11, 2001

"The only thing we have to fear is fear itself."
President Franklin D. Roosevelt, 1934

"The intended purpose of terrorism is to create [fear]."
Brian M. Jenkins, 1996

"Freedom and fear are at war."
George W. Bush, September 11, 2001

Tom Clancy's novel *The Teeth of the Tiger* is a story about Islamic terrorists' plans to attack the United States and the country's efforts to prevent those enemy strikes against American civilians. In one chapter Clancy's description of a terrorist incident is eerily similar to real events. Simultaneously, in a number of cities across the U.S. heartland (Des Moines, Salt Lake City, and Denver), almost two dozen Islamic terrorists, armed only with automatic weapons, kill scores of civilians in shopping malls before they are themselves killed by the police. One of Clancy's protagonists, an FBI agent, says of the attack: "They wanted to sting us cleverly. The objective here manifestly is to strike at Middle America. They think they can strike fear in our hearts by showing us they can attack us anywhere, not just at obvious targets like New York" (Clancy 2003, 261).

Mohammed, the cultured, highly educated Islamic leader of the terrorists who struck in these cities, agrees with the FBI agent's assessment:

> [He] hoped for hundreds of dead Americans, instead of several dozen. . . . But the strategic objective had been achieved. All Americans now know that they were not safe. No matter where they might live, they could be struck by his Holy Warriors, who were willing to trade their lives for the Americans' sense of security. . . . So now Americans would know fear as they'd not known it before. It was not their political capital or their financial capital that was at risk. It was all of their lives. The mission had been designed from the beginning mainly to kill women and children, the most precious and most vulnerable parts of any society. (Clancy 2003, 265–266)

Clancy's fictional terrorist is not really fiction. Respected scholars of terrorism believe that the most dangerous terrorist in the twenty-first century is the fundamentalist religious terrorist. Such a person declares holy war on the infidels and justifies the most horrible attacks on civilians in the name of Allah. For American leaders, and the leaders of other free societies, the issue immediately becomes one of protecting the national security and, in so doing, dampening the community's *fear* of attack, a major weapon in the arsenal of America's terrorist enemies.

The Al Qaeda terrorist attacks of September 11, 2001, on the Twin Towers in New York City and the Pentagon just outside Washington, D.C., saw almost 3,000 persons—mostly civilians—slaughtered by religious fundamentalists whose leaders had declared a holy war against the "Great Satan," the United States of America. (A fourth hijacked airplane, headed for Washington, D.C., crashed in Pennsylvania after passengers tried to overcome the hijackers.) In response, U.S. president George W. Bush declared to the world that the United States was formally engaged in a "war against terrorism."

President Bush, however, was not the first leader in world history to make that declaration. The terrorists in Clancy's novel are not merely criminals on a killing rampage; they are soldiers engaged in warfare, and the strategic use of terror in war—primarily against civilians—is as old as the most ancient civilizations, Eastern and Western, Chinese, Greek, and Roman.

The use of terror against innocents during a war has been a reality since men first went to war against other men. Terrorism is warfare deliberately waged against civilians, by generals such as Union Civil War general William Tecumseh Sherman on his march to Savannah. (The general told a reporter in September 1861: "We don't want the truth told about things here [on the battlefield].") In the twenty-first century, terrorism is being waged by religious radicals such as Al Qaeda's Osama bin Laden as well as Clancy's fanatical Muslims. Terrorism, fundamentally, is employed by armies of all kinds and sizes for "*the purpose of destroying [the civilian population's] will to support either leaders or policies that the agents of such violence find objectionable*" (Carr 2003, 6; my emphasis).

The state's response to war, threats of war, terrorism, and threats of terrorism is generally—and necessarily—harsh and unremitting investigation and apprehension of the terrorist enemy, including those who act, conspire to act, materially support terrorist activities, or are only suspected of these actions. When the nation responding to such acts of war is a democracy, a set of consequential and controversial issues emerges: balancing matters of common defense and national security with the freedoms and liberties possessed by all persons—citizens and resident aliens—living in that nation. As President George W. Bush put it a few days after the terrorist attacks of 9/11, in those cases "freedom and fear are at war."

This sentence has a double meaning, and both are of critical importance in the effort to understand the context out of which the USA Patriot Act of 2001 emerged. (The full title of the legislation is **U**nited and **S**trengthening **A**merica by **P**roviding **A**ppropriate **T**ools **R**equired to **I**ntercept and **O**bstruct **T**errorism Act of 2001.) The first meaning, the one Bush probably intended, is that the declared war between the United States and the Islamic fundamentalists is, at bottom, a war between the fear created by Al Qaeda terrorists and the freedoms that are the bedrock of a democratic society.

The second meaning is the one critics of Bush's national security policy use. The liberties and freedoms possessed by all persons living in the United States, citizens and aliens alike, are being successfully attacked by governmental policies created in light of the fears triggered by Al Qaeda actions. For these critics, as we will see in Chapter Three, the USA Patriot Act of 2001 seriously

threatens the liberties of ordinary citizens much more than it min-
imizes the terrorist threat of Osama bin Laden and his small
bands of zealous minions. As these critics see it, the 2001 act is
only the latest in a series of repressive actions taken by U.S. government leaders when they believe the nation is imperiled by war
and terrorism, at home or abroad.

In U.S. governmental efforts to defend against acts of war by
terrorists, important due process rights such as *habeas corpus* have
historically been set aside. Ironically, at such times in U.S. history,
the general public is likely to acquiesce to the temporary repression of some of these rights and liberties. Poll after poll taken
after enemy attacks on the United States—after Peal Harbor on
December 7, 1941; after the Oklahoma City bombing in 1996; and
after 9/11/2001—showed broad though somewhat reluctant
public support for governmental "emergency measures" that
included restrictions on individual travel, greater power to law
enforcement agencies, and incarceration of suspected enemies,
even if they were U.S. citizens (More than 70,000 Japanese Americans were incarcerated during World War II.) These steps are jus-
tified in the name of national security, but they also restrain or
take away fundamental civil rights and liberties in the name of
national security (Griset and Mahan 2003, 86).

During such epochs of "national emergency," national law
enforcement agencies such as the Department of Justice (DOJ) are
given broad powers, ones that tend to threaten civil liberties.
Legislators pass restrictive legislation in the effort to defeat
America's enemies. Presidents and their political allies in the
executive branch use presidential powers to take action against
perceived terrorist threats, regardless of the impact on the freedoms of innocent persons residing in the United States.

Viewing American history, one sees such onerous incidents
where the federal government, claiming the existence of an
imminent threat to national sovereignty by enemy forces, acts in
a manner that punishes persons for using freedoms ostensibly
protected by the U.S. Constitution. Examples of such governmental behavior unfortunately abound (White 2003, 209).

The Alien and Sedition Acts of 1798 were passed because of
America's poor, almost warlike relations with France at that time.
The legislation was an effort by the Federalists, in control of both
Congress and the White House, to restrict the actions of new
immigrants from Europe—as well as to silence the voices of
American dissenters, chiefly Democrat-Republican opponents of

the Federalists. The Federalists were gravely concerned that the thousands of European immigrants to the United States were a threat to order in the new nation.

The Alien Act of 1798 gave President John Q. Adams the power to seize, detain, and deport any noncitizen judged by the government to be "dangerous to the peace and safety of the United States." Aliens so targeted had no right to an attorney, nor did they have any right to present evidence on their behalf. Under the other half of the "emergency" measures taken by the Federalist government, the Sedition Act of 1798, the publication of "any false, scandalous, and malicious writing" against the government of the United States, the Congress, or the president, with the intent to defame them or bring them into "contempt or disrepute" was prohibited. (Under this act, the Federalists arrested twenty-five Democrat-Republicans; there were fifteen indictments; ten cases went to trial, all resulting in convictions. All were freed when Thomas Jefferson entered the White House in 1801. The legislation was never challenged in the federal courts.)

The most dramatic and dangerous challenge to the government of the United States took place between 1861 and 1865, when the Southern states, the Confederacy, tried to secede from the Union. By suspending the writ of habeas corpus and declaring martial law in Maryland, Abraham Lincoln enabled his generals to arrest and hold in Union prisons many thousands of men and women who were "sympathetic" to the Southern cause. Over the course of the long and bloody four-year Civil War, Lincoln suspended the writ of habeas corpus no less than eight times. The most extreme instance came in 1862, when the suspension was nationwide and stated that "all persons guilty of any disloyal practice are subject to martial law."

Even before America's entry into World War I, in his 1915 State of the Union message, Democratic president Woodrow Wilson attacked unidentified foreigners in the United States, stating that "such creatures of passion, disloyalty and anarchy must be crushed." After the United States entered the war in 1917—a decision that faced strong domestic opposition from many minority radical groups in America—the Espionage Act was passed, narrowing the rights of German aliens residing in the United States. The act allowed the U.S. postmaster general to ban all "seditious" literature from the mail. All publications of the Socialist Party and its even more radical labor group, the International Workers of the World (IWW, known as the Wobblies), were banned in the legislation.

A year later the Sedition Act of 1918 was passed. Much like the Alien and Sedition Acts of 1798, it allowed the government to suppress "disloyalty and subversion." The act made it a criminal offense for any person to use any disloyal, profane, scurrilous, or abusive language about the form of government of the United States or the Constitution of the United States, or the flag of the United States, or the uniform of the Army or Navy; any language (that brought these institutions) into contempt, scorn, or disrepute.

Between 1942 and 1945, almost 125,000 enemy aliens and (mostly, i.e., about 70,000) American citizens of Japanese origin were interned without any charges ever brought against any of them. Similarly, more than 11,000 Americans of German and 3,000 Americans of Italian origin were detained during World War II (Feinstein 2001).

During the half-century-long Cold War against the Soviet Union (1947–1990), the government used the 1940 Alien Registration Act (referred to as the Smith Act), lists of allegedly subversive organizations compiled by the U.S. attorney general, and legislative investigating committees (congressional and state)—in one word, McCarthyism—to arrest and convict citizens for what they said or what organizations they belonged to. The Cold War was the first prolonged "war" in America's history. Threats to the integrity and sovereignty of the United States existed from afar (the military strength of the Soviet Union and its allies) and from within (the fear of internal domestic subversion of the U.S. government by Communists planted deeply in both governmental and nongovernmental sectors of American society, such as the theater, movies, and media). Blacklisting of suspected enemies was a common and destructive weapon in the Cold War: Countless millions of innocent American civilians were adversely affected by these governmental activities.

During the 1960s and early 1970s, the Vietnam War era, the actions of military intelligence, the CIA, and the FBI were directed against alleged enemies of the United States. Vietnam was the first U.S. military engagement that eventually—and bitterly—divided the nation. Both Democratic president Lyndon Baines Johnson (1963–1969) and Republican president Richard M. Nixon (1969–1974) introduced national security policies that denied to war protestors the freedoms they had in the Bill of Rights.

All these episodes are clear examples of very aggressive steps that the U.S. government took to defeat a perceived "enemy" but that effectively eliminated some basic freedoms of all persons residing in America. As Senator Diane Feinstein (D–CA) noted in a speech during one of the handful of debates surrounding passage of the 2001 Patriot Act, in all the above historical events, civil liberties "took a back seat to the imperative of national security" (Feinstein 2001). Again, ironically, according to some observers of U.S. national security actions, these governmental efforts were not successful in eliminating terrorist actions against the United States either at home or abroad.

What outrages observers of these repressive governmental actions is the loss of individual freedoms in a democratic society built on the foundation of individual liberty. It is one thing for a tyrannical government such as that of Saddam Hussein in Iraq to deny rights; it is quite another if the repression occurs in a free society. This is the heart of the dilemma manifested in the need to pass antiterrorist legislation after the tragic events of 9/11. What limits are there—are there any limits?—when democratic leaders confront enemies who have entered society's gates?

National Security Measures versus Individual Liberties: Some Major Incidents in American History

Pre– and post–Civil War acts of terrorism against the government and the American people must include John Brown's raid on Harper's Ferry, Virginia, in 1859 and the rise of the Ku Klux Klan after the Civil War ended in 1865. (The government responded rapidly to these threats, by the use of troops in the former case and by the passage of the 1871 Ku Klux Klan Act to deal with the growth of Klan violence.) The invention of dynamite in the mid-nineteenth century was a critical development in the history of war and acts of terror in war. One person with a suitcase loaded with dynamite could cause havoc and great destruction when the bag was detonated in a crowd of innocent civilians.

The Haymarket Square bombing in Chicago in 1886, a clash between labor unions and police, was one of the first uses of dynamite by those opposed to the country's capitalist system. This event—and the government's harsh response—led to the immediate growth of America's xenophobic fear of left-wing class terrorist groups. Anarchists, socialists, labor organizations in their infancy, nationalist groups, and ultranationalist political organizations labeled themselves as enemies of the brutal capitalist system and planned and implemented violent activities against U.S. government and private industry.

The nineteenth- and early-twentieth-century responses to the growth of unionism, anarchism, socialism, and communism in the United States were repressive. A common criticism of observers was that the government was ignoring the key First Amendment freedoms of speech, press, religion, and assembly that were the possession of all persons in the United States. Still another basic condemnation was that the U.S. government failed to follow the principles of due process in its zeal to stop the threat of violent, bloody attacks by these "deviant" groups.

The second half of the twentieth century saw government leaders trying to react to suspected threats to U.S. national security by Communists, socialists, and their "fellow travelers." In addition, from the middle of the century, but especially during the 1950s to 1980s, there were perceived threats to the nation's national security from domestic radical organizations such as the Puerto Rican nationalist group; the Weather Underground; the Black Panthers; other antigovernment movements; nationalist/ separatist movements; survivalist militias; religious extremists; alienated, solitary terrorists; and antiabortion terrorists.

In the 1950s and 1960s, the nation experienced the birth of the civil rights movement as well as the exponential growth of the anti–Vietnam War movement. These two major events led to reactions good and bad from the government as well as private groups who were opposed to the messages of these two groups. It led to congressional passage of major civil rights and voting rights legislation. It also led to the third incarnation of the Ku Klux Klan, especially in the Deep South. The government used less than positive ways to deal with anti–Vietnam War terrorism and the Klan; among its most controversial tactics was COINTELPRO, the covert, unconstitutional FBI operation run against a number of radical domestic organizations, including the Black Panthers and the Nation of Islam, for over a dozen years.

The New Reality: The Declaration of a "Holy War" against the "Great Satan" by Al Qaeda, 1980s–present

In the 1980s, Islamic religious terrorists, having declared a holy war, or jihad, against the Great Satan, America, began to target U.S. facilities and personnel abroad (Hudson et al. 2002, 9). The first major terrorist attack on Americans overseas occurred on October 23, 1983. In part of a simultaneous suicide-bomb attack by the militant religious terrorist organization Islamic Jihad against both the U.S. and French compounds, 241 U.S. Marines were killed when a truck containing 12,000 pounds of high explosives rammed into marine headquarters at the international airport in Beirut, Lebanon. In the second attack a 400-pound high-explosives truck bomb destroyed the French base, killing fifty-six French troops.

A total of 1,500 U.S. Marines, in the company of French Legionnaires and British and Italian soldiers, had been sent to Lebanon, a nation ravaged by civil war. The Lebanese prime minister, Bashir Gemayel, had been assassinated in September 1982, and the country had recently been invaded by Syria. On April 18, 1983, the Islamic Jihad, at war with the Western democracies that attempted to bring stability to the volatile Middle East, had set off a 400-pound bomb at the U.S. embassy in Beirut. Sixty-three persons, including the CIA's director of Middle East operations, were killed and 120 were injured. Immediately after the October Islamic Jihad attack, President Ronald Reagan withdrew U.S. forces.

On December 21, 1988, Pan American Airlines Flight 103, en route from London to New York City, was blown up over Lockerbie, Scotland, by a bomb placed on the plane in Europe. All 259 passengers were killed, and the falling debris killed eleven persons on the ground. In November 1991 a grand jury of the U.S. District Court for the District of Columbia issued an indictment charging two Libyan nationals with the crime. The two were arrested and detained by Libyan police. They were eventually brought to trial and convicted in a European court for their action.

In August 1989, in Executive Order 12686, President George Bush created a seven-member Presidential Commission on

Aviation Security and Terrorism. In May 1990 it presented its 182-page report critical of the nation's aviation security system; the commission recommended top-to-bottom revamping of the government's airline security program.

On January 17, 1991, fundamentalist Islamic terrorists were outraged anew by the actions of the United States in the Middle East. Under the leadership of President Bush and the U.S. military, a multinational coalition (thirty nations in the military coalition; another eighteen nations providing humanitarian, economic, and other assistance), an operation called Desert Storm forced the Iraqi military from neighboring Kuwait, which Iraq had invaded and quickly occupied in August 1990. A few days after Desert Storm, President Bush deployed U.S. military to Saudi Arabia to prevent an Iraqi attack on that kingdom.

On April 14, 1993, Iraqi dictator Saddam Hussein's intelligence service operatives attempted to assassinate former president George Bush during his visit to Kuwait. They were unsuccessful.

In the early 1990s these warlike Islamic terrorist attacks came to U.S. soil. The attacks reflected a new and extremely dangerous phenomenon: small bands of radical Islamic terrorist cells, not linked to any nation-state but functionally united in anti-American hatred, all of them at war against the "Great Satan." Up to this time, wrote one observer, "Americans were secure in the knowledge that, at least at home, they were safe from international terrorists. Then Islamic fundamentalists sent a shocking wake-up call—the bombing of the World Trade Center in New York" (Cooper 1995, 1).

On February 26, 1993, the World Trade Center (WTC) in New York City, which 100,000 workers and visitors passed through daily, was badly damaged when a truck bomb loaded with 1,200 pounds of explosives was detonated in the underground parking garage. The blast left six people dead and over 1,000 injured. It created a crater 200 by 100 feet wide and five stories deep.

The men who carried out the attack were followers of a radical, blind Islamic Egyptian cleric, Omar Abdel Rahman. The strategist was Ramzi Yousef, who fled the country but was apprehended in 1995. He and his collaborators, who had links with Al Qaeda, were convicted or conspiring to commit acts of terrorism; each received a 240-year prison sentence and a $500,000 fine. For the first time since their unconstitutional actions of the late 1960s and early 1970s, CIA officers—who were by the 1947 statute creating the institution prohibited from engaging in domestic activities—were added to the Joint Terrorism Task Forces created after the WTC bombing.

Federal authorities called the bombing of a federal office building in Oklahoma City in 1995 "the deadliest terrorist event ever committed on U.S. soil. (It was superseded, of course, by the tragedy of 9/11 six years later.) In a blast felt over nearly thirty blocks, a truck bomb killed 169 persons (including nineteen children) and injured almost 1,000 more. The explosion left a 30-foot wide, 8-foot deep hole at the front of the building, which had to be torn down after the attack. The event shocked the federal government as well as a frightened American public even more than the 1993 World Trade Center bombing. New York was a great city; it was the cosmopolitan heart of America and the world's financial capital. Oklahoma City was in America's heartland; no one, except perhaps novelists such as Tom Clancy, suspected that terrorists would attack and murder hundreds of civilians, including infants and small children, in Oklahoma.

The bombing of the nine-story Murrah Federal Building on April 19, 1995, however, was not the work of Islamic terrorists. (Not surprisingly, the initial government and public assumption was that it was another attack in the holy war against the United States. Even in 2004 there are some who still believe that the building's destruction was the doing of a combined force of terrorists, including Islamic fundamentalists.) Through some lucky police work within hours of the detonation, right-wing extremists Timothy McVeigh (a veteran of the first Gulf War, Operation Desert Storm) and Terry Nichols were identified as those responsible.

McVeigh was embittered by the actions of the federal government in its stand-off against the Branch Davidians in Waco, Texas, in April 1993, which killed as many as eighty members of the extremist religious sect. He also blamed the federal government "for all the problems in the world." McVeigh was convicted on eleven counts of murder and conspiracy, sentenced to death, and executed on June 11, 2001. His coconspirator, Nichols, was convicted of conspiracy to use a weapon of mass destruction and eight counts of involuntary manslaughter. He was sentenced to life imprisonment.

After the 1996 Oklahoma City bombing, the image of the suicide bomber took on a more ominous and threatening character in the United States and the rest of the world. The *intifada*, the Palestinian uprising against Israeli occupation, continued with increased violence in a new form. Suicide bombers blew themselves up in nightclubs, buses, shopping centers, and other public places in order to make the dramatic case for a separate Arab state as well as to try to weaken U.S. efforts to bring Israel and the Palestine Liberation Front together in an effort to end bloodshed in that part of the Middle East. For these suicide bombers, the destruction of Israel and its replacement with an Arab Palestine was the primary reason for their martyrdom.

On June 26, 1996, Islamic fundamentalists, angered at the presence of U.S. military on Arab soil, attacked the Khobar Towers, a major U.S. military compound in Dharan, Saudi Arabia. The massive truck-bomb blast, containing between 5,000 to 20,000 pounds of explosives, killed nineteen Americans and wounded another 500 persons, including American, British, and French air force personnel assigned to Operation Southern Watch, a coalition air operation over southern Iraq. The Saudi Hezbollah was the Islamic terrorist cell that carried out the attack, evidently with support from Iran. However, by this time, U.S. military and CIA intelligence officers had surmised that this event, like the 1993 WTC bombing, was an Al Qaeda–initiated attack on the United States and U.S. nationals.

At the Olympics held in Atlanta, Georgia, in 1996, at about 1:30 A.M. on July 27, a pipe bomb went off at Centennial Olympic Park. Thousands of people were gathered at the site at the time. Two died and over 100 were injured by the blast. A combined federal-state Bomb Task Force immediately began the laborious work of gathering information to find the terrorist. In October 1998 the DOJ charged Eric Robert Rudolph—an angry "survivalist"—for the bombing as well as two 1997 bombings in Atlanta. (In May 2003 Rudolph was apprehended by the FBI; he is awaiting a criminal trial in federal court.)

On August 7, 1998, under the leadership of Osama bin Laden, Al Qaeda planned and executed simultaneous bombings of U.S. embassies in Kenya and Tanzania in eastern Africa. The Nairobi bombing killed twelve Americans, thirty-two Foreign Service nationals, and almost 250 Kenyan nationals. Over 5,000 civilians were injured by the blast, and the embassy building sustained extensive structural damage. About ten minutes later, another car bomb exploded in front of the U.S. embassy in Dar es Salaam, Tanzania, killing a dozen persons and injuring almost

100 others. Retaliating with military force, on August 20, 1998, President Bill Clinton ordered the launching of missile strikes against bin Laden's training bases in Afghanistan.

On October 12, 2000, Osama bin Laden's terrorists, riding in a small fishing boat loaded with explosives, rammed the destroyer U.S.S. *Cole*, docked at the harbor in Aden, Yemen. Seventeen U.S. sailors were killed and another thirty-nine were injured in the bomb blast, the first terrorist attack on a U.S. naval warship.

Ultimately, Al Qaeda's holy war against the United States led to the traumatic, deadly attacks on two symbols of the United States' financial and military strength, the September 11, 2001, attacks on the World Trade Center in New York City and the Pentagon in Virginia. The third target was America's political heart, Washington, D.C. The hijacked plane never made it to the nation's capital because of the heroic actions of its passengers.

U.S. Governmental Efforts to Protect National Security Prior to September 11, 2001

From the first Islamic terrorist actions against the United States and other Western democracies in the 1980s and into the twenty-first century, Congress filled the Federal Criminal Code with definitions of terrorism. This was an important first step, as before this period there were no definitions in federal, state, or local criminal statutes. In 22 USC 2656 f (d) Congress stated that "'terrorism' means premeditated, politically motivated violence perpetrated against noncombatant targets by sub-national groups or clandestine agents, usually intended to influence an audience." The FBI definition describes two types of terrorism: domestic and international:

> Domestic terrorism involves groups or individuals whose terrorist activities are directed at elements of our government or population without foreign direction [such as Timothy McVeigh's action].
>
> International terrorism involves groups or individuals whose terrorist activities are foreign-based and/or directed by countries or groups outside the United

States or whose activities transcend national boundaries.

Terrorism is the unlawful use of force or violence
against persons or property to intimidate or coerce a
government, the civilian population, or any segment
thereof, in furtherance of political or social objectives.

Although such definitions appeared in statutes, executive
orders, and federal regulations passed, issued, and created in the
effort to respond to the new type of warfare against the United
States, national security leaders, including presidents, did not
elevate the fight against terrorism to the highest priority until
after 9/11. As noted in the next section, Presidents Clinton and
Bush did not spend much time worrying about domestic acts of
terrorism until it was too late.

Congressional Hearings and Legislation up to 9/11

In the mid-1970s, after President Nixon was forced to resign
from office because of the Watergate cover-up, congressional
hearings took place on actions of the CIA and other intelligence-
gathering agencies that violated congressional constraints placed
on them. At one point during the public sessions, Senator Mark
Hatfield (R-OR) called the CIA a "rogue elephant." These hearings (named after the co-chairs of the special committee: Senator
Frank Church [D-ID] and Congressman Otis Pike [D-NY]) led to
the creation of additional limits on America's intelligence-
gathering agencies. One former high-level CIA official said the
hearings "permanently changed the way Clandestine Services
operated. It changed the rules of the game for us" (Posner 2003).
The CIA's plans for covert actions had to be approved by a committee chaired by the president; if they were approved, the president had to inform Congress within sixty days. Permanent oversight committees were formed in both houses of Congress. (And
the new president, Gerald Ford, issued Executive Order 11905,
forbidding all governmental agencies from undertaking assassi-
nations.)

Many of the legislative actions taken in the 1990s were, for
the most part, reactive statutes, ones that called for changes in
national security matters *after* a terrorist attack occurred. In
November 1990, for example, in response to the 1988 Lockerbie

tragedy, Congress passed the Aviation Security Improvement Act.

On November 20, 1993, a joint resolution of Congress stated: "It is the sense of Congress that the President should strengthen Federal interagency emergency planning by FEMA, and other appropriate Federal, State, and local agencies for development of a capability for early detection and warning of and response to: potential terrorist use of chemical or biological agents or weapons."

Another congressional statute, the Defense Against Weapons of Mass Destruction (WMD) Act of 1996, (also known as the Nunn-Lugar-Domenici Act), followed a number of terrorist events at home and abroad, including the bomb blast at the 1996 Olympics in Atlanta. The statute established a long-term effort to prepare a coordinated domestic response to the increased threats from terrorist organizations. A domestic agency, the Federal Emergency Management Agency (FEMA), was given the task of starting the planning; after three years the lead could be transferred to the Department of Defense if the president authorized such a change. In 1999 President Clinton transferred the lead to the DOJ, specifically, to the Office of State and Local Domestic Preparedness (relocated within the cabinet-level Department of Homeland Security with its creation on November 25, 2002).

The most important piece of legislation produced prior to 9/11 was the Antiterrorism and Effective Death Penalty Act of 1996, written in direct response to the April 19, 1995, bombing of the Murrah Federal Office Building in Oklahoma City.

The day after the Oklahoma City tragedy, President Clinton told the shocked and frightened nation: "[The bombing] was an act of cowardice and it was evil. . . . And I will not allow the people of this country to be intimidated by evil cowards." Clinton's deputy U.S. attorney general, Jamie S. Gorelick, said: "I think it is important to put the bombing in perspective. This is only the most recent in a disturbing and escalating trend of terrorist attacks, inside and outside the United States" (Cooper 1995). And as has been the case throughout U.S. history, the administration proposed new legislation giving federal agencies almost unrestricted power to battle these terrorists. Until the 1995 Murrah Building bombing, most federal laws dealing with foreign agents and terrorists were aimed at preventing terrorists from entering the country in the first place. A few statutes increased the criminal penalties for terrorist acts in the United States to include the death penalty if civilians were killed. After the Oklahoma City bombing, new legislation extended the powers of law enforcement dealing with suspected terrorist actions to their limit, including authorization for the use of roving wiretaps and sections that made it extremely difficult for persons to enter the United States.

The 1996 Antiterrorism Act was quickly introduced and passed in a strong showing of bipartisanship. Some of the key titles in the more than 100-page, nine-section act are:

Title III. Authorized the U.S. State Department to create a system of both designating foreign organizations as terrorist organizations and prohibiting monetary and other assistance to "terrorist" states. (See Chapter Six for the State Department's list of "Designated Foreign Terrorist Organizations.")

Title IV. Addressed the specifics of removal (deportation); new visa application protocols; modification of political asylum procedures; and new procedures for handling criminal aliens.

Title VII. Increased penalties in the criminal law to counter terrorism and terrorists, including penalties for the dissemination of certain information. It also assigned the death penalty for certain criminal actions.

Title VIII. Provided assistance to law enforcement agencies for antiterrorism training; enhanced overseas training; as well as special protection for federal buildings in the District of Columbia.

As soon as President Clinton signed the 1996 legislation into law, civil liberties groups began to condemn it. Additionally, there was the strange combination of conservative Republicans and liberal Democrats sitting in Congress who were opposed to the legislation. These two sets of critics argued that the law was unconstitutional because its sections conflicted with due process of law. As examples, they noted that the statute expanded the government's authority to conduct telephone wiretaps of suspected terrorists and enabled the military intelligence agencies to assist the FBI and other domestic law enforcement agencies in the investigation of crimes involving chemical or biological weapons. The congresspersons opposed to the act worried that the legislation expanded the powers of the federal agencies to a point that constitutional barriers were in danger of being disregarded.

"There are two very serious constitutional infirmities in the legislation," argued David Cole, a law school professor. "One is imposing guilt by association on individuals for their support of nonviolent activities of disfavored groups. The second is the provision that permits the government to rely on secret evidence to deport immigrants accused of being associated with terrorist activities" (Cole 2002, 955).

Donald M. Haines, legislative counsel for the American Civil Liberties Union, speaking before the U.S. Senate Judiciary Committee in May 1995, voiced the concerns of civil liberties groups about the loosening of FBI wiretap powers:

> The ACLU strongly opposes virtually every one of the electronic surveillance and intelligence gathering proposals presented by the Administration. These . . . particularly intrusive investigatory techniques . . . are unnecessary and, in fact, not related to the events of Oklahoma City. They will not make the American people any safer. . . . [These proposals] will expose all Americans to the increased danger that our government will violate our . . . Fourth Amendment . . . rights— thereby turning into a reality a feeling about their government that many Americans already have.

(Chapter Three's examination of the critics of the Patriot Act of 2001 will show that the essential concerns raised after the bill was signed in late October 2001 were raised a half decade earlier *by the same critics.*)

When the 9/11 tragedy occurred, there had been no federal court decisions regarding the constitutionality of the 1996 Antiterrorism and Effective Death Penalty Act. The USA Patriot Act of 2001 refined some of the titles in the 1996 statute, for the most part expanding the powers of federal agencies to hunt, arrest, indict or deport, and try suspected terrorists. And as was the case with the 1996 act, within days of President Bush's signing of the 2001 Patriot Act, civil liberties organizations began their still ongoing campaign to have the legislation declared unconstitutional.

Executive Orders and Presidential Decision Directives

Many executive orders and presidential decision directives also addressed the threat of terrorism to America. They were issued by Presidents Ronald Reagan, George Bush, Bill Clinton, and George W. Bush between 1984 and September 11, 2001.

During the Reagan administration there were efforts to provide the federal government's national security agencies with greater power to stem the flood of illegal aliens—some of them fanatical religious extremists—entering the United States. Executive Order 12472 of April 3, 1984, entitled "Assignment of National Security and Emergency Preparedness Telecommunications Functions," was an effort to further improve the nation's vast communications system so that the president's functions as commander-in-chief and chief executive could be carried out in the event of a terrorist attack.

In 1986 another Reagan executive order authorized the formation of an interagency task force, the Alien Border Control Committee (ABCC), to block entry of *suspected* terrorists and to deport those already in the country either illegally or who had overstayed their temporary visas. (Both the FBI and the CIA were involved in the work of the ABCC.)

However, civil liberties groups and sympathetic members of Congress viewed the ABCC's actions, with CIA involvement, with great concern. Congressman Barney Frank (D–MA) introduced an amendment to the Immigration and Nationality Act so that a visa applicant's membership in a terrorist organization alone was no longer sufficient to deny a visa. After the Frank Amendment's passage, the Immigration and Naturalization Service (INS) could deny a visa only if the federal government could prove that the applicant had committed an act of terrorism.

Another executive order, 12656, dated November 18, 1988, was called the "Assignment of Emergency Preparedness Responsibilities." Its purpose was to assign to various federal departments and agencies, on a functional basis, the "national security" emergency preparedness responsibilities of the government (excluding natural disasters and other, technological emergencies). Still another, issued the same day, EO12657, "FEMA Assistance in Emergency Preparedness Planning at Commercial Nuclear Power Plants," enabled FEMA initially to coordinate federal response activities when state and local commitments are either absent or inadequate.

In response to the Libyan terrorists' December 1988 destruction of Pan American Flight 103, EO 12686, "President's Commission on Aviation Security and Terrorism," was issued. The commission was tasked to conduct a comprehensive study and appraisal of the practices and policy options with respect to preventing terrorist acts involving aviation. The unclassified final report of the commission was presented to President Clinton on February 12, 1997.

In July 1999 President Clinton issued EO 13129, "Blocking Property and Prohibiting Transactions with the Taliban." The introductory passage stated that because

> the actions and policies of the Taliban in Afghanistan, in allowing territory under its control to be used as a safe-haven and base of operations for Osama bin Laden and the Al Qaeda organization who have committed and threaten to continue to commit acts of violence against the United States and its nationals, constitute an unusual and extraordinary threat to the national security and foreign policy of the United States, . . .[the president did] hereby declare a national emergency to deal with that threat. (*Federal Register*)

EO 13223, "Blocking Property and Prohibiting Transactions with Persons Who Commit, Threaten to Commit, or Support Terrorist Acts," was issued on September 21, 2001, by President George W. Bush. It came only ten days after 9/11 and was the first post-9/11 effort to list specific persons involved in terrorist attacks on American nationals. EO 13224, announced two days later, authorized the creation of one of four counterterrorism lists, the very important "terrorist financing" list. The executive order enables the government to block a designee's assets in any financial institution in the United States or held by any U.S. resident.

Presidential decision directives and presidential national security decision directives (NSDD) were based on recommendations from the president's National Security Council (NSC) staff respecting national security. Some major NSDD's include:

NSDD 30, "Managing Terrorism Incidents," April 1982

NSDD 138, "Preemptive Strikes Against Terrorists," April 1984

NSDD 179, "Task Force on Combating Terrorism," July 1985

NSDD 207, "National Program for Combating Terrorism," January 1986

PDD/NSC-63, "President's Commission on Critical Infrastructure Protection," May 1998

As was the case during the Cold War between the United States and the Soviet Union, in the 1990s the federal government established four counterterrorism lists as tools in the government's fight against terrorism. The U.S. State Department, specifically, the U.S. secretary of state, was authorized to create these lists, which name

- State Sponsors of Terrorism
- Foreign Terrorist Organizations (FTOs)
- Terrorist Financing (EO 13224)
- Terrorist Exclusion (2001 Patriot Act)

According to the government, all these lists "serve to *prevent* terrorism, *punish* terrorists and their supporters, and *pressure* changes in the behavior of designated states and groups" (www.doj.gov/). Designation on any of the lists "allows the U.S. government to:

- target a country for other sanctions/laws that penalize persons and countries engaging in certain trade with state sponsors;
- block designees' assets in U.S. financial institutions;
- criminalize willing provision of material support for designated groups;
- block visas for members of FTOs without having to show that the individual was involved in specific terrorist activities.
- block tens of millions of dollars intended to bankroll the murderous activities of Al Qaeda and other terrorist groups;
- exclude or deport aliens who provide material assistance to, or solicit it for, designated organizations" (www.lifeandliberty.gov).

Documents/Reports

Toward the end of the Clinton administration, from August 1999, through the first year of the Bush administration and the events of 9/11/2001, a number of reports were commissioned by the White House, Congress, and private think tanks that focused on the new terrorist "war" against America. Chief among these reports were:

- The quintet of Gilmore reports, published in December 1999, 2000, 2001, 2002, and 2003;
- Three Hart-Rudman Commission reports, published in August 1999, April 2000, and January 2001;
- The L. Paul Bremer Commission report, published in June 2000;
- A report entitled "Defending America in the 21st Century: New Challenges, New Organizations, and New Policies," published in December 2000 by the Center for Strategic and International Studies; and
- A number of General Accounting Office (GAO) reports, published between September and December 2001.

The Gilmore reports were annual reports to the president and Congress by the Advisory Panel to Assess Domestic Response Capabilities for Terrorism Involving Weapons of Mass Destruction. J. S. Gilmore III, former governor of Virginia, was the chair of the panel, created in 1999. The RAND Corporation provided staff support to the commission.

The first two reports were published before 9/11. These initial reports examined the threat that WMD in the hands of terrorists posed to American citizens, problems associated with existing policies focusing on terrorist actions, and the need for the government to develop a national strategy to address domestic responses to terrorism. In the first report, the panel assumed that a terrorist attack "could be designed to cause a limited number of casualties, but at the same time cause mass panic" (Gilmore 1999; Natural Hazards Research Working Paper).

In its second report, December 2000, the panel shifted from threat assessment toward "specific programs for combating terrorism and larger questions of national strategy and federal organization." For example, it recommended that "the next President [Bush] should develop and present to the Congress a *national* [not a federal] strategy for combating terrorism within one year of assuming office." In addition, the panel recommended the establishment, on "a statutory basis," of a "national office for Combating Terrorism in the Executive Office of the President" (Gilmore 2000).

The third report was prepared after the terrorist attacks on 9/11/01 and focused on the "functional challenges" to protecting the United States against terrorism in five specific areas:

- Improving state and local response capabilities,
- Improving health and medical capabilities,
- Strengthening immigration and border control,
- Enhancing security against cyberattacks, and
- Clarifying the roles and missions on the use of the military (Gilmore 2001).

The last Gilmore Commission report appeared on December 15, 2003. Its focus was on the capability of the newly created cabinet-level Department of Homeland Security, headed by former Pennsylvania governor Tom Ridge. Its title: "Forging America's New Normalcy: Securing Our Homeland, Protecting Our Liberty." The commission's press release summed up its findings:

The United States needs an improved homeland security strategy to strengthen security in communities facing the greatest risk, improve the use of intelligence, increase the role of state and local officials, and sharpen disaster response capabilities, a federal commission said today. . . .

The commission . . . says the creation of the Department of Homeland Security has resulted in improved planning and readiness. But the report concludes that the overall national homeland security strategy should be directed by a White House-level entity that "must have some clear authority over the homeland security budgets and programs throughout the federal government." . . .

The Gilmore Commission says that an existing entity—the Homeland Security Council—is best equipped to craft a new strategic policy that could then be carried out by the Department of Homeland Security, other federal agencies, and a host of state, local, and private groups that also must be involved.

The Homeland Security Council is made up of the secretaries and heads of federal departments and agencies with homeland security responsibilities, supported by its own staff in the White House. . . .

The commission says that by providing long-term guidance to federal, state, and local government officials, an improved homeland security strategy can help create a "new normalcy" that acknowledges the threat of terrorism will not disappear, but still preserves and strengthens civil liberties. . . .

The commission calls on the president to create an independent, bipartisan oversight board to provide counsel on homeland security efforts that may impact civil liberties, even if such impacts are unintended.

The commission says the board is needed because of *the potential chilling effect of government monitoring conducted in the name of homeland security. . . .*

The report expresses concern about protecting freedoms guaranteed by the First Amendment to the Constitution, which could be violated by government's increased reliance on sophisticated technology that has vast potential to invade personal privacy (my emphasis).

According to the report, too little intelligence information is shared with state and local officials, despite improvements in the ways the government handles such information. The RAND survey found that only about half of local law enforcement agencies and half of state and local emergency management organizations have received guidance from the FBI about the type of information they should collect about suspected terrorist activity and pass on to the FBI. . . .

The Gilmore Commission recommends that to improve intelligence sharing, the president should: designate a federal authority that can speed up the granting of security clearances for state, local, and private officials; provide training to allow these officials to use intelligence information; and overhaul the current classification system to improve the dissemination of critical intelligence. . . .

The commission also reiterates its recommendation of
a year ago that the president establish a Terrorist Threat
Integration Center independent of the FBI, CIA, or the
Department of Homeland Security to coordinate intelli-
gence about potential terrorist attacks in the United
States. (Gilmore 2003)

Governor Gilmore, in his cover letter to the president and
congressional leaders, warned of the continuing dilemma of terrorism and of the need to balance homeland security actions with
civil liberties rights of all persons living in the United States. Furthermore, he noted, as did all the committees and commissions
created after 9/11, that "there will never be a 100 percent guarantee of security for our people, the economy, and our society. . . .
We must resist the urge to seek total security—it is not achievable
and drains our attention from those things that can be accomplished."

"As more terrorist attacks occur," wrote Gilmore, *"the pressure
will rise to lessen civil liberties, albeit with different labels"* (my emphasis). This concern voiced by a governmental commission in
2003 is one of the basic concerns of the critics of the Patriot Act
and other actions taken by the Bush administration since 2001.

The U.S. Commission on National Security/21st Century
was an independent commission of twelve senior national security experts and the two cochairs, former U.S. senators Gary Hart
and Warren Rudman. (In addition, dozens of staffers worked for
the commission.) It was created by Congress in 1997 under the
Federal Advisory Commission Act and was jointly sponsored by
congressional leaders, the White House, and the Department of
Defense. Its dual charge was to "do the most comprehensive reassessment of the structure and processes of the American
national security system [for the next twenty-five years] since the
passage of the National Security act of 1947" and to recommend
a "national strategy" for combating the terrorist threat to Americans at home and abroad (Hart and Rudman 2002, 1–2; Natural
Hazards Research Working Paper).

The first Hart-Rudman Commission report described two
contradictory trends in the world community: the enormous
strength of the U.S. economy, "its continued dominance in terms
of military power; power to shape the world politics, and world
culture through the year 2025." However, ominously, there are
also in the twenty-first-century global village "powerful forces of

social and political fragmentation, [with] . . . cultural affinities different from our own. Our adversaries—rogue states and non-state terrorists—will resort to [various] forms and levels of violence [using WMD]."

Given these two trends, the panel predicted—two years *before* 9/11/01—that the United States "will become increasingly vulnerable to hostile attacks in our homeland and that our military superiority will not entirely protect us." Also, the panel concluded,

> The emerging security environment in the next quarter century will require different military and other national capabilities; there will be a blurring of boundaries between homeland defense and foreign policy; between sovereign states and a plethora of protectorates and autonomous zones; and between the pull of national loyalties on individual citizens and the pull of loyalties both more local and more global in nature.

Its final words in this preliminary report were chilling: "*Americans will likely die on American soil, possibly in large numbers*" (my emphasis). There was, however, absolutely no press coverage of the findings of this report; further, the Clinton administration ignored the first two Hart-Rudman reports entirely.

The second Hart-Rudman report, published in April 2000, called on the political leaders in the White House and Congress to balance the two contradictory trends identified in the first report. These were "enhancing freedom" for people in the global village while at the same time striving "to dampen the forces of global instability so that those benefits can endure." One of its somber conclusions was a warning that if the U.S. government "*loses the capacity to respond to dynamic change [in the world] the day will come when Americans will regret it dearly*" (my emphasis).

Senators Hart and Rudman sent out thousands of press releases and gave hundreds of copies of their second report to legislators and reporters in an effort to light a fire under the Clinton administration's policymakers before a catastrophic event occurred. As happened after their first report was released to the public, there were no stories in the press, on television, or in news weekly magazines such as *Time* and *Newsweek*. One reporter for a national newspaper told a frustrated Senator Hart: "This isn't important, none of this is ever going to happen." Hart himself commented in December 2001: "The national media just didn't pay attention [to our warnings]" (quoted in Hart and Rudman 2002).

The final report, issued on February 15, 2001, was another lengthy one, containing no less than fifty recommendations for improving the nation's capability to respond to the threat of international terrorism. The hope was that the new Bush administration would pay attention to the commission's findings and advice. The commission sharply stated that "significant changes must be made in the structures and processes of the U.S. security apparatus." Among its conclusions were the following recommendations for immediate and wholesale change in five key areas of the U.S. national security philosophy and policies:

- Ensuring the security of the American homeland,
- "Recapitalizing" U.S. strengths in science and education,
- Redesigning key security institutions of the executive branch,
- Overhauling the U.S. government's military and civilian personnel systems, and
- "Reorganizing Congress's role in national security affairs."

In the first twenty-five years of the twenty-first century, concluded the report, the "distinction between domestic and foreign no longer apply." A year before the creation of the Office of Homeland Security in the White House, the commissioners called for the establishment of an independent National Homeland Security Agency (NHSA) built upon four existing federal executive agencies, the FEMA, the U.S. Coast Guard, the U.S. Customs Service, and the U.S. Border Patrol. Two years before President Bush elevated the Office of Homeland Security to Cabinet status, the commission recommended that the "Director of the NHSA would have Cabinet status and would be a statutory advisor to the National Security Agency." The commissioners, mindful of the natural tension between national security and individual liberties, asserted that "the legal foundation for the NHSA would rest firmly within the array of Constitutional guarantees for civil liberties."

Both former senators met with Secretary of Defense Donald Rumsfeld, Secretary of State Colin Powell, and National Security Adviser Condoleezza Rice to go over, in some detail, the highlights of their report. Hart and Rudman met with the same lack of interest they experienced with Clinton administration national security and foreign policy leaders.

In April 2001 Hart and Rudman testified before the U.S. Senate's Judiciary Committee Subcommittee on Terrorism and Technology. They warned again: "The prospect of mass casualty terrorism on American soil is growing sharply and [because of this reality] the United States must embrace homeland security as a primary national security mission" (Hart and Rudman 2002).

Ignominiously, shortly after the two former senators met with Bush's top leaders, the White House tabled the final commission report. Further adding insult to the work of the Hart-Rudman Commission, in May 2001 President Bush gave Vice-President Dick Cheney the task of studying the problem of international terrorism and providing the White House with recommendations for improving U.S. national security. (The events of 9/11 short-circuited Cheney's report to the White House.)

The actions of the Bush administration were taken as if the Hart-Rudman Commission, with its dozen members and dozens of bright staffers examining the threat of terrorism for over two years, had never existed. The two chairmen, especially after 9/11, were crestfallen. After the attacks Senator Rudman said, bitterly, "We tend not to do what we ought to do until we get hit between the eyes" (quoted in Posner 2003).

Hart and Rudman were not the only frustrated chairs. Earlier in 2000, the National Commission on Terrorism, referred to as the (L. Paul) Bremer Commission, issued its report on the future of U.S. national security in light of the terrorist events that had taken place over the preceding two decades. Bremer, the chairman of the commission, had been ambassador-at-large for counterterrorism during the Reagan administration (1981–1989). (In May 2003 Bremer was appointed by President Bush to direct the rebuilding of Iraq.) The Bremer Commission report, as well, was ignored by the Clinton White House.

In a June 7, 2000, report titled "Countering the Changing Threat of International Terrorism," the National Commission on Terrorism, the Bremer Commission, made recommendations similar to those of other reports prepared in the decade before 9/11/01. The report can be found at www.fas.org/irp/threat/commission. The commission saw the need for (1) an "aggressive strategy against terrorism"; (2) "improved information sharing" between domestic and foreign law enforcement and information-gathering agencies, that is, the FBI and the CIA; and (3) if there was a catastrophic terrorist attack, the assignment of the U.S. Department of Defense as the lead federal bureaucracy in the U.S. response.

In December 2000 the privately funded Center for Strategic and International Studies (CSIS), published its report, "Defending America in the 21st Century: New Challenges, New Organizations, and New Policies." Its recommendations differed from those of the Hart-Rudman and Bremer studies. The CSIS recommended that the vice-president be head of homeland defense and that a National Emergency Planning Council, located in FEMA, be created to take the lead for coordination of federal, state, and local agencies charged with law enforcement and response to terrorist incidents.

Finally, in 2001 and 2002 the U.S. General Accounting Office produced many reports that critically examined a variety of issues dealing with national security and analyses of the 9/11 events.

Department/Agency Actions

As early as 1940, in the Smith Act, a law passed by Congress to deal with internal subversive activities that threatened the sovereignty of the United States, the FBI was given the authority to investigate subversive activities and to use wiretaps in these investigations without seeking a federal court order. Initially, the Smith Act aimed at hunting down, catching, indicting, convicting, and sentencing Nazi "fifth-column" subversive planning and actions against the United States.

By the end of World War II, a fundamental shift in focus took place; the hunted subversives became Communists, allies of the Communists, and fellow travelers. And the FBI continued to use the expanded powers it was granted in 1940. It was not until the post-Watergate days (1974–1975) that U.S. Attorney General Edward Levi, appointed by President Gerald Ford, issued new guidelines that limited the FBI's authority to gather domestic intelligence through unrestrained wiretapping.

In 2003 the FBI's new list of priorities was posted on the Internet. Its "first responsibility" was "to protect the United States from terrorist attack." The FBI's second priority was to "protect the United States against foreign intelligence operations and espionage." Its third major task was also related to the Bush war on terrorism: to "protect the United States against cyber-based attacks and high-technology crimes." Only after these three prime charges, note the critics of the Patriot Act, is there, in fifth position, the responsibility to "protect civil rights" ("New Agenda for FBI," at www.lifeandliberty.gov).

The second duty of the FBI brings that organization into contact with the CIA, the other premier intelligence-gathering agency of the federal government. The FBI's jurisdiction after the 2001 Patriot Act extended to domestic and foreign threats. The act also formally expanded the role of the CIA, which was charged with using a variety of methods to collect information on foreign threats to U.S. national security, working in cooperation with the FBI in the war on terror.

However, from the beginning of governmental efforts to keep tabs on suspected terrorist cells in the late 1970s, these two federal bureaucracies were at odds with each other and did not share information. This led, in post-9/11 jargon, to "dots not being connected" in the investigation of terrorist organizations. For example, in 1983, after the U.S. embassy was destroyed by a bomb blast, both agencies sent groups to Beirut to investigate. According to one agent who was there, "the two [groups] sometimes got into screaming and shoving matches" (Brown 2003). For the CIA, the FBI was too cautious and unwilling to take appropriate risks in the effort to gather information about terrorist activities. For FBI officials, the CIA was overly aggressive and a major risk-taking operation.

The low point in the relations between the FBI and the CIA probably came in the weeks before the December 11, 1988, bomb explosion that killed all 269 people aboard Pan American Flight 103. Weeks before the terrorist action, the Mossad, Israel's intelligence service, warned the CIA that a Pan Am flight from Frankfurt, Germany, to the United States would be destroyed. Flight 103 was on a route from Hamburg to New York. The CIA never passed the information they received from Mossad to the FBI and other federal agencies.

By 1990 the internal battling, the distrust, and the lack of cooperation between the two agencies was very visible and palpable. The primary beneficiaries of these battles were the terrorists bent on taking violent actions against innocent American civilians. The tensions between the FBI and the CIA continued to fester and were not resolved until, after 9/11, sections of the Patriot Act specifically addressed this endemic problem.

But the two foremost intelligence-gathering organizations were hardly alone in their bureaucratic fights. At the time of the

Oklahoma City bombing, at least twenty-five domestic federal law enforcement agencies were involved in terrorist investigations, including the Bureau of Alcohol, Tobacco, and Firearms (ATF), the Customs Service, and the Federal Aviation Administration (FAA). Clashes and conflicts between the FBI and these other smaller and less visible law enforcement agencies were rampant. It was not until 1984, during the Reagan administration, that there was an executive branch effort to end these internecine battles. President Reagan approved the creation of the Restricted Interagency Group for Terrorism. The CIA's director of covert operations chaired the group, which included one representative each from the CIA, FBI, and National Security Council (NSC). (The NSC representative was a then unknown U.S. Marine lieutenant colonel, Oliver North.) In 1986 Reagan authorized yet another interagency group, the Counter-Terrorism Center (CTC). Only after 1996 was there a federal effort to coordinate the actions and information sharing of domestic federal agencies, but very little headway had been made by 9/11.

Regarding the government's inability to (1) recognize the primacy of the terrorist threat and (2) develop and implement a policy to deal with it, one critic observed:

> The failure to have prevented 9/11 was a systemic one. Investigators did not get a lucky break early on, and there were many blunders in the immediate run-up to the attack.
>
> The seeds of failure, however, were sown repeatedly in the almost twenty years of fumbled investigations and misplaced priorities. (Posner 2003, xii)

Terrorists working and living in America, and traveling into and out of the country without any difficulty early on realized how porous American national security was and took enormous advantage of governmental weaknesses. While it is uncertain whether 9/11 events would have taken place if there had been, for example, greater cooperation between the FBI and the CIA, it is clear that the 9/11 treachery occurred because of the existing systemic breakdown of U.S. intelligence-gathering machinery.

However, according to many observers of American preparedness against acts of terrorism, by the end of July 2001 concern about terrorist activities against the United States had peaked. After July, until the events of 9/11, the general perception in the Bush White House, the Congress, and the press was that, contrary to the conclusions in the Bremer and Hart-Rudman reports, a domestic terrorist attack was not a "clear and present danger" to the United States.

In June 2001 the DOJ indicted thirteen Saudi citizens and one Lebanese for the 1996 attack on the U.S. military compound in Saudi Arabia. And it was not until September 4, 2001, that the Bush administration conducted its very first counterterrorism planning meeting. In attendance were Secretary of State Powell, Paul Wolfowitz representing Secretary of Defense Rumsfeld, CIA director George Tenet, Chairman of the Joint Chiefs of Staff Richard Myers, National Security Adviser Rice, and the head of the Counter-terrorism and Security Group (CSG), Richard Clarke. A summary of what took place at this meeting was on President Bush's desk—unread—when the planes crashed into the World Trade Center and the Pentagon on the morning of 9/11/01.

The next chapter examines the events of 9/11 and the belated efforts of U.S. leaders to address the reality of this new, asymmetric holy war declared by radical Islamic terrorists against the most powerful nation-state in world history, the "Great Satan," the United States of America.

For Further Reading

Brown, Cynthia, ed. *Lost Liberties: Ashcroft and the Assault on Personal Freedom.* New York: New Press, 2003.

Carr, Caleb. *The Lessons of Terror: A History of Warfare Against Civilians.* New York: Random House, 2003.

Clancy, Tom. *The Teeth of the Tiger.* New York: G. Putnam and Sons, 2003.

Cole, David. "Enemy Aliens." 54 *Stanford Law Review,* 953, 2002.

Cooper, Mary H. "Combating Terrorism." *CQ Researcher,* July 21, 1995, pp. 1–19.

Feinstein, Diane. 2001. Floor debate in the U.S. Senate on the proposed Patriot Act of 2001, October 24. Taken from www. cdt.org/security/011025senate.txt.

Friedman, Thomas. Editorial. *New York Times,* January 2004.

Friedman, Thomas L. "War of Ideas," part 1, *New York Times,* January 8, 2004.

Gilmore, J. S., et al. *First Annual Report to the President and the Congress of the Advisory Panel to Assess Domestic Response Capabilities for Terrorism Involving Weapons of Mass Destruction-I. Assessing the Threat.* December 15, 1999, 123 pages, p. 4. www.rand.org/nsrd/terpanel/terror.pdf.

————. *Second Annual Report to the President and the Congress of the Advisory Panel to Assess Domestic Response Capabilities for Terrorism Involving Weapons of Mass Destruction-II. Toward a National Strategy for Combating Threat.* December 15, 2000, 191 pages, at www.rand.org/nsrd/terpanel/terror3-screen.pdf.

————. *Third Annual Report to the President and the Congress of the Advisory Panel to Assess Domestic Response Capabilities for Terrorism Involving Weapons of Mass Destruction-III. For Ray Downey.* December 15, 2001, 270 pp. 2–6, passim.

————. *Fourth Annual Report to the President and the Congress of the Advisory Panel to Assess Domestic Response Capabilities for Terrorism Involving Weapons of Mass Destruction-IV. Implementing the National Strategy.* December 15, 2003, 205 pages, p. 2, www.rand.org/nsrd/terpanel/terror-4.pdf.

Griset, Pamela L., and Sue Mahan. *Terrorism in Perspective.* Thousand Oaks, CA: Sage Publications, 2003.

Gutman, Roy, and David Rieff, eds. *Crimes of War.* New York: W. W. Norton, 1999.

Hart, Gary, and Warren Rudman. *America Still Unprepared—America Still in Danger.* Washington, DC: Council on Foreign Relations, 2002.

Hudson, Rex A., and staff of the Federal Research Division of the Library of Congress. *Who Becomes a Terrorist and Why: The 1999 Government Report on Profiling Terrorists.* Guilford, CT: Lyons Press, 2002.

Journal of Supreme Court History, 28, no. 3, 2003. Special Issue: "Civil Liberties in Wartime."

Kushner, Harvey W. *Encyclopedia of Terrorism.* Thousand Oaks, CA: Sage Publications, 2003.

Leone, Richard C., and Greg Anrig Jr., eds. *The War on Our Freedoms: Civil Liberties in an Age of Terrorism.* New York: Public Affairs, 2003.

Natural Hazards Research Working Paper #107. *Major Terrorism Events and their U.S. Outcomes (1988–2001), Appendix B: Major Reports.* www.Colorado.edu.

Posner, Gerald. *Why America Slept: The Failure to Prevent 9/11.* New York: Random House, 2003.

Rehnquist, William H. *All the Laws but One.* New York: Random House, 2003.

Stern, Jessica. *The Ultimate Terrorists.* Cambridge, MA: Harvard University Press, 1999.

White, Jonathan R. *Terrorism: An Introduction.* 4th edition. Belmont, CA: Wadsworth/Thomson Learning, 2003.

2

September 11, 2001, and the Passage of the USA Patriot Act of 2001

"In the world after September 11, it is both appropriate and necessary for our country to re-examine the balance between rights of individuals, the values we cherish as an American community, and the need to secure our nation from the threat of transnational terrorism."
John Podesta, September 2003

The United States had been in an undeclared war against terror for decades prior to the September 11, 2001, attacks by Al Qaeda terrorists. Throughout the 1980s and 1990s, as Chapter One illustrated, three presidential administrations—Republican (Ronald Reagan, 1981–1989; Bush, 1989–1993) and Democratic (Bill Clinton, 1993–2001)—had to respond to attacks against Americans, both at home and abroad, carried out, for the most part, by small numbers of foreign extremist religious groups who had declared a holy war against the United States (White 2003, 204–205).

However, the overall response from the White House and America's intelligence-gathering agencies (the FBI and the CIA) was at best tepid and at worst, incompetent. As one critic noted, the federal government "did not notice when some of the most prominent radicals moved to this country and set up operations just across the river from the World Trade Center. These early militants, ignored in their new chosen homeland, would become the role models and inspiration for some of the World Trade Center and Pentagon hijackers in 2001" (Posner 2003, 3).

Senator Bob Graham (D–FL,) spoke about this systemic failure from the Senate floor a few days before President Bush signed the 2001 Patriot Act.

> For 40 years [the CIA] intelligence community was focused on one target: the Soviet Union and its Warsaw Pact allies. We knew that community. . . . It was a homogeneous enemy. . . . It was an old style symmetrical enemy: We were matching tanks for tanks, nukes for nukes. With the fall of the Berlin Wall [in 1989], the world changed in terms of intelligence requirements. Suddenly, instead of one enemy, we had dozens of enemies. . . . And instead of symmetrical relationships, we now have small groups of a dozen or a hundred or a thousand or so against a nation the size of the United States of America. So our intelligence community has been challenged to respond to this new reality. (Congressional Record, October 20, 2001)

For the first time, the United States was caught up in a new kind of warfare: asymmetrical war. The enemy at America's gates was not the massed army of Russians or Chinese, traditional nation-state foes of the United States in the twentieth century. Instead, the "enemy" was three terrorists, members of a militant Islamic fundamentalist organization called Al Qaeda that had declared war against the "Great Satan." They rode in a bomb-laden motor launch that rammed the U.S.S. *Cole*, causing death and injury to dozens of U.S. naval personnel.

The "enemy" was nineteen terrorists who, on September 11, 2001, hijacked four commercial airliners and turned them into subsonic guided missiles that flew into buildings, killing thousands of innocent civilians. As President George W. Bush said in his 2002 State of the Union message: "America is no longer protected by vast oceans. We are protected from attack only by vigorous action abroad and increased vigilance at home" (www.whitehouse.gov).

This was the new deadly reality for U.S. military, foreign intelligence-gathering, and law enforcement organizations. Above all, it was a looming reality that called for the United States to reassess its national security strategy, one created at the beginning of the Cold War in the late 1940s. Facing the enemy at that time, the Soviet Union and its Eastern European allies, the U.S. national security policy called for the creation of nuclear stockpiles that would deter the Communists from threatening the peace and security of the United States and its allies. However, "mutually assured destruction," the phrase coined to describe America's Cold War foreign and military policy, is inapposite when the enemy is not a nation-state but less than two dozen committed terrorists carrying on a holy war against the United States and its allies.

U.S. Secretary of Defense Rumsfeld, on October 16, 2003, perplexed with this new reality of asymmetrical warfare, raised troublesome but critical—and critically revealing—questions in a memo to his chief subordinates. In part (the full text of the Rumsfeld memo is found in Chapter Six) it asked:

> Is DoD changing fast enough to deal with the new 21st century security environment? . . . Does DoD need to think through new ways to organize, train, equip and focus to deal with the global war on terror? Does the US need to fashion a broad, integrated plan to stop the next generation of terrorists? . . . The cost-benefit ratio is against us! Our cost is billions against the terrorists' costs of millions. Do we need a new organization?

Although Al Qaeda and other radical terrorist groups declared war against the United States as early as the 1980s, and terrorist warfare against the United States had occurred in America and overseas since then, a thorough reassessment of U.S. national security policy was forced on the foreign and national security policymakers early in the morning of September 11, 2001.

As Attorney General Ashcroft said in a speech to the U.S. Mayors Conference a day before the president signed the Patriot Act, "On September 11, the wheel of history turned and the world will never be the same. A turning point was reached, as well, in the administration of justice. The fight against terrorism is now the first and overriding priority of the Department of Justice."

September 11, 2001: A Second "Day of Infamy" for America

In the early morning of September 11, 2001, a beautiful fall day, two hijacked commercial airliners crashed into the twin towers of the World Trade Center in New York City. Thousands died when the towers collapsed more than an hour after the jets, each loaded with over 30,000 pounds of jet fuel, rammed into the structures at speeds in excess of 300 miles per hour. (The following account is based on reports, between September and November, 2001, in the *New York Times*, the *Washington Post*, and other broadcast venues, especially O'Harrow 2002.)

At about the same time, a third hijacked airliner smashed into one wing of the Pentagon and a fourth airliner, bound for another target in the Washington, D.C., area, crashed in Somerset County, Pennsylvania, after passengers attempted to overpower the hijackers.

As soon as officials realized what was happening, actions were taken to try to prevent further death and destruction. The Federal Aviation Administration suspended all air traffic in the United States and diverted international flights to Canada. Federal offices and public buildings in Washington, D.C., New York, and other large cities were immediately closed.

Secretary of State Powell instructed U.S. embassy officials around the globe to close their facilities or suspend operations if they believed the threat level warranted such action. More than 25 percent of the embassies ceased operations for a short time.

President George W. Bush was in Florida at the time of the attacks. He flew to Louisiana and then to Nebraska before returning to Washington, D.C., in the early evening of September 11, 2001. Speaking to the nation that evening, Bush said that "the full resources of our intelligence and law enforcement communities" would be used to find the terrorists and bring them to justice. "We will make no distinction between the terrorists who committed these acts and those who harbor them" (O'Harrow 2002).

In a speech to the nation Bush declared that a war against terror had begun and that he would take all necessary actions to preserve democracy and vanquish the terrorist enemy. He and his close advisers, especially Vice-President Cheney, viewed the attacks as acts of war by foreign aggressors rather than heinous criminal actions.

The following day, September 12, 2001, Bush sent a letter to the Speaker of the U.S. House of Representatives. "Yesterday," he wrote, "evil and despicable acts of terror were perpetrated against our fellow citizens. Our way of life, indeed our very freedom, came under attack. Our first priority is to respond swiftly and surely. . . . Congress must act. [Pursuant to section 251 (b)(2)(a) of the Balanced Budget and Emergency Deficit Control

Act of 1985], I ask the Congress to immediately pass and send to me the enclosed request for $20 billion in FY 2001 emergency appropriations to provide resources to address the terrorist attacks on the United States that occurred on September 21, 2001, and the consequences of such attacks" (O'Harrow 2002).

That same day, the Congress met in joint session and approved a joint resolution pledging support to President Bush in his efforts to find and pursue the terrorist organization that committed the attacks. By this day, intelligence sources had identified the group responsible for the attacks: the Al Qaeda organization, led by the Saudi Arabian national Osama bin Laden. As President Bush told the Congress one week later, "Our war on terror begins with Al Qaeda. But it does not end there. It will not end until every terrorist group of global reach has been found, stopped, and defeated" (www.washingtonpost.com).

After meeting with his national security, state, and defense department leaders, Bush reaffirmed the nation's four-part counterterrorism policy:

I. Make no concessions to terrorists and strike no deals,
II. Bring terrorists to justice for their crimes,
III. Isolate and apply pressure on states that sponsor terrorism to force them to change their behavior,
IV. Bolster the counterterrorism capabilities of the United States and those countries that work with America and require assistance.

Within days of 9/11, Congress introduced legislation that gave the government new powers to hunt down and seize suspected terrorists. One bill, which had languished in the legislature in the past because of its threat to individual rights, was re-introduced and passed by voice vote in both houses. It was the Combating Terrorism Act, and it proposed expansion of the government's power and authority to trace telephone calls to include e-mail. Its quick passage was a harbinger of the way in which the Congress would respond to the administration's proposal for the Patriot Act.

President Bush's military response came very soon after the 9/11 attacks. In his capacity as commander-in-chief, he took steps to protect the homeland and prevent additional threats. In its "Authorization for Use of Military Force," Public Law No. 107–40, Section 2 (a), 115 Stat 224, Congress backed his use of

force against "the nations, organizations or persons he determines planned, authorized, committed, or aided the terrorist
attacks . . . or harbored such organizations or persons." Congress
emphasized that the forces responsible for the 9/11 attacks "continue to pose an unusual and extraordinary threat to the national
security." The president, it continued, "has constitutional authority under the Constitution to take action to deter and prevent acts
of international terrorism against the United States."

By the time the USA Patriot Act was signed into law in late
October 2001, the Department of Justice announced that almost
1,500 persons had been secretly detained or arrested by the FBI
and immigration authorities. Attorney General Ashcroft told the
press that these actions had been taken within the "framework of
the law" and that the alien detainees' rights were being respected.
However, there were no facts presented, and the names of the
detainees were not released. (Legal challenges to the INS and DOJ
secrecy policy were brought before federal judges in 2002. The
courts upheld the secrecy, accepting the national security argument of the government. In January 2004 the U.S. Supreme Court
denied certiorari to an appeal challenging governmental secrecy.)

In the weeks and months after 9/11, President Bush, helped
by his close advisers, quickly proposed new legislation and
issued executive and military orders. On October 10, 2001, Bush
issued Executive Order 13229, which established the Office of
Homeland Security and the Homeland Security Council, chaired
by former Pennsylvania governor Tom Ridge. (Little more than a
year later, the office became the cabinet-level Department of
Homeland Security and Ridge became the secretary of homeland
security.) On November 13, 2001, Bush announced a military
order that called for the creation of secret detentions and secret
military tribunals for noncitizens involved in terrorist activity.
The Department of Defense was responsible for conducting these
trials and establishing the criteria for them. (On March 21, 2002,
the DOD made public the military commission regulations, the
"Crimes and Elements" instructions it intended to implement
when conducting these military trials.)

But the major focus of the administration after 9/11 was
pushing through the Congress an omnibus piece of legislation
that would provide law enforcement and investigating agencies
with nearly unrestrained power and authority to combat the terrorists in the United States and abroad. President Bush, after his
return to the capital late on 9/11, quickly met with his attorney

general, John Ashcroft, to discuss the need to introduce legislation that would enable the federal government's intelligence and
law enforcement agencies, especially the CIA and the FBI, to
work more closely together to deal with the war on terror. In less
than two weeks, Ashcroft would present the legislature with the
proposal worked up by the Justice Department, labeled the Anti-
Terrorist Act of 2001. After arguments between the DOJ and congressional leaders, the draft proposal, with but a handful of substantive changes, became the U.S.A. Patriot Act of 2001.

The draft legislation presented to Congress was a reflection
of the beliefs and visions of President Bush's contentious attorney general. Ashcroft's view about the terrorist threat was clear,
controversial, and consistent.

> The terrorist enemy that threatens civilization today is
> unlike any we have ever known. It slaughters thou-
> sands of innocents—a crime of war and a crime against
> humanity. It seeks weapons of mass destruction and
> threatens their use against America. No one should
> doubt the intent, nor the depth, of its consuming
> destructive hatred. Terrorist operatives infiltrate our
> communities—plotting, planning, and waiting to kill
> again. They enjoy the benefits of our free society even as
> they commit themselves to our destruction. They
> exploit our openness—not randomly or haphazardly—
> but by deliberate, premeditated design. (www.usdoj.
> govag/testimony/2001)

Likewise, Ashcroft's view of the role of the Department of
Justice was equally clear and consistent. "We have embarked on
a wartime reorganization of the DOJ [reflected in part in the
Patriot Act]," he said.

> It has been and will be the policy of this Department of
> Justice to use the same aggressive arrest and detention
> tactics in the war on terror. Let the terrorists among us
> be warned: If you overstay your visa—even by one
> day—we will arrest you. If you violate a local law, you
> will be put in jail and kept in custody as long as possi-
> ble. We will use every available statute. We will seek
> every prosecutorial advantage. We will use all our
> weapons within the law and under the Constitution to
> protect life and enhance security for America.

One leading liberal senator who chaired the Judiciary Committee, however, was concerned about the proposed legislation's trampling of civil liberties of persons in the United States. But in the end, even Senator Patrick Leahy (D–VT) spoke in favor of the bill as it emerged after six weeks of hardball politics. On the Senate floor the day that body voted overwhelmingly in favor of the Patriot Act, Leahy said:

> This is a whole new world. It is not similar to the days of the cold war where we worried about armies marching against us or air forces flying against us or navies sailing against us. This is not that world. . . . But as the Presiding Officers and everyone else [in the Senate] knows, a small dedicated group of terrorists, with state-supported efforts, can wreck havoc in an open and democratic Nation such as ours. . . . We have the ability, with our intelligence agencies and our law enforcement, to seek out and stop people before [they attack us]. . . . We are giving powers to the administration; we will have to extend some trust that they are not going to be misused. The way we guarantee that is congressional oversight [of the FBI and other law enforcement and intelligence-gathering agencies of the federal government]. . . . *We will entrust but with oversight.* (www.usdoj. govag/testimony/2001; my emphasis)

The Six-Week Battle Royal over the DOJ Draft of "An Act to Deter and Punish Terrorist Acts in the United States and Around the World," September 12, 2001–October 26, 2001

The savage attacks on the morning of September 11, 2001, observed a *Washington Post* reporter, "didn't just set off a national wave of mourning and ire. They re-ignited and reshaped a smoldering debate over the proper use of government power to peer into the lives of ordinary people." (O'Harrow 2002).

The ensuing debate, which had subsided after passage of the 1996 Antiterrorism Act (the congressional response to the bombing of a federal building in Oklahoma City one year earlier), was between civil libertarians and advocates for greater governmental powers. The controversial issue was how to strike a balance between government power and individual rights in a time of war.

What is the proper balance between national security and the privacy rights of millions of persons living in the United States? In the first decade of the twenty-first century, these people generate personal information (telephone records, e-mails, etc.) that is already more widely available than ever before. The government wanted access to all of it to hunt down terrorists—as well as those suspected of terrorist activities—before they struck again.

The Bush administration's position in the debates was contained in a lengthy, ten-section, hundred-plus-page draft proposal entitled "Uniting and Strengthening America by Providing Appropriate Tools Required to Intercept and Obstruct Terrorism Act of 2001," otherwise known as the Anti-Terrorism Act (ATA) of 2001. The draft proposal was introduced by Attorney General Ashcroft just eight days after the 9/11 terrorist attacks on the World Trade Center and the Pentagon. Clearly, there was no time for the administration's law enforcement leaders to analyze the failure of U.S. criminal justice and intelligence agencies' anti-terrorism activities in the wake of the events of 9/11.

Instead, the ATA draft the U.S. Department of Justice gave to the Congress was a compilation of controversial ideas about combating terrorist actions that had been kicking around the Department of Justice for years, especially during the Reagan and first Bush administrations (1981–1993). The draft legislation enhanced and modified over one dozen existing federal criminal statutes such as Title III of the Omnibus Crime Control Act of 1968, the Pen Register and Trap and Trace Statute, the Electronic Communications Privacy Act of 1986, the Bank Secrecy Act, the Money Laundering Act, the Immigration and Nationality Act, the Right to Financial Privacy Act, and the 1978 Foreign Intelligence Surveillance Act (FISA).

The ATA draft also proposed the establishment of new crimes and provided federal law enforcement agencies such as the FBI with additional powers to find and apprehend terrorists bent on warlike actions against the United States, at home and abroad.

The draft act was an effort to increase America's capacity to deal with the realities of asymmetrical warfare in the highly technological and interconnected world of the twenty-first century. Its stated purpose was to "enable law enforcement officials to track down and punish those responsible for the attacks and to protect against any similar attacks." Central to the act's effectiveness were the three C's: coordination, communication, and cooperation in the effort to constrain acts of terror against Americans. Again and again during the six weeks of hardball politics, the administration's spokespersons addressed the importance of the new legislation in bringing together disparate (by law) federal organizations in the critically important task of defeating the terrorist enemies of the state.

The central ingredients of the draft were the sections focusing on:

- improving criminal and foreign intelligence investigations;
- ending money-laundering schemes that funneled large amounts of money to terrorist organizations at war with the United States;
- establishing procedures and new powers to enable law enforcement agencies to deal with border protection and the detention and removal of alien terrorists or suspected alien terrorists;
- the terrorists' victims;
- new crimes and penalties for the commission of terrorist actions or for conspiring to commit them.

Key legislators in Congress made Herculean efforts to try to address some of the balance problems with the proposed legislation. Leahy, the liberal chair of the Senate Judiciary Committee, was one of the legislators engaged in intense negotiations with the Justice Department in the effort to achieve greater balance in the proposed legislation. In the House of Representatives, Congressmen Jim Sensenbrenner (R–WI), the chair of the House Judiciary Committee, working closely with the ranking Democrat on the committee, John Conyers (D–MI), also participated in negotiations with the DOJ that led to improvements in the USA Patriot Act, as did a concerned, conservative Speaker of the House, Dick Armey (R–TX).

The major players for the administration in the negotiations with congressional leaders were Attorney General Ashcroft and Assistant Attorney General Viet Dinh. Their fundamental goal was to rapidly pass legislation that gave government all the powers—new and those that expanded on earlier legislation—necessary to protect the nation's security. According to Dinh, Ashcroft's charge was "very, very clear": "[Do] all that is necessary for law enforcement, within the bounds of the Constitution, to discharge the obligation to fight this war on terror" (O'Harrow 2002).

Ashcroft wanted, for example, the ATA to include new governmental powers to secretly detain and hold suspected terrorists for unspecified periods of time—without legal protections such as assistance of counsel and habeas corpus. For the conservative attorney general, such powers were vital to U.S. national security.

The draft ATA contents in part suggested that 9/11 may have occurred because the federal government's national security agencies—especially the FBI and the CIA—were restrained from "speaking" to each other because of existing laws. Such constraints led to gaps in intelligence sharing and interpretation in the months before 9/11. It was imperative that modifications in existing statutes such as the 1947 National Security Act, NSA (which created the CIA), and the 1968 Omnibus Crime Control and Safe Streets Act, especially Title III, had to be made quickly.

This was not a new idea; the Clinton administration, in response to the 1993 bombing of the World Trade Center, supported the 1994 amendments to the 1978 FISA, modifications of the 1947 NSA to give the CIA the authority to collect information abroad for use by federal agencies in domestic trials, and the 1996 Antiterrorism and Effective Death Penalty Act (after the bombing of the federal building in Oklahoma City). These earlier executive and legislative actions allowed the use of sneak-and-peek searches (that violated the Fourth Amendment) and the use of secret evidence to deport suspected aliens.

The 1947 NSA drew a clear line between the activities of the CIA and those of the FBI in order to protect civil liberties of persons living in the United States. The CIA and military intelligence were prohibited from "exercising any police, subpoena, law-enforcement powers, or internal security functions." The CIA was confined to gathering foreign intelligence abroad, often secretly and illegally, regarding the intentions and the capabilities of foreign government policymakers for use by U.S. policymakers. The FBI was responsible for law enforcement and counterintelligence activities inside the United States. Unlike the CIA's operations, the FBI's law enforcement information acquisition efforts had to follow due process guidelines or else the information could not be used against a defendant in a U.S. courtroom.

Title III placed great restrictions on governmental use of electronic eavesdropping—wiretapping. The FBI could track phone messages under the act, but what about tracking the destination and origin of e-mail, voice mail, and faxes? What information could be shared by foreign-intelligence-gathering investigators (CIA) and criminal investigators (FBI)?

Furthermore, the restrictive 1978 FISA legislation, the consequence of Senator Church's lengthy investigation of domestic spying by the FBI (its CONINTELPRO program, for example) and other federal agencies such as the CIA was another target of Ashcroft and the DOJ. As Senator Feinstein reminded her colleagues in a speech she gave just before the final Senate vote on the Patriot Act, "[We] should recall our nation's unfortunate experience with domestic surveillance and intelligence abuses that came to light in the mid-1970s." She went on:

> Until Watergate and the Vietnam War, Congress allowed the Executive Branch virtually a free hand in using the FBI, the CIA, and other intelligence agencies to conduct domestic surveillance in the name of national security. It was the Cold War. Members of Congress were reluctant to take on FBI Director J. Edgar Hoover, and oversight was non-existent. [The methods used during this period by the CIA, army intelligence, and the FBI] have no place in a free society. (www.epic.org)

Because of the serious domestic intelligence abuses of both the Johnson and Nixon administrations, Congress created "a wall of separation between law enforcement [FBI] and [secret] intelligence gathering in order to protect civil liberties." The Bush administration was adamantly opposed to such a separation: FISA had to be modified by tearing down the barriers between federal agencies. Powers had to be authorized to enable the FBI and other domestic-crime-fighting federal agencies to be able to work much more closely with secret intelligence-gathering agencies such as the CIA and the various military intelligence-gathering units.

For the administration, the primary weapon in the war on terror was not the troops fighting in Afghanistan to defeat the

Taliban, for example, but rather the intelligence gathered inside the United States about terrorist plans. All federal agencies had to freely gather information about terrorists and suspected terrorists, even if such freedom threatened civil liberties.

The FISA created a supersecret Foreign Intelligence Surveillance Court. The court operated through the actions of seven judges, scattered across the country, two of whom lived in the Washington, D.C., area. Federal authorities had to go to this secret court for permission to use wiretaps on foreign agencies and individuals. They had to show that the sole purpose of their request for surveillance was foreign intelligence. Because of the prior ugly history of domestic spying by federal agencies, FISA restricted the use of foreign national wiretapping for domestic criminal investigations and possible prosecutions. This constraint, argued the DOJ vigorously, had to be lifted in the face of the realities of the new kind of warfare the United States faced.

By the end of the six weeks of political hardball, Attorney General Ashcroft successfully pressured the Congress to pass the administration's version of the Patriot Act quickly because, he claimed, additional terrorist actions were imminent. For Senator Leahy, the chair of the Senate's Judiciary Committee, these six weeks were the most challenging and emotional ones he had experienced as a legislator. "What made this most intense," he said, "were not just the issues, but the great sorrows I felt" (O'Harrow 2002).

Because of the stress of the discussions, he would take long walks on the paths adjacent to the Congress. "I saw the same faces as I did when I was a law school student [in D.C.] and President Kennedy had been killed. I saw the same shock, and I wanted to make sure our shock didn't turn into panic." He was deadly afraid that the Bush administration's proposal was a "knee-jerk reaction" to 9/11, one that would, in the end, do more damage to Americans than the bombers accomplished (O'Harrow 2002).

Legislators such as Leahy were irritated by the DOJ's threats that "we were going to have another attack if we did not agree to this [draft] immediately." He and his staff, joined by other concerned senators, began drafting what turned into a 165-page alternative to the administration's proposal. It was called the "Uniting and Strengthening America" act. However, because of the rapidity of the administration's actions, the alternative legislation was never fully examined to counter the DOJ version.

On September 19, 2001, Ashcroft, Dinh, along with Bush White House counsel Alberto Gonzales, in a joint session with Senate leaders Leahy, Orrin Hatch (R–UT), Richard Shelby (R–AL), and others and House leaders Dick Armey, John Conyers, and others, presented and defended its draft of the Patriot Act. At the same meeting, Leahy handed out a preliminary version of his alternative to the DOJ draft legislation.

While similar in some respects (both dealt with e-mail and Internet messages, for example), the DOJ version clearly went much further in granting expansive powers to the government, such as indefinite detention of noncitizens the attorney general "has reason to believe may further or facilitate acts of terrorism." Also proposed was the unrestricted sharing of grand jury and eavesdropping data throughout the government and the ability of Internet service providers to voluntarily allow the FBI to tap e-mail messages. The FISA language was modified so that foreign-intelligence-gathering was only "a" purpose of wiretapping, not "the" sole purpose.

Section 215 of the DOJ draft greatly expanded the powers of federal investigators to obtain records of suspected terrorists—whether citizens or aliens—from Internet service providers, libraries, hardware stores, bookstores, and almost all other businesses. Furthermore, to the chagrin of Leahy and other legislators, it would remove the requirement that the target of the records search be "an agent of a foreign power."

For the concerned legislators, such changes gave the FBI and the CIA "unchecked access" to the FISA court and threatened to destroy vital individual protections contained in the Constitution's Fourth Amendment, which prohibits "unreasonable" searches and seizures and mandates that law enforcement authorities show "probable cause" to an impartial magistrate before they can obtain a search warrant. Immediately after the conference ended, Leahy said that "there were a lot of people in the room, both Republican and Democrat, who were not about to give the unfettered power the attorney general wanted." He went on, "We're trying to find a middle ground, and I think we can. We probably agree on more than we disagree on. [But] we do not want the terrorists to win by having basic protections taken away from us."

Ashcroft, however, did not want to find the middle ground between security and liberty in the war on terror. There was simply no time for fine-tuning the legislation. After Leahy thrashed out compromises with DOJ surrogates, the attorney general quickly disavowed the "deal" Leahy thought he had struck with the administration. Leahy felt he had been "blind-sided" and said so to Ashcroft in an October 2, 2001 meeting. "I said, 'John, when I make an agreement, I make an agreement. I can't believe you're going back on your commitment'" (O'Harrow 2002).

Ashcroft indirectly responded to Leahy at a press conference held after the bitter meeting. "I think it is time," he said, "for us to be productive on behalf of the American people. Talk won't prevent terrorism." Senator Hatch, standing next to Ashcroft, added: "It's time to get off our duffs and do what's right" (O'Harrow 2002).

By October 12, 2001, both houses of Congress had passed nearly identical antiterrorism bills. The House bill, however, because of Speaker Armey's influence, contained a handful of sunset and court-oversight provisions that Leahy was unable to get through the Senate. The Bush administration very reluctantly agreed to a four-year sunset provision for some sections of the act. After working out the modifications, on October 24–25, 2001, both houses of Congress passed and sent the "clean bill" to the president.

With the sunset and judicial review additions, the ATA bill introduced by Ashcroft and Dinh on September 19, 2001, became the U.S.A. Patriot Act. Only sixty-six representatives voted against the act; only three of the dissenters were Republican Party legislators. The final House vote, on October 24, 2001, was 357–66, with nine representatives not voting. The final Senate vote, taken on October 25, 2001, was even more lopsided: 98–1, with one senator not voting (Mary Landrieu [D–LA]). Senator Russ Feingold (D–WI was the only dissenting vote. He argued that the act contained provisions that "were some of the most radical changes to law enforcement in a generation," specifically pointing to Section 215. On the Senate floor, Feingold spoke out angrily against the act:

> There is no doubt that if we lived in a police state, it would be easier to catch terrorists. If we lived in a country where the police were allowed to search your home at any time for any reason; if we lived in a country where the government was allowed to open your mail, eavesdrop on your phone conversations, or intercept your e-mail communications, ... the government

would probably discover and arrest more terrorists, or would-be terrorists. . . . But that would not be a country in which we would want to live.

In the end, most of the congressional legislators lauded the Patriot Act. Few of their comments reflected the grave concern legislators voiced when Ashcroft presented the DOJ version, the proposed ATA. What follows are some of the comments made by senators and representatives after the votes were cast in their respective chambers:

> "The FBI could get a wiretap to investigate the Mafia, but they could not get one to investigate terrorists. To put it bluntly, that was crazy! What's good for the mob should be good for terrorists."
>
> *—Senator Joe Biden (D–DE)*

> "We simply cannot prevail in the battle against terrorism if the right hand of our government has no idea what the left hand is doing."
>
> *—Senator John Edwards (D–NC)*

> "With the passage of this legislation, terrorist organizations will not be able to move funds as easily and they will not be able to have their people move within our country with bank accounts that we cannot penetrate, with major sources of funding transferred to them from the Middle East or elsewhere to empower them to be able to do the things they did on September 11th."
>
> *—Senator John Kerry (D–MA)*

> "I am most pleased that this bipartisan compromise knocks down current legal barriers that prevent the FBI, the CIA, and other law enforcement officials from sharing information with one another. . . . Our goal must be stopping terrorists . . . rather than wasting time, energy, and resources fighting bureaucratic legal hurdles."
>
> *—House Speaker Dennis Hastert (R–IL)*

> "The attacks of September 11, 2001, marked the beginning of a new era in history. We're at war, and we need to give those who are fighting it the tools they need to win."
>
> *—Representative Joseph Pitts (R–PA)*

"When we are facing a war where it is more likely that more civilians will die than military personnel, the home front is a warfront. The old high wall between foreign intelligence and domestic law enforcement has to be modified. The bill does a good job of that."
— *Senator Chuck Schumer (D–NY)*

Barney Frank (D–MA) was one of the representatives who voted against the Patriot Act. During the final discussion of the bill, just before the House voted, he spoke from the floor about his "deep disappointment in the procedure" followed by the House:

[No] member has been allowed to offer a single amendment. At no point in the debate on this very profound set of issues have we had a procedure whereby the most democratic institution in our government, the House of Representatives, engages in democracy. Who decided that to defend democracy we had to degrade it? Who decided that the very openness and participation and debate and weighing of issues, who decided that there was a defect at a time of crisis? (www.lifeandliberty. gov)

In less than one month's time, the Congress passed and sent to the president an omnibus bill that would enable the government to effectively fight the war against terrorism. It was also a bill that greatly concerned many Americans.

The USA Patriot Act of 2001, October 26, 2001

On October 26, 2001, President Bush signed the USA Patriot Act into law (Public Law 107–56). Addressing the nation on the occasion, he said:

The changes, effective today, will help counter a threat like no other our nation has ever faced. We've seen the enemy. . . . They have no conscience. The terrorists cannot be reasoned with. . . . But one thing is certain. These terrorists must be pursued, they must be defeated, and they must be brought to justice. And that is the purpose of this legislation. . . . We're dealing with terrorists who operate by highly sophisticated methods and technologies, some of which were not even available when our existing laws were written. The bill before me takes account of the new realities and dangers posed by modern terrorists. It will help law enforcement to identify, to dismantle, to disrupt, and to punish terrorists before they strike. . . . This government will enforce this law with all the urgency of a nation at war. The elected branches of our government, and both political parties, are united in our resolve to fight and stop and punish those who would do harm to the American people. (www.whitehouse.gov)

The act has ten sections, or titles, almost all of them reflecting the views of President Bush, Attorney General Ashcroft, and Ashcroft's DOJ subordinates. As passed by the Congress, the Patriot Act:

1. granted federal officials greater powers to trace and intercept terrorists' communications, for both law enforcement and foreign intelligence purposes;
2. reinforced federal anti–money-laundering laws and regulations in an effort to deny terrorists the resources necessary for future attacks;
3. tightened immigration laws to close U.S. borders to foreign terrorists and to expel those thought to be terrorists;
4. created new federal crimes, such as outlawing terrorist attacks on mass transit, and increased penalties for other crimes; and
5. introduced procedural changes in existing statutes, such as a longer statute of limitations for terrorist crimes.

In light of congressional concerns about the intrusion into the civil liberties of those who live in the United States, the act also contains sunset provisions (December 31, 2005) for some—but not all—of the controversial wiretapping and foreign intelligence amendments in the legislation. Because of the efforts of Leahy, Armey, and other legislators, the act includes as well judicial safeguards for the monitoring of e-mail and grand jury disclosures. As discussed in Chapter Three, however, while there are some sunset safeguards built into the act, critics maintain that the

Patriot Act's provisions still go too far in encroaching on the civil liberties of all persons living in the United States.

In summary fashion (excerpts from the USA Patriot Act are found in Chapter Six), the ten titles of the act are:

Title I. Enhancing Domestic Security Against Terrorism. This section creates a counterterrorism fund and provides increased funding to the FBI for the enhancement of its technical support center. It also broadens the attorney general's authority to request assistance of the secretary of defense and the DoD in emergency situations involving weapons of mass destruction. Part 106 grants the president the power to confiscate and take possession of property when the United States is engaged in military activities and enables courts to consider classified evidence, without making it public, in lawsuits that challenge the government's seizure of property.

Title II. Enhanced Surveillance Procedures. The second section provides federal agencies with authority to intercept wire, oral, and electronic communications relating to terrorism or relating to computer fraud and abuse offenses; share criminal investigation information; employ translators; seize voice-mail messages pursuant to a warrant; issue subpoenas for records of electronic communications; delay notice of the execution of a warrant (sneak and peek), and the authority to serve, nationwide, search warrants for electronic surveillance. Additionally, the 1978 FISA was changed to enable closer wiretap and other electronic coverage by the FBI of suspected terrorists. The sharing, among federal agencies, of wiretap information, secret grand jury testimony regarding foreign intelligence and counterintelligence, is also permitted in this section.

Title III. International Money Laundering Abatement and Anti-Terrorist Financing Act of 2001. Financing terrorist activities is a central problem the government had to end in order to limit the terrorists' war against America. This money-laundering section provides governmental agencies, especially the U.S. Department of the Treasury (Subtitle A), with powers to maintain long-term jurisdiction over foreign money matters as well as to oversee correspondent activities and private banking accounts in order to deter money laundering. Subtitle B, the Bank Secrecy Act Amendments and Related Improvements, makes it easier for federal agencies to examine and report "suspicious activities" by securities brokers and dealers and by "underground banking systems" and to create more pervasive anti–money-laundering schemes. Subtitle C, "currency crimes and protection," is an effort to address the problem of bulk cash smuggling into and out of the United States by terrorist cells in their effort to wage terrorist war against U.S. citizens.

Title IV. Protecting the Border. In order to protect the nation against the threat of terrorists who enter the country, this title triples the number of Border Patrol personnel and provides the Department of State and the INS access to certain identifying information in the criminal history records of visa applicants and applicants for admission to the United States. Subtitle B enhances the powers of the INS and other federal agencies, including the Office of Homeland Security, to impose mandatory detentions for suspected terrorists without giving them due process rights. Foreign students are also monitored under this subtitle. The attorney general is required to detain aliens whom he certifies as threats to national security. The definition of terrorist activity is broadened to include all dangerous devices in addition to firearms and explosives.

Title V. Removing Obstacles to Investigating Terrorism. Under this title the DOJ and the Department of State are authorized to pay rewards to combat terrorism. The jurisdiction of the Secret Service is extended to investigate offenses against government computers, and the FBI can apply for an ex parte court order to obtain educational records that are relevant to an authorized investigation or prosecution of a grave felony or an act of domestic or international terrorism.

Title VI. Providing for Victims of Terrorism, Public Safety Officers, and Their Families. Among other things, this section adds amendments to the Victims of Crime Act of 1984 by establishing a crime victims fund, setting compensation guidelines, and providing assistance to crime victims and victims of terrorist activities.

Title VII. Increased Information Sharing for Critical Infrastructure Protection. This portion of the act expands the regional information-sharing system to facilitate federal-state-local law enforcement responses related to terrorist attacks.

Title VIII. Strengthening the Criminal Laws Against Terrorism. This section of the Patriot Act defines domestic terrorism, terrorist attacks, cyberterrorism, and other acts of violence against mass transportation systems. It also prohibits any person from harboring aliens or those engaged in sabotage against the United States and from providing "material support" to individuals and organizations that commit terrorist crimes. A separate offense created by this act punishes those persons harboring terrorists— Americans or foreigners. This title also provides for extraterritorial jurisdiction to cover terrorist actions committed against U.S. facilities abroad. This section enables the U.S. government to seize the assets of all foreign terrorist organizations. Finally, the section underscores the severity of terrorist actions with harsh penalties for terrorist conspiracies.

Title IX. Improved Intelligence. This section of the Patriot Act expands the responsibilities of the director of the CIA regarding foreign intelligence collected under the FISA of 1978. Amending the National Security Act of 1947, this title requires the CIA director to assist the attorney general in the generation and dissemination of information regarding terrorism. It also creates the Foreign Terrorist Asset Tracking Center and the National Virtual Translation Center and provides for the training of governmental officials regarding identification and use of foreign intelligence.

Title X. Miscellaneous. This section includes creation of an independent oversight review agency, within the Department of Justice, for the FBI as well as other definitions and clarification of terms used in the act

A Legal Analysis of the USA Patriot Act of 2001 by the Congressional Research Service (CRS)

"Restrictions on intelligence gathering within the United States *mirror American abhorrence of the creation of a secret police,* coupled with memories of intelligence gathering practices during the Vietnam conflict which some felt threatened to chill robust public debate" (my emphasis). This was not part of the Feingold speech given on the Senate floor the day of the 98–1 Senate vote. These words were part of an independent governmental report written less than one year after the Patriot Act was signed into law.

In April, 2002 the Congressional Research Service (CRS) of the Library of Congress published its report for Congress analyzing the Patriot Act. Authored by Charles Doyle, a senior specialist in the American Law Division of the Library of Congress,

"The U.S.A. Patriot Act: A Legal Analysis" was a seventy-five-page examination of the controversial legislation prepared because Senator Leahy and other critics "suggested that [the Patriot Act] may go too far . . . [and that many of its] features are troubling to some." Doyle noted:

> The Act itself responds to some of these reservations. Many of the wiretapping and foreign intelligence amendments sunset on December 31, 2005. The Act creates judicial safeguards for e-mail monitoring and grand jury disclosures; recognizes innocent owner defenses to forfeiture; and entrusts anti–money laundering powers to those regulatory authorities whose concerns include the well being of our financial institutions. (3)

However, because of the continuing legislative concerns as well as the chorus of protest from civil rights groups, domestic and international alike, the legal analysis was undertaken.

The analysis consists of five detailed sections that contain the central features of the Patriot Act: criminal investigations, foreign intelligence investigations, money laundering, alien terrorists and victims, and other crimes, penalties, and procedures. Each section examines the prior laws dealing with the subject and how the Patriot Act modifies, changes, or adds to the legislative record; it also indicates the various provisions built into the act to protect U.S. citizens and legal aliens residing in the United States.

Each of the sections is also a functional assessment of the major governmental powers granted by the act. For example, in discussing criminal investigations, the report examines the portions of all ten titles that touch on the subject matter. For the most part, the report tends to minimize the act's threats to the civil liberties of legitimate businesses, ordinary citizens, and resident aliens.

"Criminal Investigations: Tracking and Gathering Communications" is the first substantive segment of the report. In the U.S. criminal justice system, there is a three-tier system "erected for the dual purpose of protecting the confidentiality of private telephone, face-to-face, and computer communications while enabling authorities to identify and intercept criminal communications."

The highest tier is the Fourth Amendment itself, as inter-preted by the U.S. Supreme Court along with legislative actions taken in concert with Supreme Court decisions, especially Title III of the Omnibus Crime Control and Safe Streets Act of 1968. Court orders issued under Title III must contain instructions describing the permissible duration and scope of surveillance as well as the conversations that may legally be seized.

The second tier of privacy protections covers some of the matters the Supreme Court "has described as beyond the reach of the Fourth Amendment protection—telephone records, e-mail held in third party storage, and the like." Federal laws permit law enforcement access, via use of a warrant or court order, in connection with any criminal investigation but without the "extraordinary levels of approval and constraint that mark a Title III interception" (5).

The lowest tier of privacy protection is the procedure that governs court orders approving the government's use of trap-and-trace and pen register devices. (These electronic aids are "a kind of secret 'caller-id,' which identify the source and destina-tion of calls made to and from a particular telephone." A pen reg-ister collects outgoing phone numbers placed from a specific phone line while a trap-and-trace device captures the incoming phone numbers placed to a specific phone line.) The court order is available when the government certifies—not when a court notes probable cause—that there are "reasonable grounds" to believe that the use of the device is likely to produce information relevant to the investigation of any crime.

According to the CRS report, the Patriot Act modifies the procedures in each of these three tiers of existing privacy protec-tions in the following ways:

- The act permits trap-and-trace and pen register orders for electronic communications (e-mail, cable company customer records, etc.). (See Sections 126, 209, 210, 216, 220.)
- It authorizes nationwide execution of court orders for use of the devices.
- It treats stored voice mail akin to stored e-mail commu-nications.
- It adds terrorist, production/distribution of chemical weapons, and computer crimes to Title III's "predicate

offense" list. (See Section 201 [cybercrime], 202.) Terrorist crimes include use of chemical weapons, acts of violence committed against Americans abroad, use of weapons of mass destruction (WMD), terrorist acts transcending national boundaries, financial transactions with countries that support terrorists, providing material support to terrorists and/or terrorist organizations.

- The act encourages cooperation between law enforcement and foreign intelligence investigators. (See Section 218.)
- It terminates the authority of many of these changes in several ways: (1) Disciplinary action is possible when government officials intentionally violate proscriptions of Title III (see Section 121, 223), and there is asunset clause safeguard (Section 224). (2) There are protections for service providers who assist government investigators to track and gather communications information. (See Sections 212, 222, 815.)

As already noted, until passage of the Patriot Act of 2001, criminal investigations and foreign intelligence investigations were separated by law. The former seek information about unlawful activity, while the latter capture data about other countries and their citizens. According to Doyle in the part of the CRS report entitled "Foreign Intelligence Investigations," "Foreign intelligence is not limited to criminal, hostile, or even governmental activity. Simply being foreign is enough."

However, existing legislation did not ban foreign intelligence gathering in the United States. In 1978 Congress passed the FISA, "something of a Title III for foreign intelligence wiretapping conducted in this country, after the Supreme Court made it clear that the President's authority to see to national security was insufficient to excuse warrantless wiretapping of suspected terrorists who had no identifiable foreign connections." FISA was directed at foreign governments, international terrorists, and their agents, spies, and saboteurs.

The Patriot Act eases some of the FISA restrictions on foreign intelligence gathering. As well, it allows the intelligence community (the CIA, for example) greater access to information gathered during a criminal investigation by the FBI or other domestic criminal investigation agencies. In addition to expanding governmental authority, the act "establishes and expands safeguards against official abuse," concluded Doyle in this section of the CRS report.

Specifically, in the foreign-intelligence-gathering sections, the act:

- Permits "roving" surveillance and the sharing of information between governmental agencies such as the FBI and the CIA. A roving wiretap allows the interception of any communication made to or by an intelligence target without specifying the particular phone line, computer, or other device to be monitored. (See Sections 203, 358, 905, 907.)
- Increases the number of FISA judges from seven to eleven. (See Section 208.)
- Allows FISA orders when gathering foreign intelligence is "a significant reason" for the application rather than "the reason."
- Permits tracking and tracing of e-mail as well as telephone conversations. (See Section 214, 505.)
- Carries a sunset provision.
- Expands the prohibition against FISA orders based solely on an American's exercise of First Amendment rights. (See Section 214.)
- Establishes a claim against the United States for privacy violations by government personnel.

The third segment of the CRS report examined another important aspect of America's war against terrorism, money laundering. Existing statutes had defined money laundering as actions involving "the flow of cash or other valuables derived from, or intended to facilitate, the commission of a criminal offense." Federal authorities, under existing statutes, battled money laundering through (1) U.S. Treasury Department regulations, (2) international cooperation, (3) criminal sanctions, and (4) forfeiture. The passage of the Patriot Act, said the CRS report, "bolsters federal efforts in each area."

Treasury Department regulations imposed reporting and record-keeping standards on all financial institutions, especially with regard to anti–money-laundering matters. Legislation such as the Currency and Financial Transaction Reporting Act and the Bank Secrecy Act contained these reporting standards that institutions had to follow. Sections 321, 351, 355, 356, and 357 of the

Patriot Act expands the authority of the secretary of the treasury over these reporting requirements.

The act also establishes other regulatory mechanisms "directed at the activities involving U.S. financial institutions and foreign individuals or institutions." (See Sections 313, 325, and 326.) Section 314 encourages financial institutions and law enforcement agencies "to share information concerning suspected money-laundering and terrorist activities," while Section 319 (b) requires financial institutions to provide governmental agencies with anti–money-laundering records (within 120 hours) and/or records concerning foreign deposits (within seven days).

International cooperation involves the strengthening of U.S. capability to trace money transfers to the United States from abroad. The act (in Section 328) instructs the secretary of the treasury, the secretary of state, and the U.S. attorney general to "make every effort" to encourage foreign nations to require identification of the originator of international wire transfers. Section 330 expresses the sense of Congress that the administration seek to negotiate international treaties and conventions that would enable U.S. law enforcement officials to track the financial activities of foreign terrorist organizations, money launderers, and other criminals.

The Patriot Act as passed contained a number of new money-laundering crimes as well as modifications and increased penalties for existing crimes. The newly added predicate offenses, contained in Section 315, include crimes in violation of the laws of other nations when the proceeds are involved in foreign transactions in this country, crimes of violence, public corruption, smuggling, and offenses condemned in treaties to which the United States was a party. This section was added, in the words of a House committee report, "to send a strong signal that the United States will not tolerate the use of its financial institutions for the purpose of laundering the proceeds of foreign crimes" (Doyle 2002, 4). Other sections, 374 and 375, of the act increased the penalties for counterfeiting.

Forfeiture is "government confiscation of property as a consequence of a crime." Under the 1997 International Emergency Economic Powers Act (IEEPA), as modified by Section 106 of the Patriot Act, the president or the president's delegate may confiscate and dispose of any property "within the jurisdiction of the United States, belonging to any foreign national, foreign entity, or foreign country whom they determine to have planned, authorized, aided, or engaged in an attack on the United States by a foreign country or foreign nationals." Under Section 806 of the act, the government is authorized to confiscate all property, regardless of where it is found, of any individual, entity, or organization engaged in domestic or international terrorism against the United States, Americans, or their property. If the governmental action is subject to judicial review, the Patriot Act allows the government to present, secretly (ex parte and in camera), classified information upon which the forfeiture was based (see Section 106). However, under Section 316, property owners may institute a challenge to a confiscation by filing a claim under applicable rules.

Neither Section 106 nor 806 "require[s] conviction of the terrorist property owner. Both call for forfeiture of the terrorist's property, without requiring any nexus to the terrorist's offenses other than terrorist ownership." In a word, both are punitive measures. However "broad the President's war powers may be," observed Doyle, "they would hardly seem to provide a justification for Section 806, which embraces domestic terrorism and is neither limited to foreign offenders nor predicated upon war-like hostilities. . . . These forfeiture sections," he concluded, "all raise constitutional points of interest."

"Alien Terrorists" is the fourth segment of the CRS report. One of the central concerns of the Bush administration was the entry into the United States of alien terrorists, particularly through Canada. The Patriot Act was intended to prevent that from occurring as well as to grant government officials the authority to detain and deport suspected alien terrorists and those who support them. Sections of the act provided increased border protection and much stronger detention and removal powers for INS agents.

Border protection provisions, in part, included:

- Tripling the number of Border Patrol, Customs Service, and INS personnel stationed along the border with Canada. (See Section 401.)
- Funds for upgrading border surveillance equipment. (See Section 402.)
- Funds for the INS and the State Department to create a criminal record identification information system relating to visa applications for admission to the United States. (See Section 403.)

- Expansion of the student visa monitoring program. (See Section 416.)
- Authorization for the sharing of the State Department's visa lookout data and related information with other nations to prevent terrorism, drug trafficking, slave marketing, and gun running. (See Section 413.)

Detention of suspected alien terrorists (or alien seditionists) by the attorney general, for up to seven days without any charges, was a new power given to the government in Section 412 of the Patriot Act. Within that time, the DOJ must initiate removal or criminal proceedings or release the alien.

The Patriot Act also contained provisions for stronger governmental denial, detention, and deportation powers applicable to foreign nationals. Section 411 added three categories to the existing terrorism-related grounds for denial of admission of aliens to the United States:

1. espousing terrorist activity,
2. being the spouse or child of an inadmissible alien associated with a terrorist organization, and
3. intending to engage in activities "that could endanger the welfare, safety, or security of the United States."

"Other Crimes, Penalties, and Procedures" is the last segment of the CRS assessment of the Patriot Act. It describes new crimes the act created for

- terrorist attacks on mass transportation facilities (Section 801);
- biological weapons offenses (Section 817);
- harboring terrorists (Section 803);
- affording terrorists material support and misconduct associated with money-laundering schemes (Section 805);
- running a business engaged in interstate commerce that supports the commission of terrorist acts (Section 813); and
- fraudulent charitable solicitations (that are allegedly used to support terrorist activities in the United States and elsewhere) (Section 1011).

These new crimes "generally supplement existing law, filling gaps and increasing penalties," concluded the CRS report. Accompanying them in the Patriot Act were the sections that provided increased maximum penalties for the commission or conspiracy to commit these new crimes (see Sections 810, 811, and 814).

In this last segment the CRS report examined other "procedural adjustments" designed to facilitate criminal investigations. These adjustments included the highly controversial Section 213 authorizing governmental investigators to use sneak-and-peek search warrants, which enable government agents to "secretly enter—physically or virtually—conduct a search, observe, take measurements, conduct examinations, smell, take pictures, copy documents, download or transmit computer files, etc., and depart without taking any tangible evidence or leaving notice of their presence."

This "adjustment" concerned Doyle. The Fourth Amendment, he wrote, "clearly requires officers to knock and announce their purpose before entering to execute a warrant, but with equal clarity recognizes exceptions for exigent circumstances such as where compliance will lead to destruction of evidence, flight of a suspect, or endanger the officers." However, he concluded that, legally, based on federal court opinions, "there is no doubt that the Fourth Amendment imposes no demands where it does not apply."

Another controversial "adjustment" is found in Section 219 of the Patriot Act. That section allows a "neutral magistrate" to issue a search warrant "to be executed *within or outside the district* [in which a crime of terrorism has occurred] in domestic and international terrorism cases" (my emphasis). Furthermore, the act (Section 503) authorizes the attorney general to collect DNA samples from prisoners convicted of any crime of violence or terrorism.

Ashcroft and Dinh, in their Antiterrorism Act draft, had an adjustment that would have eliminated the statute of limitations in *all* terrorism cases. "The Act takes less dramatic action in Section 809," observed Doyle's report. That section eliminates the statute of limitations for any crime of terrorism that risks or results in a death or serious bodily injury. Absent these criteria, all terrorism offenses become subject to the eight-year statute of limitations unless already covered by the ten-year statute for explosive and arson offenses.

However comforting the CRS report on the USA Patriot Act may have been to apprehensive legislators, there has been a continuing firestorm of protest by civil liberties organizations against the USA Patriot Act of 2001 ever since its passage. "Before the ink was dry on the Patriot Act," pressure group spokespersons from both the right and left ends of the political spectrum had First, Fourth, Fifth, Sixth, and Tenth Amendment objections to it. Additionally, for the critics, the USA Patriot Act "breaks down the wall of separation between intelligence and criminal investigations" (Lichtblau 2003, 1).

Before the ink was dry, Attorney General Ashcroft and the DOJ took actions to implement the legislation, including guidelines for the ninety-four U.S. Attorney's Offices and the fifty-six FBI field offices "directing them to begin immediately implementing this sweeping legislation." By November 5, 2001, less than two months after 9/11, the DOJ had under secret detention 1,147 persons, most of them of Arab or South Asian origin. (Many of them remained under detention as of May 2004.)

Since President Bush signed the USA Patriot Act in October 2001, there have been eleven executive orders issued and ten new interim federal agency regulations and two final sets published and implemented. Also, as mentioned earlier, the Office of Homeland Security, created by the president after 9/11, was elevated to Cabinet-level status in November 2002. Clearly, the federal government has been extremely busy in the effort to minimize the threat of terrorism against Americans.

The next chapter presents and analyzes the arguments against the 2001 Patriot Act that came to light in October 2001 and are still being argued today.

For Further Reading

Beale, Jon, and Eric Felman. "The Consequences of Enlisting Federal Grand Juries in the War on Terrorism: Assessing the USA Patriot Act's Changes to Grand Jury Secrecy." 25 *Harvard Journal of Law and Public Policy*, 699, Fall 2002.

Best, D. *Intelligence and Law Enforcement: Countering Transnational Threats to the U.S.* CRS Report No. RL 30252, December 5, 2001. Washington, D.C.: GPO, 2001.

Cole, David. "Enemy Aliens." 54 *Stanford Law Review,* 953, 2002.

Doyle, Charles. "The U.S.A. Patriot Act: A Legal Analysis." Congressional Research Service (CRS) of the Library of Congress, April 2002.

House Committee on the Judiciary. *Bush Administration Draft Anti-Terrorism Act of 2001: Hearing Before the House of Representatives Committee on the Judiciary*, 107th Congress, 1st session, September 20, 2001.

Joo, Thomas. "Presumed Disloyal: Executive Power, Judicial Deference, and the Construction of Race Before and After September 11." 34 *Columbia University Human Rights Law Journal*, 1, 2002.

Kerr, Orrin S. "Internet Surveillance Law After the Patriot Act: The Big Brother That Isn't." 97 *Northwestern University Law Review*, 1, 2003.

Lichtblau, Eric. "U.S. Uses Terror Law to Pursue Crimes from Drugs to Swindling." *New York Times*, September 27, 2003, A1, 14.

O'Harrow, Robert Jr., "Six Weeks in Autumn," *The Washington Post*, October 27, 2002, 14–20.

Podesta, John. "Bush's Secret Government." *American Prospect*, September 2003.

Posner, Gerald. *Why America Slept: The Failure to Prevent 9/11*. New York: Random House, 2003.

White, Jonathan R. *Terrorism: An Introduction*. Belmont, CA: Wadsworth/Thomson Learning, 2003.

3

The Critics of the 2001 Patriot Act: Civil Liberties Endangered by the Imperatives of National Security

"Those who would give up essential liberties to purchase a little temporary safety, deserve neither liberty nor safety."

Benjamin Franklin, An Historical Review of the Constitution and Government of Pennsylvania, 1759

"This Administration is using fear as a political tool."

Al Gore, November 9, 2003

Shortly after 9/11, the FBI arrested as a "material witness" a San Antonio, Texas, radiologist, Albader Al-Hazmi, who had a name similar to two of the 9/11 hijackers and who had tried to book a flight to San Diego for a medical conference. The FBI held the radiologist incommunicado for six days before his lawyers could get access to him. He was finally released after a few more days. After his release, Al-Hazmi's lawyer said, "This is a good lesson about how frail our processes are. It's how we treat people in difficult times like these that is the true test of the democracy and civil liberties that we brag so much about throughout the world" (Feinstein 2001). On the Senate floor, Senator Russ Feingold spoke about the incident, one of many hundreds that occurred after 9/11:

As it seeks to combat terrorism, the Justice Department is making extraordinary use of its power to arrest and detain individuals, jailing hundreds of people on immigration violations and arresting more than one dozen "material witnesses" not charged with any crime. . . . The government has not brought any criminal charges related to the attacks with regard to the overwhelming majority of these detainess.

These comments reflect the concern of a host of organizations about the adverse impact of the Patriot Act on the freedoms and civil liberties of persons residing in the United States—citizens and aliens alike. The Bush administration maintains that the FBI and all other federal agencies involved in homeland and national security must have these "extraordinary" powers in order to destroy terrorists.

When, on October 26, 2001, President George W. Bush signed the Patriot Act, he stated that the purpose of the legislation was the pursuit, the defeat, and the bringing to justice of the terrorists who declared war on the United States. His message was a reflection of the new national security policy: preventive action against U.S. enemies.

U.S. Attorney General John Ashcroft, speaking one day earlier at the annual U.S. Mayors Conference, was even more direct—and more aggressive. On September 11, he said, "A turning point was reached . . . in the administration of justice. The fight against terrorism is now the first and overriding priority of the Department of Justice. But our war against terrorism is not merely or primarily a criminal justice endeavor—our battle is the defense of our nation and its citizens." Ashcroft compared the war against terrorism with another attorney general's confrontation "with a different enemy within our borders":

> Robert F. Kennedy came to the Department of Justice at a time when organized crime was threatening the very foundations of the republic. . . . Then, as now, the enemy that America faced was described bluntly—and correctly—as a conspiracy of evil. Then, as now, the enemy was well-financed, expertly organized and international in scope. Then, as now, its operations were hidden under a code of deadly silence.

Ashcroft then said that just as Kennedy did four decades earlier in his war against the Mafia, the Bush administration has "launched an extraordinary campaign against [terrorists]." And

Ashcroft's Justice Department, like Kennedy's, is "directed toward one overarching goal: to identify, disrupt, and dismantle the enemy."

> Attorney General Kennedy made no apologies for using all of the available resources in the law to disrupt and dismantle organized crime networks. . . . Kennedy's Justice Department, it is said, would arrest mobsters for "spitting on the sidewalk" if it would help in the battle against organized crime. It has been and will be the policy of this Department of Justice to use the same aggressive arrest and detention tactics in the war on terror. Let the terrorists among us be warned. . . . We will seek every prosecutorial advantage. We will use all our weapons within the law and under the Constitution to protect life and enhance security for America.

The Bush administration's offensive against terrorism is reflected in the 2001 Patriot Act. The legislation, said the attorney general, "embodies two over-arching principles: The first principle is airtight surveillance of terrorists." Once the act was signed into law, Ashcroft said before the event,

> I will direct investigators and prosecutors to begin immediately seeking court orders to intercept communications related to an expanded list of crimes under the legislation. . . . Agents will be directed to take advantage of new, technologically neutral standards for intelligence gathering. . . .
> Investigators will be directed to pursue aggressively terrorists on the internet.

The second principle Ashcroft named "is speed in tracking down and intercepting terrorists." As soon as possible, Ashcroft told the mayors, "law enforcement will begin to employ new tools that ease administrative burdens and delays in apprehending terrorists."

Finally, regarding the perennial and quintessential question of civil liberties versus homeland security, Ashcroft said:

> Some will ask whether a civilized nation—a nation of law and not of men—can use the law to defend itself from barbarians and remain civilized. Our answer, unequivocally, is "yes." Yes, we will defend civilization,

and yes, we will preserve the rule of law because it makes us civilized. . . . Terrorists live in the shadows, under the cover of darkness. We will shine the light of justice on them. Americans alive today and yet to be born and freedom-loving people everywhere will have new reason to hope because our enemies now have new reason to fear.

At the heart of the actions of the president and his advisors is an executive branch understanding of justice, one assumed by chief executives in U.S. history since George Washington and John Adams. In time of danger to the nation, imminent or otherwise, the president acts on the basis of the concept of preventive justice. In so acting, the administration diminishes the constitutionally mandated concept of criminal justice. In replacing the notion of due process with the concept of preventive justice, secrecy replaces transparency, and administrative proceedings replace criminal proceedings. As a consequence, the liberties outlined in the Constitution and the Bill of Rights are lost.

As early as the passage and signing of the Enemy Alien Act of 1798, to the passage of the Alien Registration Act of 1940, to the Patriot Act of 2001, persons in the United States have been arrested for what they say and for their association with organizations or nations perceived to be enemies of the United States. This is the essence of the concept of preventive justice: Use the latest technology, identify "suspected enemies/terrorists," arrest them for suspicion of "materially supporting" the enemy (the language of the Patriot Act), detain them without the aid of lawyers, and deport them in secret hearings closed to the public if the suspected enemies are illegal aliens or, if they are not, hold them in detention indefinitely without filing charges against them (Cole 2003, 14–15).

Needless to say, as soon as President Bush signed the 2001 Patriot Act, critics condemned the legislation, arguing that the Bush administration, like earlier administrations in their efforts to overcome enemies of the state, was aggressively undermining the very foundations of a democratic political system. For these critics, Ashcroft's utterance that the government "will seek every prosecutorial advantage" and "will use all our weapons within the law and under the Constitution to protect life and enhance security for America" contained a very frightening message: Civil liberties are in great jeopardy.

Former vice-president Al Gore (1993–2001), the Democratic candidate for president in the controversial, contested 2000 presidential election, for one, categorically disagreed with both Bush and Ashcroft. In a speech delivered at Constitution Hall in Washington, D.C., on November 9, 2003, Gore clearly presented the case against the Bush administration and the 2001 Patriot Act:

> The true relationship between freedom and security may be the most important issue we face today as a people. The Bush Administration's implicit assumption [seen in the 2001 Patriot Act] is that we have to sacrifice traditional freedoms in order to be safe from terrorists. This is simply untrue. It makes no more sense to launch an assault on civil liberties in order to get at terrorists, than it did to launch an invasion of Iraq in order to get Osama Bin Laden.

The Patriot Act of 2001, Gore exclaimed, was the Bush administration's weapon of choice in its assault on American freedoms and the concept of liberty.

> Under the Patriot Act, federal agents have been given authority to secretly enter your home and search it, even when there is no connection to terrorism. And for the first time in our history, American citizens have been seized and imprisoned indefinitely, with no charges filed and no right to a trial, or even to see a lawyer. . . . And just this month, Ashcroft issued new guidelines, permitting FBI agents to run credit and background checks on anyone of "investigatory interest," without any evidence of criminal behavior, let alone terrorism. (Doty 2003)

These are comments made by three patriotic men. The words of President Bush, Attorney General Ashcroft, and former vice-president Gore place the following two sections of this chapter into sharp focus.

For the first two men, defeating terrorists requires aggressive, no-nonsense actions of federal, state, and local law enforcement authorities—as well as vigilance on the part of the general public. (Ashcroft in 2003 announced a new program involving civilians. It was labeled Operation TIPS and called for ordinary persons to report to federal authorities "suspicious activities" of their neighbors and friends. The ensuing firestorm of protest against TIPS forced Ashcroft to quickly cancel the program.)

For Gore and critics of antiterrorism programs and statutes created after 9/11, these governmental actions are, noted Gore, "terrible mistakes." The Patriot Act contains serious errors that flaunt "the rule of law as embodied in our Constitution. . . . The Patriot Act must be repealed. . . . Our choice is clear" (quoted in Doty 2003).

The Critics of the Patriot Act

As was the case after the passage of the 1996 antiterrorism legislation, immediately after passage of the 2001 Patriot Act hundreds of pressure groups condemned the law because of its capacity to diminish civil liberties protections in the name of national security against terrorism.

However, it was not only groups that rose up in arms after passage of the law. Legislators, individuals, the press, even the Inspector General's Office within the Department of Justice and local communities issued reports, appeared before congressional committees, and took other actions that expressed their grave concern about the Patriot Act's potential to diminish the civil rights and liberties of all Americans. Given the past record in American history, these critics were not sanguine about the future of civil liberties in the new age of asymmetrical warfare against terrorists.

A number of the organizations opposed to the 2001 Patriot Act and other actions of the Bush administration asked federal courts to review these statutes' constitutionality as well as the behavior of federal administrators in the war on terror. By the middle of 2003, a number of federal appeals courts issued rulings that blunted the aggressive efforts of the Bush administration. Also, in November 2003, the U.S. Supreme Court took a number of cases that raise an important jurisdictional question, one that may ultimately pit the executive branch against the federal judiciary. It heard oral arguments in April 2004; decisions were expected sometime in late June 2004.

Interest Groups and Organizations

Among the groups that saw the 2001 Patriot Act as a serious threat to civil liberties were everything from business and technology organizations to social action groups, including some very conservative, libertarian groups. Many that had almost nothing in common with each other in the past became "strange bedfellows" (Tomasky 2003, 47ff.).

In late June 2003, for example, Laura Murphy, the director of the Washington, D.C., legislative office of the American Civil Liberties Union (ACLU), met with Bob Barr, the former conservative Republican congressman from Georgia. Barr, who holds the Twenty-First-Century Liberties Chair at the American Conservative Union (ACU), joined Murphy in Houston, Texas, in order for the two of them to convince the conservative editorial board of the *Houston Chronicle* of the "potential dangers" of the Patriot Act.

The two were successful. On July 11, 2003, the *Chronicle* ran the editorial "Heightened Alert: Increased Government Intrusion Is Not Patriotic." It read in part:

> U.S. Attorney General John Ashcroft and other Justice Department officials assure Americans that their liberties and privacy are not in jeopardy. They say the antiterrorist Patriot Act passed after 9/11 does not apply to American citizens. Ashcroft is wrong, and he knows he is wrong. In the alternative, he lacks the reading comprehension and legal skills required for his office. . . . It doesn't make sense for the U.S. government to endanger [our] freedom in the name of the war on terrorism. (17)

Barr's participation in the attacks on the Patriot Act is fascinating because as a congressman he voted for the act in October 2001 (as did all but three Republicans in Congress). He now admits that his vote was a mistake: "The [Bush] Administration has not at all been forthcoming since then in explaining in a clear and open way how that act would be used and is being used. The lack of being forthcoming about discussing that has bothered me" (quoted in Tomasky 2003).

He has been joined by other conservatives in and out of Congress who have openly expressed concern about the loss of liberties as government agencies begin to implement the Patriot Act. Some of these are Dick Armey; Grover Norquist; Phyllis Schlafly; Timothy Lynch, director of the conservative think-tank Cato Institute; and the American Conservative Union's David Keene. Conservative Republican congressman Don Young (R–AK), who also voted for the act, afterward called it "the worst piece of legislation we've ever passed. It was what you call *emotional voting*" (Tomasky 2003).

In November 2001 the Federalist Society, a prominent conservative organization, published a white paper, "The USA PATRIOT Act of 2001 Criminal Procedure Sections." (Shortly thereafter the Federalist Society published another white paper on "the most important changes related" to the laws on wiretapping and surveillance.) The report focused on "significant changes to criminal procedure" in the act, specifically, sections of Title II (sharing of grand jury information, sneak-and-peek warrants, nationwide search warrants); Title IV (changes in the INS statute that now requires the attorney general to take into custody aliens, as well as limiting judicial review in such actions); Title V (expansion of the law allowing collection of DNA samples from federal prisoners convicted of violent crimes from murder, rape, kidnapping, and burglary to terrorism, sabotage, and assassination); and Title VIII (which expands U.S. maritime and territorial jurisdiction and extends the statute of limitations for certain terrorist actions).

The Federalist Society, along with other conservative, libertarian groups, concluded that some of the provisions "do raise constitutional issues" that will have to be examined by the federal courts. In particular, the paper zeroed in on the "indefinite detention" and "evidentiary" standards for detaining aliens, found in Section 412. Also of concern to the authors of the white paper was the authority given to the attorney general and "how much deference must be paid to the Attorney General's conclusion that he has reasonable grounds to believe that an alien is a terrorist" (Strossen 2003, 3, 12–14).

It is less surprising that liberal social action groups such as the National Association for the Advancement of Colored People (NAACP) and the ACLU have been critical of the Patriot Act. In a recent essay in *Crisis* (the monthly journal published by the NAACP since 1910), "The Color Line: Watch Out America, the White House Is Seeking to Expand the Patriot Act," the author pointed out that

> the arguments used to justify the FBI's harassment and intimidation of African Americans during the Civil Rights Movement are disturbingly similar to those put forward to justify post–September 11 antiterrorism policies that today erode basic civil liberties in the pursuit of

national security. Both eras illustrate the ease with which our freedoms and civil rights can be usurped under the banner of national security. . . . That threats of terrorism are being misused to justify the registration, monitoring, arrest and deportation of people based on the color of their skin or the nature of their faith, should be of direct concern to African Americans when considering the impact of these post–September 11 security measures. (Edgar 2003, 7)

The ACLU has been in the vanguard of critics of the 2001 Patriot Act. Nadine Strossen, the national organization's president, recently wrote:

New immigration regulations and tracking laws, applied almost exclusively to immigrants from largely Muslim countries, treat certain groups as separate and quasi-criminal elements of society, without making us safer, as terrorists will find ways to circumvent them. . . . Terrorists are hardly likely to report to the Bureau of Citizenship and Immigration Services (BCIS) as the INS was renamed after its absorption into the Department of Homeland Security (DHS). (Strossen 2003, 2, 10)

The ACLU has focused extensively on the mistreatment of aliens by the Department of Justice. The organization has testified before the Judiciary Committees in both houses of Congress, has worked with other organizations to educate media leaders about the serious danger to civil liberty posed by the act, and has also gone to federal court to challenge some of the provisions of the act. Strossen (quoting from the DOJ inspector general's internal report about the agency's implementation of the Patriot Act) often talks of the "indiscriminate and haphazard" rounding-up of immigrants as terror suspects. The Bush administration, she argues constantly, "has made immigrants a proxy for terrorists—threatening to turn the war on terrorists into a war on immigrants" (www.aclu.org/safeandfree/cfm).

On July 30, 2003, the ACLU filed the first constitutional challenge to the USA Patriot Act. Lawyers for the Michigan ACLU affiliate went into a U.S. district court in Detroit, arguing that Section 215 of the Patriot Act violated the Constitution. That section of Title II allows the FBI to order any organization to turn over tangible thing" as long as the FBI claims that it is "sought ʌ" an ongoing foreign intelligence or terrorism investigation. For the ACLU, this section

> gives the government access to all sorts of extremely personal information, including medical records, e-mails, library records, bookstore purchases and even genetic information. There is almost no limit to the kinds of information the FBI can access. . . . There are few safeguards in the law. Section 215 doesn't require the FBI to have 'probable cause'—or even to believe that its surveillance target is engaged in criminal activity, terrorism, or espionage (www.aclu.org/safeandfree/cfm).

The lawsuit charges that the section violates both the First and the Fourth Amendments of the Bill of Rights. It breaches the First Amendment in two ways: (1) The FBI can investigate individuals based on the exercise of their freedom of speech, free association, and freedom of religion; and (2) it prohibits any person from telling another person that the FBI has sought records or any other personal information. The section ignores the Fourth Amendment in two ways: (1) The FBI is authorized to conduct personal investigations without a showing of "probable cause," and (2) the FBI is allowed to conduct sneak-and-peek searches without ever making the target aware of the privacy violation.

The In Defense of Freedom Coalition is a group of over 140 organizations that formed even before the Patriot Act became law in late October 2001. Its member groups, from the entire range of the political spectrum have joined together to blunt the act's corrosive potential. The statement presented by one of its spokespersons to the Congress reflects its core view about liberty and national security:

> This tragedy [9/11] requires all Americans to examine carefully the steps our country may now take to reduce the risk of future terrorist attacks. We need to consider proposals calmly and deliberately with a determination not to erode the liberties and freedoms that are at the core of the American way of life. We need to ensure that actions by our government uphold the principles of a democratic society, accountable government and international law, and that all decisions are taken in a manner

consistent with the Constitution. We can, as we have in the past, in times of war and of peace, reconcile the requirements of security with the demands of liberty. We should resist the temptation to enact proposals in the mistaken belief that anything may be called antiterrorist will necessarily provide greater security. We must have faith in our democratic system and our Constitution, and in our ability to protect at the same time both the freedom and security of all Americans. (Halperin 2001)

Still another pressure group that has spoken before Congress against the Patriot Act is the Center for National Security Studies (CNSS), a civil liberties organization created in the late 1960s. Its two chief spokespersons: director Kate Martin, and a senior fellow of the Council on Foreign Relations and the chair of the CNSS advisory board, Morton H. Halperin. Halperin has personal memories of unconstitutional governmental invasion of personal privacy. During the administration of Republican Richard M. Nixon (1969–1974), he served as deputy undersecretary of state when Henry Kissinger was Nixon's secretary of state. Unbeknown to Halperin at the time, his telephones—in his office and in his home—were bugged by White House operatives who were, at the direction of the president, using wiretaps to find out who was leaking information to the press and others.

In the late 1970s, the CNSS was very active in the successful effort to structure the Foreign Intelligence Surveillance Act so that personal liberty and national security were carefully balanced. After 9/11 the group's plaintive plea was to pursue national security "in a way that protects our liberties as well as our security."

Appearing before the Senate Permanent Select Committee on Intelligence on September 24, 2001, Martin and Halperin testified as to the importance of correctly balancing individual freedom and liberty with national security. Acting correctly, for the pair, meant proceeding "calmly and deliberately" in the legislative process. Like so many other organizations that testified before Congress or acted in other ways to voice their alarm about the Patriot Act, the CNSS was worried about the treatment of aliens, the use of wiretap evidence, significant changes in FISA, and threats to the Bill of Rights protections.

On October 3, 2001, testimony given before Senator Feingold's Subcommittee on the Constitution, Federalism, and

Property Rights of the Senate Judiciary Committee, Halperin tried to provide legislators with ideas that could be used to moderate the grave problems in the administration's proposed Patriot Act. He once again directed his concern to changes proposed in the legislation that would, he believed, adversely affect the FISA (Halperin 2001).

In January 2002 Martin offered testimony before the House Committee on the Judiciary. Her comments focused on the treatment of aliens and immigrants to the United States, especially the detention, without charges filed, of more than 1,100 individuals.

> We are most concerned that these measures [in the Patriot Act] target immigrants and other foreigners in violation of our most fundamental values—equal treatment of all individuals before the law—and our unique history as a country of immigrants, knit together not by race, ethnicity, or religion, but by a commitment to the Constitution and the rule of law. (Martin 2002)

Martin pointed to the "excessive secrecy" of the DOJ in the implementation of the act, the policy of eavesdropping on attorney-client conversations, and the secret detention policy. In its "Memorandum to Interested Persons," CNSS devoted space to discussing the FBI's new and dangerous wiretapping authority, as well as its new sneak-and-peek authority. There has been no public discussion in the media or the legislature about these unilateral and secret policy initiatives. The Department of Justice and Attorney General Ashcroft, Martin said, "continue to stonewall" (Martin 2002).

The Center for Democracy and Technology (CDT) is another, more specialized group that has spoken out against the excesses its members believe the act contains. On January 24, 2002, James X. Dempsey, deputy director of the CDT, gave testimony before the House Judiciary Committee. His focus was on the problems associated with the FBI's counterintelligence investigations and their "relevance to the government's response of September 11" (Dempsey 2002). As Dempsey and his organization saw it, 9/11 put a democratic government in a tough predicament:

> Terrorism poses a devilish problem, for politics or religion or ideology are not entirely irrelevant to terrorism investigations. After all, terrorists carry out criminal acts for ideological reasons. The challenge of terrorism

investigations is how to separate the few who would commit violence from the many who share an ideology. To make the problem more difficult, the government's main goal is to identify those planning violence before they take any violent action; to interdict them before they hijack the plane or set off the bomb.

But Dempsey objected to the Patriot Act's weakening of the FISA "particularity" requirement, allowing the FBI to use intelligence taps and searches to collect criminal evidence without "probable cause," and enabling the DOJ to seize "any tangible things (including books, records, papers, documents, and other items)" where they are sought for a criminal investigation "to protect against international terrorism or clandestine intelligence activities." The implications of the act's changes to existing statutes, Dempsey said, "are enormous." The Patriot Act, he argued, permits the FBI "to cast its net far wider than ever before" in its effort to prevent further terrorist attacks against Americans. There is, he concluded, the need to retain

> limits on government surveillance not merely to protect individual rights but to focus government activity on those planning violence. The criminal standard and the [FISA] principle of particularized suspicion [both loosened greatly by the Patriot Act] keep the government from being diverted into investigations guided by politics, religion, or ethnicity.
> We should focus on perpetrators of crime, avoid indulging in guilt by association, maintain procedures designed to identify the guilty and exonerate the innocent, insist on limits on surveillance activity, and bar political spying.

Yet another group opposed to the Patriot Act is the Center for Constitutional Rights (CCR), founded in 1966 by attorneys working on behalf of civil rights in the Deep South. The center is a nonprofit legal and educational organization whose mission is the protection and advancement of the rights guaranteed by the U.S. Constitution and the Universal Declaration of Human Rights. Like all the other groups, the CCR has worked to ensure that government responses to terrorism do not erode "the rights and liberties that define America." Along with the ACLU, the CCR has filed lawsuits (seven as of mid-2004) challenging governmental actions based on the Patriot Act and on executive orders with respect to treatment of the alleged terrorist detainees at Guantanamo Bay, Cuba.

The CCR has also published reports and prepared information packets for the media regarding the government's operations against terrorism and their impact on personal rights and liberties. In one report, "The State of Civil Liberties: One Year Later—The Erosion of Civil Liberties in the Post 9/11 Era," the CCR argues that to retain civil liberties in the post–9/11 era, several basic principles must be followed to retain the balance between national security and individual freedoms:

- Punishment imposed only after the conclusion of fair, open, transparent, and objective procedures designed to protect the rights of the accused and determine innocence or guilt. [These include] the right to be free from coerced interrogation, the right to have an objective and independent judge and jury, and the right to a skillful, independent and un-intimidated lawyer.
- The government may not discriminate against individuals or groups on the basis of arbitrary categories such as race, ethnicity, religion, political belief or gender.
- The government must abide by the system of checks and balances set forth in the Constitution that prevent the aggregation of power in the hands of one person or in a single branch of government.
- People must be free to express ideas, regardless of their content, without fear of reprisal (CCR 2002).

"Since September 11th," the report said, "each of these . . . principles has been severely compromised [by the Bush administration]. In addition, our credibility in the international arena has suffered." The rationale for this report was to "detail the ways in which the actions of the Executive Branch, and more specifically the Bush administration, have threatened people's basic freedoms and the foundation of democracy in this country."

The CCR report maintained that the secret arrests and detention by the FBI and INS (now a part of the DHS) of aliens and citizens "has often reached Kafkaesque proportions for detainees and their families." Many hundreds were taken from their homes "without warning or explanation." All were held incommunicado. Family members were not notified of the location of their loved ones; "no charges or explanations for their detentions were given either publicly or in private." Many were held in solitary confinement; most were held for months before being released without explanation (CCR 2002).

As early as September 21, 2001, the chief immigration judge, Michael Creppy, issued an order to all immigration judges to close all immigration hearings. Attorney General Ashcroft rejected CCR lawyers' requests, under the Freedom of Information Act, to get information about the number of people held by the DOJ. On August 2, 2002, after the CCR challenged Ashcroft's decision in federal court, federal district court judge Gladys Kessler ordered the DOJ to release the names of all persons detained by the FBI and the INS since September 2001. In another case brought by the CCR and other organizations, on August 26, 2002, a federal appeals court ruled that the Creppy memo was unconstitutional: "Democracies die behind closed doors. . . . When the government begins closing doors, it selectively controls information rightfully belonging to the people. Selective information is misinformation" (CCR 2002, 7).

A major segment of the CCR report entitled "Governing Above the Law: The Erosion of the Bill of Rights" outlined what the organization considered "the most disturbing" aspect of Bush administration actions since 9/11. The administration's "willingness to cast aside the protections afforded by the Bill of Rights" was the gravest threat to the functioning of a democratic republic.

> Our concerns are two-fold. First, in the past twelve months, there have been widespread abuses of the rights conferred by the Constitution. These abuses have targeted mainly non-citizens, but as in the cases of citizens Jose Padilla and Yaser Esam Hamdi indicate, there is no reason to think that the threat is in any way confined to those who lack American citizenship. (In December 2003 the DOJ allowed Padilla and Hamdi to meet with attorneys.) Second, and perhaps of greater concern than specific abuses, are the ways in which civil liberties have been eroded by the introduction of sweeping new laws, and by the codification of abusive practices through executive order and interim rules.

The twenty-page report methodically examines the amendments in the Bill of Rights that have been adversely impacted by the Patriot Act and other actions of the Bush administration. Page after page in the report presents incidents where rights and liberties in the First, Fourth, Fifth, and Sixth Amendments have been routinely ignored, bypassed, and eroded by imperious acts of the Bush administration. The CCR conclusion is a sharp condemnation of these actions:

> The Bush Administration's war against terrorism, without boundary or clear end-point, has led to serious abrogation of the rights of the people and the obligations of the federal government. Abuses, of 4th and 5th Amendment rights in particular, have been rampant, but more disturbing is the attempt to codify into law practices that erode privacy, free speech, and the separation of powers that is the hallmark of our society. . . . By weakening those protections, the government has opened the doors to new encroachments on the liberties that all residents of the United States rightfully enjoy.

Legislators

In addition to the organizations that have attacked the Bush administration's actions in the name of the war on terrorism, many congressional legislators have come around to view the 2001 Patriot Act as an unjust blunderbuss that seems to be directly threatening basic freedoms and liberties of all persons residing in the United States.

As noted above, some Republican legislators in Congress, after having voted for the Patriot Act, had second thoughts about its validity, its constitutionality. Representative James Sensenbrenner (R–WI) is the chairman of the House Committee on the Judiciary. On April 18, 2003, he was quoted in the *Milwaukee Journal Sentinel* as saying that any attempt to cut the sunset provisions out of the Patriot Act would take place "over my dead body" (Tomasky 2003, 47).

Almost immediately after the act took effect, Sensenbrenner and John Conyers, the leading Democrat on the committee—which has oversight of DOJ actions—began to press the DOJ for answers to questions about how the act is being implemented by federal agencies. By the end of 2002, they and the staff of the committee prepared and delivered two lengthy sets of questions to the DOJ.

The first set of questions was mailed to the DOJ on June 13, 2002. On July 26, 2002, Daniel J. Bryant, assistant attorney general, answered forty-three of the complex questions in a twenty-five-page letter. On August 26, 2002, Bryant sent a twenty-one-page letter responding to questions he had not answered earlier. Bryant sent a third letter to the legislators on September 20, 2002, after Judiciary Committee staff requested additional information from the DOJ.

The queries focused on the controversial portions of all ten titles. One example: Section 206 of the act authorized the FISA secret court "to issue an order that can be used to obtain assistance and information from any common carrier, landlord, or custodian when the court finds that the target of the surveillance may take actions" that try to evade the order. The question: "How many times has the DOJ obtained such 'roving' orders?" The answer: "The number of times the DOJ has obtained authority for 'roving' surveillance is classified." Many of the questions posed by the congressmen led to similar answers: classified, "but will be provided in an appropriate channel."

On April 1, 2003, Congressmen Sensenbrenner and Conyers sent a further thirty-eight multifaceted questions about the DOJ's implementation of the Patriot Act. On May 13, 2003, Jamie Brown, acting assistant attorney general, sent the legislators a sixty-page letter that tried to answer their queries involving the expanded powers of the FBI to use sneak-and-peek searches, roving searches, and other criminal investigation issues.

The Senate's Judiciary Committee, chaired by conservative Republican Orrin Hatch, took a decidedly different oversight tack. Hatch has gone so far as to say that he will introduce legislation to remove all sunset provisions in the 2001 Patriot Act. He has also given his strong support to the administration's proposal for a Patriot Act II.

During summer 2003, Republican Congressman "Butch" Otter (R–ID), one of only three Republicans who voted against the Patriot Act, was able to move legislation through the House of Representatives to ban the sneak-and-peek" provision. The Otter Amendment passed overwhelmingly in the House by a vote of 309–118. It stands little chance of clearing the much more conservative Senate, especially because Senator Hatch, the chair of the Senate Judiciary Committee, remains strongly committed to providing the president with unlimited powers to deal with the terrorist threat to national security.

In the Senate a number of bills have been introduced to change some of the more egregious sections of the act. Senators Lisa Murkowski (R–AK) and Ron Wyden (D–OR) introduced the Protecting the Rights of Individuals Act. Senator Feingold, the only member of the Senate to vote against the Patriot Act, introduced a bill to "fix" Section 215 (the part challenged in court by the ACLU). Senator Hatch and other solons, however, continue to pledge to deep-six these kinds of legislative efforts that would hinder the actions of President Bush and his executive departments in the war on terrorism.

More recently, in fall 2003, some Republican senators have challenged the Republican leadership in the Senate. Senator Larry Craig (R–ID), a member of the Judiciary Committee, called for some serious changes in the 2001 Patriot Act "or see the law die in two years." He said that "we [senators opposed to the act as it now stands] are building that kind of base for it [changes in the act] in the Senate" (Holland 2003).

In early October 2003, Craig and other Republican senators, including John Sununu (R–NH), Murkowski, and Mike Crapo (R–ID), along with Democratic senators Feingold, Richard Durbin (D–IL), Jeff Bingaman (D—NM), and Wyden, introduced and/or supported revisions in the Act. Senators Durbin and Craig formally introduced the Security and Freedom Ensured (SAFE) Act. Durbin said: "I believe it is possible to combat terrorism and preserve our individual freedoms at the same time. The Patriot Act crossed the line on several key areas of civil liberties" (Holland 2003). If passed, the law would restrict the broadened powers the government was given in the Patriot Act. It would limit government's ability to use "roving" wiretaps against terrorist suspects and to execute such search warrants without immediately informing the suspect.

As introduced, the proposed changes are as follows:

- The FBI would be required to demonstrate suspicion that a person is suspected of terrorism or spying before seizing library or business records,
- The FBI would be required to get a court order to get electronic communications from a library instead of using just an administrative subpoena,
- Nationwide search warrants would be prohibited,
- "Roving" wiretaps would be required to name either the person or the place to be tapped,

- DOJ officials must inform a federal judge every seven days that telling the subject of the secret search would cause the destruction of evidence, tampering with evidence, or threaten someone's life.

Quickly responding to these proposed changes, DOJ spokesman Mark Corallo said the 2001 act, "as is, has been an important tool" in the Bush administration's war against terrorism. "Those who would seek to repeal or water down the important tools in the Patriot Act," he said, "would return America to the level of vulnerability that existed prior to September 11, 2001." According to the DOJ and administration officials, the 2001 Patriot Act has prevented a second "catastrophic terrorist attack" on innocent Americans (Lichtblau 2003).

Senator Crapo initially expressed his belief that the bill "has a good chance of becoming law," and when he introduced the proposed changes to the 2001 Patriot Act, Craig said, "We think the public has spoken very clearly on this [matter]." However, on January 30, 2004, President Bush announced that he would categorically veto such legislation (SAFE) if it ever reached his desk. And in April 2004 the legislation was still in the Senate Judiciary Committee. Given the views of conservative chair Hatch, there is little likelihood the act will ever see the light of day.

The U.S. General Accounting Office

As noted earlier, the investigative arm of the Congress, the General Accounting Office (GAO), has periodically published reports about the impact of the 2001 Patriot Act. It has been consistently critical of the federal executive branch's efforts to implement the legislation.

In December 2003 the GAO published the latest of its reports on the implementation of the act by the DOJ and other federal agencies. This report focused on the continuing problem of tracking down and halting the movement of financial assets to terrorist organizations such as Al Qaeda. According to the GAO report, federal authorities as yet do not have a clear understanding of how terrorists move their financial assets. These federal agencies are still struggling, the GAO concluded, to prevent the flow of money to terror groups.

The GAO also found that the Internal Revenue Service has not yet developed a formal plan for sharing financial information with state authorities about charities under federal investigation. It further noted that the Treasury and Justice Departments have fallen nearly a year behind in developing a plan for attacking money laundering and issues like terrorists' use of black-market gems and gold. And "some agencies have failed to make terrorism financing a high priority or have set unrealistic goals for overhauling their tactics" (Lichtblau and O'Brien 2003, 1). Senator Durbin called the GAO report a "real eye opener. . . . This is an indication that we were naïve to believe that all of our attention had this problem under control. I don't think we're close, and this report says that terrorists are going to continue to have resources at their disposal" (Lichtblau and O'Brien 2003, 1).

Office of Inspector General, DOJ

Ironically, the DOJ's own internal agency, the Office of the Inspector General (OIG), has been critical of the DOJ's actions in the war against terrorism. On June 2, 2003, the OIG published its 198-page report entitled "The September 11 Detainees: A Review of the Treatment of Aliens Held on Immigration Charges in Connection with the Investigation of the September 11 Attacks." In a cover letter attached to the report, Glenn A. Fine, inspector general of the DOJ, wrote: "While our review recognized the enormous challenges and difficult circumstances confronting the DOJ in responding to the terrorist attacks, we found significant problems in the way the detainees were handled" (ii).

Among the specific findings in the OIG report were the following:

> *Arrest, Charging and Assignment to a Detention Facility.*
> - The FBI in New York City "made little attempt to distinguish between aliens who were subjects of the FBI terrorism investigation (PENTTBOM) and those encountered coincidentally to a PENTTBOM lead."
> - The INS "did not consistently serve the September 11 detainees with notice of the charges under which they were being held with the INS's stated goal of 72 hours. The review found that some detainees did not receive these charging documents for more than a month after being arrested."
> - "FBI agents responsible for clearance investigations often were assigned other duties and were not able to

focus on the detainee cases. The result was that detainees remained in custody—many in restrictive conditions of confinement—for weeks and months with no clearance investigations being conducted. . . . The FBI clearance process took an average of 80 days."

Bond and Removal Issues.

- DOJ "instituted a 'no bond' policy for all September 11 detainees as part of its effort to keep the detainees confined until the FBI could complete its clearance investigations."
- The detainees' conditions of confinement were, in many instances, extremely poor. "Our review found that 84 September 11 detainees were housed in the Metropolitan Detention Center (MDC) in Brooklyn under highly restrictive conditions, including 'lock down' for at least 23 hours per day; escort procedures that included a '4-man hold' with handcuffs, leg irons, and heavy chains any time the detainees were moved outside their cells; two lights illuminating the cell 24 hours a day; and a limit of one legal telephone call per week and one social call per month."
- In the Passaic, New Jersey, detention facility, more than 400 detainees were held from September 11 until May 30, 2002.

The OIG report details how DOJ and INS used the Patriot Act and federal immigration statutes to detain 762 persons, most of Arab and Asian origin. In the final count, more than 1,100 aliens were held for months without their families' knowing where they were and what "crimes" they may have committed. Those who were picked up were suspected of having ties to the 9/11 attackers or having connections to terrorist organizations in the United States and abroad or were simply rounded up in the hastily put-together FBI dragnet in response to the 9/11 attacks. It was not until the second half of 2002 that the detainees were investigated and innocent residents released.

Critics of the DOJ and other federal agencies saw their fears validated in the OIG report. By the time it was made public, many local governments had taken action, largely expressive, to indicate their disdain for the 2001 Patriot Act and for the responses of the federal agencies after the 9/11 tragedy.

States, Cities, and Towns

As of February 2004, three states and more than 240 local governments in thirty-five other states had passed resolutions or ordinances in support of preserving civil rights by ignoring unconstitutional acts that defy provisions in the Patriot Act. "Some are largely symbolic; others actually take legal steps to curb local compliance with oppressive provisions of the law or ensure adequate reporting about how the Patriot Act is being used on the street" (Edgar 2003, 17).

The Idaho County, Idaho, ordinance is typical of the hundreds of bills passed after the Patriot Act became law. In its entirety it reads as follows:

> An ordinance for the County of Idaho, State of Idaho, providing for the continued adherence to the Bill of Rights and to the Constitution of these United States of America, which is the Supreme Law of the Land. Providing that this ordinance shall be in full force and effect from and after its passage, approval, and publication, according to law, and declaring an emergency.
>
> Now, therefore, be it ordained by the Board of Idaho County Commissioners of Idaho County, Idaho.
>
> The Bill of Rights and the Constitution for these United States of America, which is the Supreme Law of the Land, shall be upheld and enforced within the boundaries of Idaho County; repugnant acts, ordinances, or regulations of government in clear contravention notwithstanding.
>
> ENACTMENT AND EFFECTIVE DATE:
>
> This ordinance shall be in full force from and after its passage, approval, and publication, according to law.
>
> Passed and approved this 23rd day of September, 2003, County of Idaho, State of Idaho.

Individuals

Many persons took it upon themselves to protest against the Patriot Act's potential for infringing on the civil rights and civil liberties of persons residing in America. Some placed advertisements in newspapers; many wrote letters to the editor critical of the act. Still others testified before congressional committees.

Some, especially lawyers, wrote essays in the *American Bar Association Journal* (*ABAJ*) and other legal publications.

Susan Herman, a law professor at Brooklyn Law School, is one example of these individual statements of opposition to the 2001 Patriot Act. Her essay in the December 3, 2001, issue of *Jurist* is entitled "The U.S.A. Patriot Act and the U.S. Department of Justice: Losing Our Balance?" Herman, like so many others, writes about the act's "force feed[ing] power to the executive branch, while limiting the judiciary, and keeping Congress in the dark" (3).

She is critical of the Patriot Act's

- surveillance provisions that allow federal agencies more power and less judicial supervision,
- increasing the authority of the attorney general to detain and deport noncitizens with little or no judicial review, and
- decreasing the vitality of the nation's separation of powers among the executive branch, the Congress, and the federal judiciary.

"Being asked to have blind faith in the Attorney General," she says, "is a difficult message for a child of the Vietnam era." Her concluding words reflect a view of all those fearful of the consequences of an "aggressive" implementation by the DOJ of the 2001 Patriot Act:

> I have found myself thinking often lately about the world of George Orwell's *1984,* and not only because Orwell's "Big Brother" has become such a pervasive metaphor for expansive governmental surveillance. The people in Orwell's totalitarian state, Ocena, . . . knew that their state was engaged in a murky foreign war, against some enemy or other—either Eastasia or Eurasia. . . . Information about the war was no more specific and no more reliable than the Newspeak about domestic affairs. I don't know whether we have lost our balance, but I do know that power is careening in one direction. That, combined with the extent of what I don't know, is reason enough to worry (4).

Many readers responded to her essay. One, a Texas attorney, Ellis L. Bert, commented: "I hate to use the term, but once in jest President Bush stated he could get things done if he were a dictator. I fear that he may be using the September 11 tragedy as his 'Reichstag fire' to curb civil liberties. . . . Battle terrorism, but preserve our rights or the terrorists will have won" ("Discussion," *Jurist,* December 2002).

Many essays in law review journals have been extremely critical of the 2001 Patriot Act. One example is a piece by Chris Mooney in *Legal Affairs,* "A Short History of Sunsets." In the piece Mooney is concerned about whether the sunset provisions in the Patriot Act will ever be used by the Congress to terminate the law's troublesome sections. Sunset provisions cause a law or a segment of it to expire after a certain number of years. The Patriot Act's sunset provisions call for expiration at the end of 2005—unless Congress passes additional legislation to void the sunset clauses. Many critics of the act believe that it will be very difficult politically for legislators to eliminate portions of a national security statute while the war on terror continues. As Wesleyan University professor John Finn put it, "What politician wants to say, 'You're right, I voted for the revocation of the USA Patriot Act and two weeks later the Sears Tower [in Chicago] got blown up'?" (quoted in Mooney 2004).

The Media

Herman's essay carried the message presented in editorials across the nation. As soon as the 2001 Patriot Act was signed into law, angry editorial essays and op-ed pieces appeared in hundreds of newspapers. These media pieces have important consequences for the continued vitality and vigor of the act and for those responsible for ensuring that another catastrophic terrorist attack does not take place.

For one example (also recall the *Houston Chronicle* editorial, mentioned above), on July 25, 2002, the *Washington Post* published an editorial called "Just the Facts, Mr. Ashcroft." The piece coincided with Attorney General Ashcroft's appearance before the Senate Judiciary Committee to talk about the FBI's dragnet operations to round up over 1,000 aliens after the 9/11 attacks. One year before the OIG report on this issue, the *Post* accused the attorney general of directing

> the roundup and jailing of hundreds of individuals and compilation of dossiers on thousands of individuals

and groups—a dragnet targeted at the Arab American, Muslim and immigrant communities. . . . [Ashcroft] has repeatedly misled the American public by suggesting that the hundreds of Arabs and Muslims who have been jailed were involved in terrorism. That isn't true; virtually none of those caught up after 9/11 has been charged with terrorism. . . . Ashcroft has boasted to Congress that the terrorism investigation has resulted in the convictions of 86 people on criminal charges. What he forgot to say was that none of the charges against the 86—virtually all of whom are Arabs and Muslims—was related to terrorism. Most of them were minor charges that might never have been filed if the individuals hadn't got caught up in the terrorism dragnet. A substantial number have been sentenced to time served, turning on its head the presumption of innocence.

The editorial concluded with harsh words directed toward Ashcroft: "[There must be] a renunciation of the Attorney General's implication that Arabs and Muslims, citizens or not, are a fifth column ready to spring into action at Al Qaeda's bidding." Editorials similar to this one were published regularly and may have forced the OIG and other investigative agencies of the federal government to carefully examine the actions of the DOJ and the INS. One organization, the Electronic Privacy Information Center (EPIC), suggested that the OIG report was "instigated by media reports and reports from human rights organizations. . . . Only after details of the abusive treatment [of detainees] emerged in the press did the DOJ begin to process the detainees more quickly" (EPIC 2003, 1).

Already some conservative legislators, led by Senator Hatch, have voiced concerns about the sunset provisions. Hatch suggested congressional repeal of these provisions, stating that "terrorists will not sunset their evil intentions" (Mooney 2004, 70). Leahy, the ranking minority member of the Judiciary Committee, threatened a floor fight and possible Democratic filibuster. He said that Hatch's proposal "would give up the ghost of any meaningful oversight about how the government is using these sweeping powers" (Mooney 2004, 70).

The Federal Courts Enter the Fray

"As more terrorist attacks occur," wrote James Gilmore III in his commission's final report published in December 2003, "the pressure will rise to lessen civil liberties, albeit with different labels" (Gilmore 2003, 117). As noted above, this is the central fear of critics of the Bush administration's behavior against international terrorism since 9/11. They claim that even though there has been no second tragic cataclysm of violence since 9/11, civil liberties and freedoms of persons living in the United States have already been lessened.

In response to this perceived threat, a basic tactic of the opposition is to use the legal process to strike down—declare unconstitutional—the laws and executive orders that are the basis for the controversial government acts. Inexorably, although President Bush is greatly opposed to this development, beginning in 2002 the federal courts have entered the debates surrounding the constitutionality of the 2001 Patriot Act and other executive actions taken since 9/11.

This legal development is not unexpected. Ever since the Supreme Court's opinion in *Marbury v. Madison* (1803), the core "province and duty" of the federal courts, especially the U.S. Supreme Court, has been, in the words of the great chief justice John Marshall (1801–1835), to determine "what the law is."

Regarding the Bush war on terror, there are "two broad categories of court cases: those the administration has taken before judges and those in which outside lawyers have challenged administration policies" (Gearan 2002, 1) The first category is a small one, for the Department of Justice has brought criminal charges against terrorists at war with America in only three cases since 9/11. The first was that of John Walker Lindh, a young man labeled the "American Taliban" who was captured in Afghanistan during the fighting; he accepted a guilty plea and was sentenced to twenty years in federal prison. The second case involves a French citizen government lawyers call the "twentieth 9/11" bomber, Zacarias Moussaoui. He was scheduled to stand trial in federal court in Virginia, charged with conspiring to commit terrorism. However, as of spring 2004 that case has still not gone to trial because of many troublesome legal complications that have been raised by his defense counsel. The third case since 9/11 involves a British citizen, Richard Reid, who was charged in federal court with attempting to blow up, using a crude shoe bomb, a passenger plane in flight over the Atlantic Ocean in December 2001. The plane was en route from Paris to Miami when passengers wrested the explosive shoe from Reid's foot after he had lit the fuse. In January 2003 a federal judge in Boston sentenced Reid to life imprisonment.

Prior to 9/11, the U.S. government brought other terrorists to trial in federal courts. During the Clinton administration, four defendants with links to Al Qaeda and led by blind Egyptian Muslim cleric Sheikh Omar Abdel Rahman were charged in the 1993 bombing of the World Trade Center in New York City. The jury found them all guilty, and each was sentenced to 240 years in prison and fined $500,000.

The second set of cases, those brought against the federal government's actions since 9/11, have been far more numerous. From the weeks after 9/11 through the spring of 2004, the federal courts had been asked to intercede by private counsel in cases involving three different sets of persons detained by the federal government in what the filed written briefs call gross violations of due process.

The first type of litigation, heard by the U.S. Supreme Court in April 2004 (see Chronology, p. 224), involves sixteen citizens (two each from Great Britain and Australia; twelve from Kuwait) who were seized in Pakistan and Afghanistan during operations led by U.S. forces against Taliban and Al Qaeda forces after 9/11. They and hundreds of others (more than 660) were then transported to the U.S. Naval Base at Guantanamo Bay, Cuba, where they have been imprisoned at Camp X-Ray, the specially built prison camp to hold the "enemy combatants" captured in that hot war against terrorism—a military campaign still going on in 2004.

U.S. district court judge Colleen Kollar-Kotelly dismissed the cases for lack of federal court jurisdiction, and a three-judge panel of the U.S. Court of Appeals for the District of Columbia Circuit unanimously upheld her ruling. By the time the U.S. Supreme Court answers the question raised in the petition submitted by family members of the captives, the sixteen prisoners will have been held for twenty-six months with no charges filed, no access to legal counsel, no trial, and no judgments about guilt or innocence. As their petition to the U.S. Supreme Court states: "The sixteen have been deprived of their liberty without due process of law." They have been held indefinitely, by executive direction, without any adequate process.

The Bush administration's justification for the indefinite detention without any process was stated by Secretary of Defense Rumsfeld at one of his many press conferences: "The asymmetrical war on terror is unlike all other wars America fought since 1789. It is an open-ended war, one that will not be over until all the terrorist leaders, groups, and cells have been identified, pursued, and destroyed. Until then, enemy combatants must be held without being released and without the opportunity to seek some sort of habeas relief."

The U.S. Court of Appeals for the District of Columbia Circuit in March 2003 ruled that no federal court has jurisdiction to consider the legality of an open-ended detention (Greenhouse 2003, 1). However, on November 10, 2003, the U.S. Supreme Court, rejecting the arguments of the Bush administration's solicitor general, Theodore B. Olson, granted certiorari in the two cases: *Rasul, Shafiq, et al. v. Bush, President of the United States, et al.* (case number 03–334) and *Al Doah, Fawzi K, et al. v. United States, et al.* (case number 03–343).

Olson's brief urged the Court not to grant certiorari because the lower federal court had properly applied a Supreme Court precedent to hold "that aliens detained by the military abroad [only have rights] determined by the executive and the military, and not the courts" (www.supremecourtoftheus.gov). Therefore, the government's brief concluded, the two cases do not merit review by the U.S. Supreme Court. Olson told the justices that the federal courts, including the U.S. Supreme Court, must avoid "judicial interference with military affairs."

It surprised many when the Court rejected Olson's argument and granted review, stating:

> The petitions for writs of certiorari are granted limited to the following question: Whether United States courts lack jurisdiction to consider challenges to the legality of detention of foreign nationals captured abroad in connection with hostilities and incarcerated at the Guantanamo Naval Base, Cuba. The cases are consolidated and a total of one hour is allotted for oral argument. (Order of the U.S. Supreme Court, January 11, 2004, www.supremecourtoftheus.gov)

The second set of cases roiling the federal government involves a challenge brought by the father of a U.S. citizen born in Saudi Arabia, Yaser Esam Hamdi, challenging Hamdi's open-ended detention in the United States as an "enemy combatant." He was captured in Afghanistan during battles between the Taliban and the coalition forces led by the U.S. military. Since April 2002 he has been held without access to a lawyer in military jails, first in Virginia and then in South Carolina.

A federal district judge in South Carolina twice ordered the military to allow an attorney to meet with Hamdi. However, in January 2003 a three-judge panel of the Fourth Circuit U.S. Court of Appeals ruled that Hamdi was not entitled to a lawyer and has no legal basis to challenge his indefinite detention. The three-judge panel determined that "the Constitution gives the executive branch the responsibility to wage war and that courts must yield to the military." The Fourth Circuit Court of Appeals, sitting en banc in July 2003, voted 8–4 to uphold the judgment of the panel.

Hamdi's father then appealed the government's refusal to allow counsel to visit and confer with his son. In August 2003 Hamdi's father asked the U.S. Supreme Court to grant certiorari to determine whether a U.S. citizen labeled as an enemy combatant and held in a military jail in the United States could be held without charges and unable to speak with an attorney. Amicus curiae briefs were filed with the Court, and the Bush administration responded in December 2003. However, on December 2, 2003—"on the eve of [the] government filing . . . at the U.S. Supreme Court," as the *Washington Post* pointed out—the Bush administration did a turnabout in the Hamdi case (Markon and Eggen 2003, 1). "As a *matter of discretion* and military policy," the Department of Defense announced that a U.S. citizen jailed after being captured with Taliban soldiers in Afghanistan would be allowed access to a lawyer. After receipt of the government's response, the justices of the Court granted certiorari and heard and decided the important constitutional issues raised, that is, fourth, fifth, and sixth amendment issues, in the litigation in June 2004 (see Chronology, p. 224).

Two other American citizens held as "enemy combatants" by the Department of Defense, Jose Padilla and Bradley University graduate Ali Saleh Kahlah al-Marri, were not affected because of the DOD's use of discretion in the Hamdi matter. Padilla was being held for allegedly plotting to detonate a "dirty bomb" in Chicago. Al-Marri was placed in military detention in June 2003 because of a government allegation that he was an Al Qaeda "sleeper" agent.

But in another one-two combination judicial hit to the Bush administration's war on terror, two federal courts on the same day, December 18, 2003, ruled against the president, his secretary of defense, and his attorney general. A divided U.S. Court of Appeals, Second Circuit, sitting in New York City, ruled that Bush lacked the authority to detain indefinitely a U.S. citizen (Jose Padilla) arrested on American soil on suspicion of terrorism by declaring him an "enemy combatant." The panel did say that while Congress might have the power to legislate in this area (the indefinite detention of a U.S. citizen), the president, on his own authority as commander-in-chief, did not:

> The President, acting alone, possesses no inherent constitutional authority to detain American citizens seized within the United States, *away from the zone of combat,* as enemy combatants. . . . Presidential authority does not exist in a vacuum and this case involves not whether those responsibilities should be aggressively pursued but whether the president is obligated [to share them with Congress]. (my emphasis) (CA2 352 *F3d* 695 [2003], at 702)

The court gave the DOD thirty days to release Padilla or take some other action. The administration appealed the ruling of the federal appeals court panel. Bush's press secretary, Scott McClellan, told reporters: "The President's most solemn obligation is protecting the American people. We believe the Second Circuit ruling is troubling and flawed. The President has directed the Justice Department to seek a stay, and further judicial review" (Sanger 2003).

On the same day, another divided appellate court, the U.S. Court of Appeals, Ninth Circuit, based in San Francisco, California, ruled that the DOD policy of denying access to a lawyer for the more than 660 enemy combatants incarcerated at Guantanamo Bay violated the U.S. Constitution as well as international law. The Bush administration appealed both rulings to the U.S. Supreme Court in 2004. (See Chronology, p. 224.)

A *New York Times* editorial dated December 19, 2003, entitled "The Padilla Decision," called the New York federal court ruling a "signal" one in the battle between national security actions and civil liberties. It labeled the Bush action in the case as "egregious presidential overreaching in the name of fighting terrorism." For the *Times,* the two appeals court decisions "could be signs that the administration's strategy of aggressively bypassing the traditional protections of the criminal justice system and meaningful judicial oversight is crumbling. At least, that is our hope" ("The Padilla Decision" 2003).

The next day, a *New York Daily News* editorial entitled "Preserving the Constitution," also heralded the ruling of the Second Circuit U.S. Court of Appeals panel:

> A federal appeals court here in New York has reaffirmed that every United States citizen is entitled to the rights that are the cornerstone of America—even a suspected terrorist when the country's very security is under assault. . . . The Bush administration may seek to have the ruling over-turned. This is within its rights. But it does not have the right to confine a U.S. citizen to legal limbo. That's not the American way. ("Preserving the Constitution" 2003)

The much more conservative *Wall Street Journal* also editorialized about the two rulings. Its piece, "September 10 Mindset," was extremely critical of the court orders. The two federal courts, said the editorial, "issued decisions ignoring the fact that the U.S. homeland was attacked on September 11."

> There are many problems with the [Second Circuit] Court's analysis, starting with the view that the U.S. is not "a zone of combat." Perhaps the Second Circuit judges should take a walk in their own downtown Manhattan neighborhood, a few blocks from where the World Trade Center once stood. The two majority judges might ask the visitors staring at the metal cross that still stands at ground zero whether or not "combat" occurred in this "zone." ("September 10 Mindset" 2003)

The third set of legal issues raised in federal courts involves the efforts of civil rights groups, as noted above, to challenge the Bush administration's decision not to release any information, including names, about the hundreds of people, most of them Arab Muslim immigrants, who were arrested in the immediate aftermath of the 9/11 tragedy. U.S. district court judge Gladys Kessler ruled that such information has to be divulged to the groups and to the media: "Secret arrests are a concept odious to a free society" (www.seattlepi.nwsource.com). She ordered the DOJ to release the names of more than 1,100 detainees. However, in June 2003 the Fourth Circuit Court of Appeals ruled that such information was exempt from disclosure. (In January 2004 the U.S. Supreme Court denied certiorari in the case, thereby letting stand the Fourth U.S. Circuit Court of Appeals decision.)

Another potential legal challenge to Bush administration actions in the war on terror revolves around the November 2001 executive order creating special military tribunals to try suspected Al Qaeda members and supporters. The four categories of persons subject to such secret military tribunals are:

- unlawful enemy combatants seized in Afghanistan or other countries outside the United States,
- prisoners of war captured in Afghanistan,
- illegal aliens in the United States or aliens who came to America legally "but with the alleged purpose of engaging in terrorism," and
- legal aliens with permanent resident status who are accused of engaging in terrorist attacks against the United States.

Until the DOD, with Secretary of Defense Rumsfeld's support, issued guidelines in spring 2002 that provided some kind of due process, the executive order, labeled "draconian" by many, threw fear in the hearts of civil libertarians around the globe (Neier 2002, 1). As announced in November 2001, the order allowed tribunals to impose penalties, including the death sentence, by a majority vote of the U.S. military officers sitting as judges and permitted a lower standard of proof and looser standards of evidence than allowed in any regular U.S. court— including military courts. It also permitted the trials to be held in secret and denied defendants the right to choose a lawyer or to appeal the verdict to a civilian federal appeals court ("What to Do with Al Qaeda Prisoners" 2002, 3). As of April 2004 there had been no special military tribunals convened; therefore, there have not been any actual legal challenges to them.

By the beginning of 2004, the major cases already heard by the federal courts, in addition to the ones mentioned above, were:

- *United States v. John Walker Lindh* (E.D. Va, October 4, 2002). American Taliban; guilty plea.

- *United States v. Satter* (S.D., N.Y., April 4, 2002). Lynne Stewart, charged with providing material support for terrorists.
- *United States v. Goba* (W.D., N.Y., October 21, 2002). Five Yemeni men from Lackawana, New York, charged with providing material support to Al Qaeda.
- *United States v. Ujaama* (W.D., Washington, August 28, 2002). A Seattle activist charged with providing material support for Al Qaeda.
- *United States v. Battle* (W.D., Oregon, October 3, 2002). A group in Portland, Oregon, charged with providing material support for Al Qaeda.
- *United States v. Koubriti* (E.D., Michigan, August 28, 2002). A group of men in Detroit charged with providing material support to Al Qaeda.

In sum, the major concerns of the critics, and the federal courts, noted above, focused on:

- Inroads into and diminution of personal rights and freedoms found in the First, Fourth, Fifth, and Sixth Amendments in the Bill of Rights. Specifically, freedom of association, freedom of information, freedom of speech, the right to legal representation, freedom from unreasonable searches, the right to a speedy and public trial, and the right to liberty are all threatened by the 2001 Patriot Act.
- The weakening of important concepts in a democratic republic: the separation of powers, checks and balances, and judicial review.
- The inability of Congress to sunset some of the provisions of the 2001 Patriot Act.
- The injustices foisted on the many hundreds of Arab and Muslim detainees by the FBI and the INS, including closed hearings held by the INS.
- Changes in FISA restraints on federal use of wiretaps.
- The aggressive, unilateral actions of the Bush administration in the detention of immigrants; the indefinite captivity, without due process rights, of U.S. citizens alleged to have Al Qaeda connections; and the indefinite holding of enemy combatants at Guantanamo Bay, Cuba, without any due process.

The Bush administration's leading spokespersons in the defense of the government's actions in the war on terror are President Bush and Attorney General Ashcroft. Both men have been uninhibited in the defense of the government's actions. As Bush sees it, the oath of office he took to protect and defend U.S. sovereignty, accompanied by his constitutional designation as commander-in-chief of the armed forces, gives him all the power he needs, acting unilaterally if necessary, to strike back and defeat America's enemies. According to Ashcroft, the DOJ is "standing firm in our commitment to protect American lives. The DOJ is waging a deliberate campaign of arrest and detention to protect American lives. We're removing *suspected* terrorists who violate the law from our streets to *prevent* further terrorist attack" (www.doj.gov).

Chapter Four examines the actions taken by the Bush administration to aggressively pursue suspected terrorists and, once caught, bring them to justice in one of a number of legal venues or hold them indefinitely—until the war on terrorism is finally won.

For Further Reading

Center for Constitutional Rights (CCR). "The State of Civil Liberties—One Year Later; Erosion of Civil Liberties in the Post 9/11 Era." September 11, 2002, 1–20, 19–20. www.ccr.org.

Cole, David. "The Course of Least Resistance: Repeating History in the War on Terrorism." In Cynthia Brown, ed., *Lost Liberties: Ashcroft and the Assault on Personal Freedom.* New York: New Press, 2003.

Dempsey, James X. Statements before U.S. House Committee on the Judiciary, January 24, 2002. www.cdt.org.

Doty, Cate. "Gore Criticizes Expanded Terrorism Law." *New York Times,* November 10, 2003, A1.

Edgar, Timothy H. "The Color Line: Watch out America, the White House Is Seeking to Expand the Patriot Act." *Crisis,* November/December 2003, 16–17.

EPIC. "DOJ Inspector General Criticizes DOJ for Treatment of Immigrant Detainees." EPIC Alert, June 17, 2003; available at http://www.epic.org.

Feinstein, Diane. Comments on the floor of the U.S. Senate. October 21, 2001. www.kdt.org.

Gearan, Ann. "Bush's War on Terror Runs Afoul of the Rule of Law." *Seattle Post-Examiner,* August 28, 2002.

Gilmore, J. S., et al. "Fourth Annual Report to the President and the Congress: Implementing the National Strategy." 2003, 117.

Greenhouse, Linda. "Justices Face Decision on Accepting 9/11 Cases." *New York Times*, November 3, 2003, A1.

Halperin, Morton H. "In Defense of Freedom." In statement on behalf of the Center for National Security Studies, before the U.S. Senate Committee on the Judiciary. September 24, 2001, 1–2. www.cnss.gwu.edu.

Halperin, Morton. *Memorandum to Interested Persons, Re: Secret Arrests and Closed Immigration Hearings.* Washington, DC: CNSS, 2002.

Herman, Susan. "The U.S.A. Patriot Act and the U.S. Department of Justice: Losing Our Balance?" *Jurist,* December 3, 2001.

Holland, Jesse J. "Senate Republicans Warn that Patriot Act Will Not Be Renewed Unless Changes are Made." AP dispatch, October 15, 2003, 1. www.SFgate.com.

Lichtblau, Eric. "Bush Administration Plans Defense of Terror Law," *New York Times*, August 19, 2003, A1.

Lichtblau, Eric, and Timothy L. O'Brien. "Efforts to Fight Terror Financing Reported to Lag." *New York Times,* December 12, 2003, A1.

Maack, Marcia T. *Memorandum to Interested Persons, Re: Material Witnesses Detained Since September 11.* Washington, DC: CNSS, 2002.

Markon, Jerry, and Dan Eggen. "U.S. Allows Lawyer for Citizen Held as 'Enemy Combatant.'" *Washington Post,* December 3, 2003.

Martin, Kate. "Civil Liberties since 9/11." House Committee on the Judiciary, January 24, 2002. www.cnss.gwu.edu.

Mooney, Chris. "A Short History of Sunsets." *Legal Affairs,* January/February 2004, 36–39.

Neier, Aryeh. "The Military Tribunals on Trial." 49 *New York Review of Books,* no. 2, February 14, 2002, 10–12.

"The Padilla Decision." Editorial. *New York Times,* December 19, 2003, A17.

"Preserving the Constitution." Editorial. *New York Daily News,* December 20, 2003, 14.

Sanger, David. "President Urging Wider U.S. Powers in Terrorism Law." *New York Times,* September 11, 2003, A1.

Scheidegger, Kent, Charles Hobson, and Maritza Meskan. *Federalist Society White Paper on the USA PATRIOT Act of 2001, Criminal Procedure Sections.* Washington, DC: Federalist Society, 2001.

"September 10 Mindset." Editorial, Review and Outlook. *Wall Street Journal,* December 19, 2003, A14.

Strossen, Nadine. "It's a War on Terrorism, not a War on Immigrants." *Civil Liberties*, Fall 2003, 2, 10.

Tomasky, Michael. "Strange Bedfellows: Conservative Civil Libertarians Join the Fight." *American Prospect*, September 2003.

U.S. Department of Justice. Office of the Inspector General. *A Review of the Treatment of Aliens Held on Immigration Charges in Connection with the Investigation of the September 11 Attacks*. Washington, DC: Department of Justice, 2003.

"What to Do with Al Qaeda Prisoners." *Economist*, January 17, 2002.

4

The Bush Administration's Aggressive Defense of the 2001 USA Patriot Act and Its "Floating" of Patriot Act II

"There is no such thing as perfect security against a hidden network of cold-blooded killers. Yet, abroad and at home, we're not going to wait until the worst dangers are upon us."
—*President George W. Bush, February 2003*

"Foreign terrorists who engage in war crimes against the United States do not deserve constitutional rights."
—*John Ashcroft, November 18, 2001*

"Terrorists don't deserve the same guarantees and safeguards of the U.S. Constitution [that citizens have]."
—*Vice President Dick Cheney, November 15, 2001*

"While the Constitution protects against invasions of individual rights, it is not a suicide pact."
—*U.S. Supreme Court justice Arthur J. Goldberg, Kennedy v. Mendoza-Martinez, 1963*

In December 2003 Ruth Wedgwood wrote an op-ed piece in the *New York Times* entitled "The Rule of Law and the War on Terror." In it she raised the essential conundrum—liberty versus security, preventive versus criminal justice—as seen from the perspective of the president and his attorney general.

> In the ongoing war with Al Qaeda, *America's civic ideals should not frustrate an effective defense*. What is the government to do, for example, when it knows of catastrophic threats or dangers to Americans through intelligence sources, yet is unable to prove its case in a criminal trial against those planning such attacks? (Wedgwood 2003, 28; my emphasis)

She looked at the case of Jose Padilla, a U.S. citizen being held as an enemy combatant in a naval brig in South Carolina. According to intelligence accounts, Padilla left the United States in 1998 and traveled to Egypt, Pakistan, Saudi Arabia, and Afghanistan. In Afghanistan he met with Abu Zubaydah, a senior Al Qaeda planner. Padilla offered to detonate a radioactive bomb in the United States, and Zubaydah sent him to Pakistan to learn how to make such a bomb.

By 2002 Padilla discussed with other Al Qaeda terrorists in Pakistan how to attack America with such a bomb. According to U.S. intelligence, Padilla was sent back to the United States to carry out reconnaissance and then to conduct an attack on a site. In May 2002 Padilla flew from Pakistan to Switzerland and then to Chicago, his hometown. However, two months earlier, in March 2002, Zubaydah had been arrested in Pakistan and was thoroughly questioned by Pakistani and CIA officers. During the questioning he spoke of Padilla's actions. Wedgwood described the situation:

> The government faced an extraordinary dilemma upon Mr. Padilla's return to the United States. Federal rules of evidence do not permit the consideration of intelligence reports as proof for criminal convictions, no matter how reliable the informant. And any effort to hold Mr. Padilla as a grand jury witness was bound to be temporary, since he could not be forced to testify without immunity. (Wedgwood 2003, 28)

Bush used two concepts to detain Padilla. There was the employment of the September 18, 2001, joint resolution of Congress, authorizing the president to use "all necessary and appropriate force against those organizations or persons he determines planned, authorized, committed, or aided the terrorist attacks on

September 11, 2001, [in order to] prevent any future acts of international terrorism against the United States." Second, Bush employed his constitutional authority as commander-in-chief to protect U.S. sovereignty in the ongoing battles with the Islamic terrorists and ordered Padilla detained in a military jail as an enemy combatant.

However, as noted in Chapter Three, a federal appeals court panel, by a 2–1 vote, disagreed with the president. The majority concluded that "an operative of Al Qaeda must be caught carrying weapons or explosives in order to be seen as actively engaged in armed conflict against the United States." Wedgwood, formerly a federal prosecutor and presently a professor of international law at Johns Hopkins University, observed:

> This sanguine view overlooks the Eichmann-like division of labor in Qaeda operations. Target spotting missions . . . are part of armed conflict. The appellate court supposes, without any basis in the record, that there was no "imminent danger" of attack. . . . It would be preferable to know everything that is important in life by standards of "beyond a reasonable doubt." But imagine if the intelligence dots had been replete and connected on September 10, 2001. What if we knew, from out-of-court sources, the names of Qaeda operatives who were planning to hijack the jet-fueled airplanes for attacks on the World Trade Center and the Pentagon? Even then, we would likely have lacked admissible criminal proof. By the logic of last week's [federal appeals court] decision, the president could not have held the hijackers as combatants—even after they had entered the United States, even with habeas corpus review of a president's decisions, until the moment they appeared at Logan Airport with box cutters. (Wedgwood 2003, 28)

For Wedgwood, such a scenario was unthinkable. The president must act to prevent Padilla and other alleged terrorists from committing terrorist acts against Americans: "The training camps of Osama bin Laden created a dangerous and far-flung network that criminal law alone may not suffice to vanquish" (Wedgwood 2003, 28). The ordinary criminal justice processes, she believes, must be set aside during times of ongoing warfare.

"Terrorism," Attorney General Ashcroft reminded the public on September 24, 2001, "is a *clear and present danger* to Americans today" (Ashcroft, "Mobilization, 2001"). Preventive justice is the only possible alternative process, and it must be the basis of governmental action until the war against terrorism ends.

The Response of the Bush Administration to Criticism of the 2001 Patriot Act, 2001–2004

The U.S. attorney general, John Ashcroft, is the Bush administration's point man in the defense of the USA Patriot Act and all other actions taken by the government since 9/11. On December 6, 2001, in one of his numerous appearances before the Senate Committee on the Judiciary, he spoke of the terrorist threat and of the need to respond harshly to it. The Al Qaeda terrorist threat, he said, "is unlike any we have ever known. It slaughters thousands of innocents—a crime of war and a crime against humanity. It seeks weapons of mass destruction and threatens their use against America. No one should doubt the intent, nor the depth, of its consuming destructive hatred." He drew a portrait of an evil "fifth column" of Islamic fundamentalists preparing for additional crimes against humanity: "Terrorist operatives infiltrate our communities—plotting, planning, and waiting to kill again. They enjoy the benefits of our free society even as they commit themselves to our destruction. They exploit our openness—not randomly or haphazardly—but by deliberate, premeditated design" (www.lifeandliberty.gov/subs/speeches).

We are at war, he reminded the senators, and the government has "embarked on a wartime reorganization" to deal with the enemy. All the efforts of the government are "targeted [at] a narrow class of individuals—terrorists. Our legal powers are targeted at terrorists. Our investigation is focused on terrorists. Our prevention strategy targets the terrorist threat."

On March 4, 2003, Ashcroft again appeared before the Senate Judiciary Committee, which was holding hearings on "the terrorist threat." As always, Ashcroft aggressively defended the actions of the Bush administration in the war on terrorism. He strongly defended the administration's use of preventive justice. "America's defense," he told the solons, " the defense of life and liberty—*requires a new culture of prevention,* nurtured by cooperation, built on coordination and rooted in our Constitutional liberties" (my emphasis). He went on: "Our survival and success in this long war on terrorism demands that we continuously adapt and improve our capabilities to protect Americans from a fanatical, ruthless enemy. I will continue to seek the assistance of Congress as we build a culture of prevention and ensure the resources of our government can be dedicated to defending Americans" (Ashcroft 2003).

The overriding priority of the DOJ is "preventing future terrorism, not just prosecuting past crime," said the attorney general. In the spring of 2003, testified Ashcroft, Americans were more secure because of the passage of the USA Patriot Act of 2001. He then presented to the senators five positive results of the Bush administration's new cooperative "integrated prevention" strategy:

> "Gathering and cultivating detailed intelligence on terrorism in the United States," including the issuance of over 18,000 subpoenas and search warrants. Human sources of intelligence and counterterrorism investigations have doubled since 2001.
> "Arresting and detaining potential terrorist threats," including the breakup of four alleged terrorist cells in Buffalo, New York; Detroit, Michigan; Seattle, Washington; and Portland, Oregon; 211 criminal charges brought to date; 108 convictions or guilty pleas, including those of Richard Reid and John Walker Lindh; 478 deportations linked to the 9/11 investigations.
> "Dismantling the terrorist financial network," including the designation of thirty-six groups as terrorist organizations; $124 million in assets frozen and over 600 accounts frozen around the world; seventy investigations into terrorist financing with twenty-three convictions or guilty pleas.
> "Disrupting potential terrorist travel," including more than fifty airport sweeps and more than 1,200 arrests for ID and document fraud and other crimes; nine major smuggling networks disrupted; hundreds of terrorists and criminals stopped through the National Security Entry-Exit Registration System (NSEERS).
> "Building our long-term counter-terrorism capacity," including a 270 percent increase in counterterrorism

funds; over 1,000 new and redirected FBI agents; 250 new assistant U.S. attorneys; fifty-six joint terrorism task forces; and new fly-away expert teams for rapid deployment to hot spots worldwide.

Ashcroft concluded his opening statement with the following observation: "Our strategy and tactics are working. . . . We are winning the war on terrorism."

When Ashcroft testified before the U.S. House Committee on the Judiciary on June 5, 2003, his message was the same combative one he had given to the senators a few months earlier. The USA Patriot Act has been the major tool in the administration's arsenal of weapons to combat terrorism. However, he pointed out that there are many groups and organizations, including members of Congress, "who suggest that we should not have a USA Patriot Act. Others, who supported the Act 20 months ago, now express doubts about the necessity of some of the Act's components." Then Ashcroft somberly stated:

> Let me state this as clearly as possible. Our ability to prevent another catastrophic attack on American soil would be more difficult, if not impossible, without the Patriot Act. . . . *Unfortunately, the law has several weaknesses which terrorists could exploit, undermining our defenses.* (www. usdoj.gov / ag / testimony / 2003; my emphasis)

With these remarks, the Bush administration began to address the need to strengthen the 2001 Patriot Act. A forthcoming section presents the arguments made by the Bush administration for a second Patriot Act. Before then, however, let us examine the efforts of the Bush administration to defend the 2001 Act and related executive orders and statutes passed subsequent to October 24, 2001.

Other Antiterrorist Executive Orders of the Bush Administration and Congressional Actions, 2001–2003

Beyond the 2001 USA Patriot Act, there have been a number of presidential executive orders and additional actions of the Congress, in conjunction with Bush administration policymakers, in response to the 9/11 attacks.

Among the executive orders and other presidential orders and directives issued by President Bush are the following:

- EO 13223, September 18, 2001: Ordering the Ready Reserve of the Armed Forces to Active Duty.
- Presidential Proclamation 7463, September 18, 2001: Declaration of National Emergency by Reason of Certain Terrorist Attacks.
- EO 13224, September 25, 2001: Blocking Property and Prohibiting Transactions with Persons Who Commit, Threaten to Commit, or Support Terrorism.
- EO 13228, October 15, 2001: Establishment of the Office of Homeland Security and the Homeland Security Council.
- EO 13234, November 15, 2001: Establishment of Presidential Task Force on Citizen Preparedness in the War on Terrorism.
- Military Order, November 13, 2001: Authorization of Military Tribunals for Non-Citizens Involved in Terrorism Activities.
- Notice of Continuation, September 13, 2002: National Emergency with Respect to Certain Terrorist Attacks.
- EO 13284, January 23, 2003: Amendment of EO's, and Other Actions, in Connection with Establishment of the Department of Homeland Security (DHS).
- Notice of Continuation, September 13, 2003: National Emergency with Respect to Certain Terrorist Attacks.
- Homeland Security Presidential Directive 6, September 16, 2003: Integration and Use of Screening Information to Protect against Terrorism.

Additionally, after the signing of the USA Patriot Act on October 26, 2001 (PL 107–56), the following pieces of legislation, prepared by the Bush White House, were passed by Congress:

- PL 107–71, November 19, 2001: The Aviation and Transportation Security Act.
- PL 107–134, January 23, 2002: Victims of Terrorism Tax Relief Act of 2001.
- PL 107–173, May 14, 2002: Enhanced Border Security and Visa Entry Reform Act of 2002.
- PL 107–188, June 12, 2002: Public Health Security and Bio-terrorism Preparedness and Response Act of 2002.

- PL 107–243, October 16, 2002: Joint Resolution to Authorize the Use of United States Armed Forces Against Iraq.
- PL 107–295, November 25, 2002: Maritime Transportation Security Act of 2002.
- PL 107–296, November 25, 2002: Homeland Security Act of 2002.
- PL 107–297, December 15, 2002: Terrorism Risk Protection Act of 2002.
- October 1, 2003: Homeland Security Appropriations Act of 2004.

Creation of the Terrorist Threat Integration Center, 2003

In his January 27, 2003, State of the Union address, President Bush announced the creation of the nation's first unified Terrorist Threat Integration Center (TTIC). It was the government's latest effort to close the "seam" between the analysis of foreign and domestic intelligence on terrorism.

The new federal entity, said the president, will "merge and analyze terrorist-related information collected domestically and abroad in order to form the most comprehensive possible threat picture." The directors of the CIA and the FBI, working with the attorney general and the secretaries of homeland security and defense, would be responsible for getting the TTIC off the ground and operational as soon as possible. Among the TTIC's major tasks were to:

- "Optimize the use of threat-related information and conduct a threat analysis.
- Create a structure that ensures information sharing across agency lines.
- Integrate threat-related data collected domestically and abroad to form the most comprehensive possible threat picture.
- Be responsible and accountable for providing terrorist threat assessments for our national leadership."

To further strengthen the government's intelligence-gathering mechanism, the secretaries of state and homeland security (but not, as was the case with the TTIC, the secretary of defense), the attorney general, and the director of the CIA signed a "Memorandum of Understanding on the Integration and Use of Screening Information to Protect Against Terrorism" on September 16, 2003.

The "Memo of Understanding," from which the following quote comes, was signed the same day Bush announced his Homeland Security Presidential Directive 6:

> Consistent with the President's direction, the Parties to this Memorandum will develop and maintain, to the extent permitted by law, the most thorough, accurate, and current information possible about individuals known or appropriately suspected to be or have been involved in activities constituting, in preparation for, in aid of, or related to terrorism.

The key structure created to implement the presidential directive was the Terrorist Screening Center (TSC). It is to become the "continuously updated, sensitive but *unclassified* subset of the Terrorist information possessed by the [top secret] TTIC, and the Purely Domestic Terrorism Information possessed by the FBI." As perceived by the government, the TSC will be the central clearinghouse for all unclassified data about those suspected of alliances with terrorist groups. It will be staffed by personnel from the FBI, CIA, DHS, and the State Department. The information in the TSC database will be shared with "state, local, territorial, and tribal authorities to support their screening processes and otherwise enable them to identify, or assist in identifying, such individuals." The "factors" that must be included in each report on an individual were also spelled out in the memorandum:

- "the nature of the person's association with terrorism;
- the quality of the data, including credibility, reliability, and extent of corroboration;
- the extent of the uniquely identifying data;
- the authority or authorities under which this data was obtained, and any restrictions on how it may be shared or used;
- the circumstances . . . under which screening will occur; and
- the action the screening entity will take if a person is identified as a person in the terrorist screening database."

There is one critical element in the "Memorandum of Understanding," added in light of the criticism the liberal community heaped on the Bush administration's efforts to fight the war on terror: the director of the TSC is charged with the establishment of

> the necessary procedures and safeguards to ensure the TSC's functions are carried out in a manner consistent with the Constitution and applicable laws, including, but not limited to, procedures to:
>
> • address the repeated misidentification of persons in any U.S. government screening process;
> • regularly review information, and to promptly adjust or delete erroneous or outdated information; and
> • protect personal privacy.

It is still too early to gauge the effectiveness of this Bush initiative in the war on terror. It is, however, the latest in a series of proposals and actions authored by the Bush administration in its fight against Al Qaeda and other fundamentalist religious groups who have declared war on America.

The Administration's Initial Defense of the USA Patriot Act, 2001–2002

In 2001 and 2002, in a series of essays on its Web page www.lifeandliberty.gov, the DOJ went on a spirited offensive to neutralize the chorus of critics who were condemning the USA Patriot Act. Under the heading "Preserving Life and Liberty," the DOJ tried to dispel myths and positively describe the Patriot Act while simultaneously debunking the critics.

For example, the DOJ presented four fundamental elements of the Patriot Act that showed how it improved "our counterterrorism efforts." First, it allowed investigators to use the tools that were already available to investigate organized crime and drug trafficking. The DOJ quoted Democratic senator Joe Biden: "The FBI could get a wiretap [roving wiretaps, delayed notification search warrants] to investigate the Mafia, but they could not get one to investigate terrorists. To put it bluntly, that was crazy! What's good for the mob should be good for terrorists."

Second, the USA Patriot Act "facilitated information sharing and cooperation among governmental agencies so that they can better 'connect the dots.'" It did so, the DOJ said, "by removing major legal barriers that prevent law enforcement, intelligence, and national defense communities from talking and coordinating their work to protect the American people and our national security." Again, the DOJ quoted a Democratic senator, John Edwards: "We simply cannot prevail in the battle against terrorism if the right hand of our government has no idea what the left hand is doing."

Third, the USA Patriot Act "updated the law to reflect new technologies and new threats, so that we no longer have to fight a digital-age battle with antique weapons." Finally, the Patriot Act "increased the penalties for those who commit terrorist crimes, especially for those who commit and support terrorist operations, both at home and abroad."

Another essay on the DOJ's Web site, "Anti-Terror Record of Accomplishments: How We Are Winning the War on Terrorism," lists six successes. First, the DOJ claims, the FBI and other law enforcement agencies are "disrupting, arresting, and detaining *potential* terrorist threats" while, second, the DOJ is "gathering and cultivating detailed intelligence on terrorism in the United States." And hundreds of "suspected terrorists" have been identified and tracked throughout the United States.

Third, according to the DOJ, the government is "gathering information by leveraging criminal charges and long prison sentences." Facing a long prison term, many individuals plead guilty and cooperate with federal law enforcement agencies. In the year following 9/11, for example, criminal plea agreements were worked out with fifteen individuals who are now cooperating with the FBI in its current terrorist operations. Through this arrangement, the FBI has uncovered Al Qaeda cells, safe houses, training camps, recruitment operatives, and tactics.

Fourth, the government is "dismantling the terrorist financial network." Dozens of investigations into terrorist financing have led to the freezing around the world of over $100 million in assets. Fifth, says the DOJ, "we are using new legal tools to detect, disrupt, and prevent potential terrorist plots." And finally, "we are building our long-term counter-terrorism capacity" with more funds allocated for hiring new FBI agents and U.S. attorneys and increases in the numbers of persons working for joint antiterrorism organizations.

Yet another broadside on its Web site, "Dispelling the Myths," identified three major—and very negative—"myths" about the Patriot Act and "dispelled" them. The first myth is the one spread by the ACLU. That organization claims that the Patriot Act's definition of "terrorism" and "domestic terrorism" expands the terms in a way that "could subject political organizations to surveillance, wiretapping, harassment, and criminal action for political advocacy." The reality, as the DOJ would have it, is that "domestic terrorism is limited to conduct that breaks criminal laws, endangering human life. 'Peaceful groups that dissent from governmental policy' without breaking laws cannot be targeted. . . . Peaceful political organizations engaging in political advocacy will obviously not come under the definition [of domestic terrorism]."

Another "myth" of the ACLU: "Many people are unaware that their library habits could become the target of government surveillance. In a free society, such monitoring is odious and unnecessary." The reality, according to the DOJ, is quite different: "The Patriot Act specifically protects Americans' First Amendment rights, and terrorism investigators have no interest in the library habits of ordinary Americans." To collect library or business information about alleged terrorists, the governmental investigating agency asks the Foreign Intelligence Surveillance Court to order the production of such information, "typically available through grand jury subpoenas." The FISC issues such an order

> only after the government demonstrates the records concerned are sought for an authorized investigation to obtain foreign intelligence information not concerning a U.S. person or to protect against international terrorism or clandestine intelligence activities, provided that such investigation of a U.S. person is not conducted solely on the basis of activities protected by the First Amendment.

The ACLU further claims that the delayed notification search warrants "would allow law enforcement agencies to delay giving notice when they conduct a search. . . . This provision would mark a sea-change in the way search warrants are executed in the United States." The DOJ counters this: "Delayed notification search warrants are a long-existing, crime-fighting tool upheld by courts for decades in organized crime, drug cases, and child pornography. The Patriot Act simply codified the authority law enforcement had already had for decades. This tool is a vital aspect of our strategy of prevention—detecting and incapacitating terrorists *before* they are able to strike."

Media Defenders of the Bush Administration's Antiterrorism Actions

For all the editorials, op-ed pieces, and feature stories that have condemned the USA Patriot Act, there have been others, including those in the *Des Moines Register,* the *Arizona Republic,* the *Winchester (Virginia) Star,* the *Baltimore Daily Record,* the *Lancaster (Pennsylvania) New Era,* the *Asheville (North Carolina) Citizen-Times,* and the *Columbus (Ohio) Dispatch,* that have extolled the counterterrorism measures of the Bush administration. These defenders of the legislation believe the civil libertarian groups and editors of liberal newspapers are crying, falsely, that the sky is falling. Rich Lowery of the *New York Post* challenged the ACLU and other critics to "name one civil liberty that has been violated under the Patriot Act" (Lowery 2003, 21):

> They can't, which is why they instead rely on hyperbole in an increasingly successful effort to make the Patriot Act a dirty phrase. . . . Opponents of the Act must explain why Mohammad Atta should have greater freedom from surveillance than Tony Soprano. . . . Critics want to eviscerate these sections of the Act (213, 215) and more. They should bundle their proposals together and call them "The Zacarias Moussaoui Protection Act," after the 20th hijacker, whose computer wasn't searched prior to September 11 due to civil liberties concerns.

"We have already forgotten the importance of aggressive, preemptive law enforcement," concluded Lowery (2003, 21).

Heather MacDonald, writing in the *City Journal,* called the critics' "rhetoric . . . both false and dangerous":

> Lost in the blizzard of propaganda is any consciousness that 9/11 was an act of war against the U.S. by foreign enemies concealed within the nation's borders. If the media and political elites keep telling the public that the campaign against these terrorist enemies is just a racist power grab, the most essential weapon against terror cells—intelligence from ordinary citizens—will

> be jeopardized. A drumbeat of ACLU propaganda could discourage a tip that might be vital in exposing an Al Qaeda plot. (MacDonald 2003, 1)

Her task, and the task of other reporters and editors, was "to demolish the extravagant lies about the anti-terror initiatives [of the Bush administration spread by left- and right-wing] libertarians. Close scrutiny shows . . . that civil liberties are fully intact" in America two years after the 2001 USA Patriot Act became law (1).

Some writers took a condescending tack toward the civil libertarian critics. There's no need for "hyperventilation," they said to them. "Civil libertarians are well-meaning folks," wrote David Yepsen in the *Des Moines Register*, "and we must always have them around to tweak our conscience. But they tend to see bogeymen, or black helicopters, where there are none" (Yepsen 2003, 1).

However, while the Bush people took encouragement from these supportive stories and editorials, the hue and cry of the critics forced the government to take to the road in defense of the Patriot Act. The major trouper was, as usual, Ashcroft.

Summer 2003: Ashcroft's "On the Road" Campaign in Defense of the 2001 USA Patriot Act

Attorney General Ashcroft spoke often about the "fear-mongering" of the critics of the USA Patriot Act. For example, in December 2001, he said: "Some of our critics, I regret to say, have shown less affection for detail. Their bold declarations of so-called fact have quickly dissolved, upon inspection, into vague conjecture. Charges of 'kangaroo courts' and 'shredding the Constitution' give new meaning to the term, 'the fog of war'" (Ashcroft, Remarks).

In one of its many critical editorials directed at the Bush administration's "aggressive" implementation of the 2001 Patriot Act and other federal statutes and executive orders, the *New York Times* accused Ashcroft of "spin-doctoring the problem" of the constitutionality of the USA Patriot Act. For the Bush administration, this was not "honest, reasoned debate" by the critics. According to the attorney general, "such condemnation of the Patriot Act only aids terrorists—for [these criticisms] erode our national unity and diminish our resolve. They give ammunition to America's enemies, and pause to America's friends. They encourage people of good will to remain silent in the face of evil" (www.usdoj.gov/ag/testimony/2002).

In the effort to defend the use of "core constitutional executive powers" in the war against terrorism, the attorney general in the summer of 2003 went on a nationwide tour as "pitchman" for the administration to counter the chorus of criticism aimed at the USA Patriot Act. As one reporter observed: "The increasingly vitriolic concerns over the [Patriot Act] and its future have thrown the administration on the defensive, according to people close to the administration. Mr. Ashcroft, though often criticized by liberal and conservative policy-makers, is seeking to solidify support for the law" (Lichtblau, "Bush Administration Plans Defense," 2003, 1).

Especially galling to the Bush administration leaders was that in early July 2003 the Republican-controlled House of Representatives, by a 309–118 majority, voted to repeal a provision of the Patriot Act that allowed law enforcement officials to execute search warrants secretly and to delay notifying the targeted individual. Although the House action was not acted on in the Senate, it was an important message to the White House. One immediate reaction was what critics labeled the Ashcroft "road show."

Ashcroft's defense of the Patriot Act was a month-long cross-country trip, with over one dozen speaking engagements scheduled only before law enforcement audiences in Iowa, Georgia, Pennsylvania, Idaho, New York, North Carolina, New Hampshire, Michigan, and Ohio. Ashcroft's basic task, said his former DOJ colleague Viet Dinh, was "to correct the misperceptions that are out there and to disabuse the American public of the misinformation they've gotten." In Washington, D.C., at a kickoff talk before his trip, Ashcroft forcefully defended the Patriot Act before a friendly audience at the American Enterprise Institute: "To abandon these tools would senselessly imperil American lives and American liberty, and it would ignore the lessons of September 11" (quoted in *Washington Post*, October 31, 2003, 1).

In Boise, Idaho, on August 25, 2003, Ashcroft gave his basic talk about the value of the Patriot Act in the fight against terrorism. Speaking to a selected audience of police and other law enforcement officers, he said:

> We have used the tools provided in the Patriot Act to fulfill our first responsibility to protect the American people. We have used these tools to prevent terrorists

from unleashing more death and destruction on our soil. We have used these tools to save innocent American lives. *We have used these tools to provide the security that ensures liberty.* (my emphasis)

Ashcroft again pointed out, as he has done since 2001, the three major goals of the USA Patriot Act: "To provide critical investigative tools to law enforcement; to bring the criminal laws up to date with modern technology; and to expand the government's capacity to build strong teams . . . dedicated to uncovering and stopping terrorists before they strike." He surmised that the critics "have forgotten how we felt" on September 11. "Just two years have passed," he said, "but already it has become difficult for some Americans to recall the shock, anger, grief, and anguish of that day" (www.lifeandliberty.gov/subs/speeches).

Ashcroft's standard speech on the tour quoted Thomas Jefferson and Abraham Lincoln—and paid homage to the fallen firefighters and police officers who died on September 11—to buttress the case for the Patriot Act. In his closing words, Ashcroft pointed to history:

> Abraham Lincoln [at Gettysburg] expressed the sense of resolution familiar to anyone who has looked into the void at Ground Zero, surveyed the wreckage of the Pentagon, or seen the gash in the earth left by Flight 93. . . . The responsibility of those who remain, said Lincoln, is to honor the dead, not with their words, but with their actions; to be "dedicated to the unfinished work which they who fought here have thus far so nobly advanced." It is now as it was then. . . . Our greatest memorial to those who have passed must be to protect the lives and liberties of those yet to come. (www.lifeandliberty.gov)

And he always ended the speech with the emphatically stated observation that "we are winning the war on terrorism."

At every stop Ashcroft was met by protesters. Many waved signs "denouncing as 'fascist' Mr. Ashcroft and the law he helped create." Other protesters chanted: "Stop Ashcroft! Defend the Constitution! Ashcroft go home. Leave our liberties alone!" (Linchtblau, "Ashcroft's Tour," 2003, 1).

The *Winchester, Virginia Star* editorialized in support of Ashcroft's "road show." In August 2003 the paper noted that "liberals are doing their darnedest to say that Attorney General John

Ashcroft's month-long nationwide tour in defense of the Patriot Act is a sure sign that public approval of the anti-terrorism legislation is crumbling" (www.lifeandliberty.gov/subs/speeches. htm).

> We say *it's about time Mr. Ashcroft took to the offensive* to combat those odious attacks on a measure intended not to run roughshod over civil liberties but to provide our protectors better tools to do their jobs in what figures to be a protracted war on terrorism. [The Patriot Act's purpose is] to help those agencies responsible for homeland security to "connect the dots" in this ongoing struggle to bring the perpetrators of terror to justice. This nation remains at war against shadowy foes—and Mr. Ashcroft is to be applauded for defending it.

But a September 21, 2003, *Washington Post* editorial entitled "Mr. Ashcroft's Tantrum," published at the end of the attorney general's trip, pummeled him once again. A few days earlier, Ashcroft reluctantly declassified data about the number of times the government had demanded library records of book borrowings. The answer was zero. The government had never used its power to seize such personal information from libraries and other sources.

Ashcroft followed that information with a "sarcastic harangue of critics of the Patriot Act," noted the *Post* editorial.

> He said: "The charges of the hysterics are revealed for what they are: castles in the air. Built on misrepresentation. Supported by unfounded fear. Held aloft by hysteria. . . . Allow me to take a moment to clarify who should, and who should not, be worried about these tools in the hands of law enforcement. If you are spending a lot of time surveilling nuclear power plants with your Qaeda pals, you *might* be a target of the Patriot Act. If your idea of a vacation is two weeks in a terrorist training camp, you *might* be a target of the Patriot Act. If you have cave-side dinners with a certain terrorist thug named bin Laden, . . . if you enjoy swapping recipes for chemical weapons from your 'Joy of Jihad' cookbook, you *might* be a target of the Patriot Act."

Ironically, the *Post* editorial condemned Ashcroft's penchant for secrecy as well as his sarcastic criticism of the administration's critics. The editorial did not criticize the Patriot Act itself. "We believe Mr. Ashcroft's defense of the infamous library provision of the Patriot Act is reasonable," it said; however, it went on,

> The attorney general of the United States has no business jeering at those who, rightly or wrongly, disagree with his policies or disfavor a particular law. [Other actions of the administration] naturally inflame suspicion. It is unfortunate that some of Mr. Ashcroft's critics are not more sober and careful in their charges. But Mr. Ashcroft's apparent disregard for civil liberties concerns—indeed, his contempt for those who have questions—does not invite sobriety or care. The attorney general ought to manage to debate important policy without selectively declassifying to serve his own interests and then throwing a temper tantrum at the controversy that results.

The critics' condemnation of the Patriot Act's potential to eviscerate the Bill of Rights continued unabated in the early months of 2004 and may very well prove to be a major issue in the 2004 presidential election. The Democratic candidate for president will certainly challenge the Bush administration's many actions taken in the war on terror. President Bush, who will seek reelection in November 2004, will certainly continue his aggressive defense of the Patriot Act of 2001. He may also push for legislation to strengthen it. His attorney general began the effort to improve the Patriot Act in early 2003.

Floating the "Domestic Security Enhancement Act" of 2003: A Patriot Act II?

In his testimony before the House Judiciary Committee in March 2001, Attorney General Ashcroft presented three basic loopholes in the existing Patriot Act:

> First, in pursuit of terrorist cells, current law makes it a crime to provide a terrorist organization with personnel or training. We must make it crystal clear that those who train for and fight with a designated terrorist organiza-

tion can be charged under material support statutes. Second, existing law does not consistently encourage cooperation by providing adequate maximum penalties to punish acts of terrorism. Some terrorist acts resulting in the death of citizens do not provide for the death penalty or even life imprisonment. Third, terrorism offenses are not expressly included in the list of crimes that allow for pre-trial detention, even though it could prevent an attack. In criminal cases where public safety is of concern—such as drug dealing, organized crime, and gun crimes—defendants in federal cases are presumptively denied pre-trial release. (Ashcroft 2003)

By January 2003 the Bush administration, against very vocal opposition to the 2001 USA Patriot Act in and out of Congress, started to take steps to fill in the perceived gaps in the 2001 act. A month later, on February 7, 2003, a "confidential" draft proposal of an eighty-six-page bill entitled the "Domestic Security Enhancement Act" of 2003, along with a section-by-section analysis of the law, was posted on the Web site of the Center for Public Integrity (CPI). Also posted was a "control sheet" indicating that the draft had been sent to House Speaker Dennis Hastert and Vice-President Dick Cheney on January 10, 2003.

The Bush Administration's Proposal to Strengthen the 2001 Patriot Act

Given the growing criticism of the 2001 USA Patriot Act in the Republican-controlled houses of Congress, along with the vitriolic attacks on the act and on the Bush administration's actions in the war on terrorism generally, the draft did not have a very receptive audience. However, it is important to examine the proposed national security enhancement bill because it will resurface during and after (if President Bush wins reelection) the 2004 presidential election.

The proposed legislation has five titles:

The first title enhances the 1978 Foreign Intelligence Surveillance Act as well as law enforcement investigative tools.

Title II takes up the protection of national security information.

Title III focuses on the augmentation of governmental
investigations of terrorist plots, specifically, through the
improvement of the Terrorist Identification Database,
the improvement of information sharing among law
enforcement agencies, and the facilitation of international terrorist investigations.

Title IV concerns the enhancement of preventing and prosecuting terrorist crimes through increased penalties and
protections against terrorist actions and incapacitating
terrorism financing.

The fifth title provides governmental agencies with
increased powers to enhance border and immigration
security.

Title I of the proposed legislation enhances, for example, the
coverage of terrorist operations to define "foreign power" to
include unaffiliated single individuals, *all* persons, who engage
in terrorist acts. Presently, "investigations of 'lone wolf' terrorists
or 'sleeper cells' may not be authorized under FISA" (Section 101;
another section, 111, amends the FISA "so that international terrorist organizations are consistently treated as *foreign powers*").

Section 121 redefines "terrorist activities" to include criminal
acts of domestic and international terrorism and specifies that
"'criminal investigations' include all investigations of criminal
terrorist activities, to make it clear that the full range of authorized surveillance techniques are available in investigations of
'terrorist activities' under the new definition."

Another proposed enhancement in Title I, Section 105,
would set aside the current prohibition on "the disclosure of
information 'for law enforcement purposes' unless the disclosure
includes a statement that the information cannot be used in a
criminal proceeding without the Attorney General's advance
authorization." The new language eliminates the requirement
that the attorney general personally approve the use of such
information in the criminal context.

Title I, Section 107, would amend the law to allow for a
lower standard for the use of pen registers on U.S. citizens. If the
proposal becomes law, "FISA pen registers would be available in
investigations of both U.S. persons and non-U.S. persons when-

ever they could be used 'to obtain foreign intelligence information.'"

Title II focuses on the matter of guarding national security information. For example, Section 201 would modify the Freedom of Information Act (FOIA) exemptions so that "the government need not disclose information about individuals detained in investigations of terrorism until disclosure occurs routinely upon the initiation of criminal charges."

And Section 202 would modify the Clean Air Act. Under Section 112 (r) of the Clean Air Act, private companies are required to submit to the Environmental Protection Agency (EPA) a worst-case scenario report detailing "what would be the impact on the surrounding community of release of the specified chemicals. Such reports are a roadmap for terrorists, who could use the information to plan attacks on the facilities." The modification to the act would allow much greater limits on who could access such information. It would enable the government to "better manage access to information contained in 'worst case scenario' reports."

Another section (203) in Title II would protect information filed with the Occupational Safety and Health Administration (OSHA) regarding the working conditions of legislative branch employees. "Terrorists may be able to obtain this information from OSHA via a FOIA request." The modification would exempt such information from disclosure under FOIA exemption 3.

Title III is a set of proposed changes in legislation, including the 2001 Patriot Act, respecting governmental investigations of terrorist plots. Section 302 would modify the Patriot Act to allow the FBI to collect DNA information from detainees suspected of terrorist acts as well as those convicted of certain crimes. The section would enable the secretary of defense or the attorney general to collect, analyze, and maintain DNA samples from

- "persons suspected of engaging in terrorism, or committing an offense proscribed in the Patriot Act, or attempting to do so;
- enemy combatants or other battlefield detainees;
- persons suspected of being members of a terrorist organization; and
- certain classes of aliens including those engaged in activity that endangers national security."

Section 311 of this Title would permit federal law enforcement agencies to share "consumer credit information, visa-related information, and educational records" with state and local government law enforcement agencies. Section 312 would impact court-ordered "consent decrees" that have "handicapped" law enforcement agencies from gathering information about organizations and individuals that may be engaged in terrorist activities and other criminal wrongdoing. The section would "terminate" most consent decrees enacted before September 11, 2001, that could impede terrorist activities conducted by federal, state, or local law enforcement agencies.

Section 321 of Title III would enable the United States to obtain search warrants in response to requests from foreign governments. At present the Patriot Act applies only to subpoena requests from foreign governments; a search warrant can be issued only if the United States entered into a treaty with a foreign government that contains such an authorizing provision.

The same treaty prescription applies to extradition proceedings. Currently, many treaties date back to the nineteenth century. Additionally, there are seventy countries that have no extradition treaties with the United States. This section would amend the law so as to:

1. "authorize the United States to extradite offenders to treaty partners for modern crimes that may not be included in our older list treaties with these countries; and
2. provide for on a case-by-case basis . . . [the] extradition from the United States for serious crimes even in the absence of an extradition treaty."

Title IV of the proposed modification of the 2001 Patriot Act is called "Enhancing Prosecution and Prevention of Terrorist Crimes." It contains nineteen sections, including criminal penalties and punishments for:

- "terrorist hoaxes" (Section 401);
- civil aviation threats (Section 409);
- "no statute of limitation for terrorist crimes" (Section 410);
- penalties for terrorist murders (Section 411);
- increasing penalties for terrorism financing (Section 421);

- "suspension of tax-exempt status of designated foreign terrorist organizations" (Section 423).

Title V of the proposed enhancement legislation focuses on improving the government's ability to counter terrorists by broadening governmental authority respecting immigration and border security. Like the previous four titles, this title deals with omissions in the hastily drawn-up and debated 2001 Patriot Act. For example, Section 501 would amend the 2001 law to make clear that just as an American can relinquish his or her citizenship "by serving in a hostile foreign army," so can citizenship be relinquished "by serving in a hostile terrorist organization." The same section would have a person "expatriated if, with the intent to relinquish nationality, he becomes a member of, or provides material support to, a group that the United States has designated as a 'terrorist organization,' if that group is engaged in hostilities against the United States."

Section 503 would give the attorney general authority to bar or remove from the United States an alien "whom the Attorney General has reason to believe would pose a danger to the national security of the United States." It would also give the attorney general "the authority to bar from the United States aliens who have been convicted of, or charged with, serious crimes in other countries."

The proposed enhancement of the 2001 law does indeed do what Attorney General Ashcroft has said it would: It closes loopholes and otherwise strengthens the government's efforts to combat terrorism.

The Critics Condemn the 2003 Enhancement Proposal

The 2001 USA Patriot Act, as discussed earlier, was quickly drawn up by the DOJ's top people (Ashcroft and Dinh), was rapidly submitted to Congress, and within six weeks was negotiated to a quick closure. The mark-up and passage of the law was so rapid that many congresspersons confessed to not having read the almost 400-page act in the final hours before voting on the legislation. However, as soon as the proposed enhancement of the Patriot Act was leaked by an alarmed Justice Department lawyer, the liberal and conservative organizations trained their sights on it (Welch 2003, 1).

The draft of the Domestic Security Enhancement Act was the equivalent of the crimson cape flaunted by the matador (Ashcroft) in front of the already enraged and wounded bull (civil liberties groups). Civil Rights groups charged that the proposed law

- "authorizes summary deportations without the non-citizen having violated any law and without ever knowing the basis for the action;
- adds more surveillance powers by [sheltering] federal agents in illegal surveillance, removes checks on local police spying, and gives the government power to access citizens' credit reports, and catalogue genetic information; and
- further criminalizes [guilt by] association [by] broadening death penalty applications that could cover acts of protest, and permits the stripping of even native-born Americans of U.S. citizenship" (Edgar 2003).

Within days of the draft's circulation, both liberal and conservative organizations began to rip the proposal apart as being even more of a bad thing. OMB Watch and others worried about the proposal's impact on the public's right-to-know: "The draft [act] is yet another development in a series of actions taken by the Bush administration to increase secrecy within the federal government and reduce public access to government information." The 2003 draft law would make it much more difficult for Americans to find out what the government is doing by barring them from using the FOIA to access information" ("Patriot Act" 2003, 1).

The CPI, the Friends Committee on National Legislation, the ACLU, the Rutherford Institute, the Cato Institute, and a host of other groups cited the more than 100 modifications to existing law in the 2003 draft as over-the-top antidemocratic governmental secrecy and interference with civil liberties and due process rights. The groups counted no less than nine major threats to personal privacy and civil liberties in this leaked draft bill:

1. increased secret surveillance;
2. increased control over immigrants;

3. establishment of new crimes;
4. addition of new death penalty crimes;
5. granting autopsy rights to the government;
6. decreased access to public information;
7. establishment of new terrorist-related DNA database;
8. allowance of extradition without treaty; and
9. altered procedure for taking away U.S. citizenship. (Edgar 2003, 1–13, passim)

While there was some support for this bill by conservative Republican senators such as Orrin Hatch, there was overwhelming concern and some vitriolic criticism of this latest effort to expand the authority of federal law enforcement agencies. Critics such as longtime civil liberties defender Nat Hentoff wrote that the eighty-seven-page proposal was "the most radical government plan in our history to remove from Americans their liberties under the Bill of Rights." And as was the case with the 2001 USA Patriot Act, liberal and conservative groups joined together to oppose the proposed bill. On March 17, 2003, for example, an open letter to Congress condemning the proposal, signed by the ACLU and People for the American Way along with conservative groups such as the Free Congress Foundation, the Gun Owners of America, and the American Conservative Union, was widely circulated (Welch 2003, 1, 3).

Within months, the proposal disappeared from public conversation. Instead, Attorney General Ashcroft took to the road in August and September 2003 in an effort to stem the tide of criticism against the 2001 USA Patriot Act. Patriot II was shortly to be replaced, in September and October 2003, by a three-part plan to enhance the act that the president proffered in a number of speeches before military and law enforcement audiences (Sanger 2003).

The Future of the 2001 USA Patriot Act

On September 10, 2003, President Bush addressed an audience of cheering FBI agents and troops from the nearby U.S. Marine training base at the FBI's training academy in Quantico, Virginia. He was there to give a speech commemorating the second anniversary of the terrorist attacks on the World Trade Center and the Pentagon. "Tomorrow's anniversary," he said, "is a time for remembrance. Yet history asked more than memory. The forces of global terror cannot be appeased, and they cannot be ignored. They must be hunted and they will be defeated" (www.whitehouse.gov).

At the core of his speech was Bush's call for a three-point plan for significant expansion of existing law enforcement powers under the USA Patriot Act. "We are winning the war against terrorism," he said, uttering the striking words of his attorney general. However, Bush bluntly argued, countering his critics' concerns, that the 2001 USA Patriot Act did not go far enough in giving law enforcement organizations the tools to defeat terrorists.

For the first time since he signed the legislation in October 2001, Bush entered the fray. He wanted Congress to amend the 2001 law to:

1. allow the FBI and other agencies to issue "administrative subpoenas" in terrorism cases without obtaining any approval from the FISC, a federal judge, or a federal grand jury;
2. expand the federal death penalty statutes to cover additional terrorism-related crimes; and
3. make it harder for suspected terrorists to be released on bail. (Sanger 2003, 1)

The president went on:

Under current federal law, there are unreasonable obstacles to investigating and prosecuting terrorism, obstacles that don't exist when law enforcement officials are going after embezzlers or drug traffickers. . . . If we can use [administrative] subpoenas to catch crooked doctors, the Congress should allow law enforcement officials to use them in catching terrorists. . . . [Regarding release on bail,] this disparity in the law makes no sense. If dangerous [Mafia] drug dealers can be held without bail in this way, Congress should allow for the same treatment for accused terrorists. (Sanger 2003; www.whitehouse.gov)

The critics resolutely challenged the president's three-part plan with the same arguments they used against the 2001 law. The *New York Times* editorial "Patriot Act, Part II" came out on

September 22, 2003. It was, as might have been expected, critical of the proposal to strengthen the 2001 USA Patriot Act. "None of these [new] tools are necessary to fight terrorism, and each *threatens* to infringe on the civil liberties of Americans."

The editorial charged that checks and balances, one of a handful of hallmark values rooted in the Constitution and evident in the American political system, are gutted even more in the new set of proposed changes to the 2001 Patriot Act. Inherent in the editorial—and in all criticism of the Bush administration's actions since 9/11—is the almost total lack of trust in the Bush White House's pledge to honor the Constitution's guarantees of due process and civil rights. One sees that distrust in the editorial's final words:

> If the administration truly had nothing to hide about its use of this power [to demand library records], it would not be arguing for the authority to put a librarian in prison for speaking publicly about receiving a subpoena. . . . The [administration's] drive to roll back civil liberties is a threat to freedom and a distraction. The administration would better use its energy on more effective law enforcement strategies to keep us safe. While this mistrust is not new in American political history, it comes at a time when the United States is fighting an asymmetrical world war unlike any other it has fought in its almost 230-year history. Throughout that history, we have seen excessive governmental actions that deprived U.S. citizens and resident aliens of their lives, their property, and their liberty for real and imaginary reasons. These uncivil and often brutal events have colored many Americans' perceptions of government requests for more power; people of goodwill are extremely wary of presidential requests to enhance law enforcement authority to fight terrorism at the expense of due process and civil rights. And the Bush administration's penchant for excessive secrecy has not placated the concerns of the critics. ("Patriot Act," 2003, A18)

It is saddening to see the estrangement between government and the governed, once again, in American history. It is always the hope that presidential administrations will learn from history; it seems that the past is not prologue to the present. Secrecy is one of the many factors in the public's loss of trust in the Bush administration's actions since 9/11. In a time of asymmetrical, open-ended war and perpetual fear of savage attacks against innocent civilians, it is understandable that the governmental leaders are wary of being too open. But one major task of the Bush administration, especially the president and his major executive department leaders, is to try to minimize the harsh condemnation by segments of the public and the Congress by being more forthcoming with the people.

There have been significant changes in law enforcement in the United States since the terrorist attacks of 9/11/01. President Bush has become a focused chief executive since that day of infamy. On September 10, 2001, he was seen by many as an illegitimate minority president, the man who lost the popular vote to Democratic Party presidential candidate Al Gore. He was the president because his brother, Jeb Bush, the Republican governor of Florida, helped him eke out a victory in that crucial state. And he was put into the White House by five conservative Republican U.S. Supreme Court justices.

September 11 dramatically turned a purportedly drifting presidency into a focused, dedicated, and aggressive one with a clearly defined goal: Fight the terrorist enemies with *all* the appropriate tools in order to protect the American public. Hunt down all enemy combatants, the terrorists and the suspected terrorists, and the organizations, at home and abroad, including the financial supporters of terrorism. Capture them, hold them as long as possible—without bail when necessary, and without the ordinary due process afforded ordinary criminal suspects. Make darn sure that 9/11 is not repeated again.

The president changed overnight. George W. Bush no longer seemed carefree; the terrorist war transformed him and his presidency. So too did change come to the federal law enforcement bureaucracy—but not nearly as quickly as it did to the White House. The FBI's primary mission is no longer crime solving; its primary mission, since 9/11, is preventing terrorists from striking innocent persons living and working in the United States.

The FBI and the CIA are talking to each other, sharing information, working side by side in the new Terrorist Screening Center. There is a new executive department, created in November 2002, to deal with all aspects of security on U.S. soil: the Department of Homeland Security. All law enforcement agencies have been given the appropriate powers to eavesdrop, sneak and peek, and conduct nationwide searches and arrests.

The critics of the strategy and tactics of President Bush's war on terror, fearing the loss of civil liberties, remain loud and constant. However, the president and his chief surrogates, especially Attorney General Ashcroft, have not backed away from the battle to make the 2001 USA Patriot Act even more effective. Bush's and Ashcroft's strong arguments for a more powerful set of law enforcement tools to battle the terrorists clash with the growing wariness of the legislators in Congress. As Eric Lichtblau observed recently: "Mr. Bush's proposal for stronger counter-terrorism laws . . . faces a hard sell in Congress, as the administration tries to persuade skeptical lawmakers in both parties that the authorities will not abuse their growing power to investigate and lock up suspects" (Lichtblau, "Bush's Counter-Terror Proposals," 2003, 1). In a strategic move, however, the attorney general, who is, Lichtblau said, a "polarizing figure," did not unveil the new proposals, ones that were markedly less onerous to the critics than those in the proposed Patriot Act II. Instead, the president has now become the spokesperson for a stronger, more effective USA Patriot Act.

It is axiomatic that Bush-as-candidate will make these enhancements of the 2001 law a significant part of his 2004 re-election campaign. As Lichtblau noted in his analysis of the president's September 10, 2003 speech, Bush "appeared undaunted by the increasing attacks from both Republicans and Democrats over the Patriot Act and the government's expanded powers" (Lichtblau, "Bush's Counter-Terror Proposals," 2003, A1). A Democratic critic of the Patriot Act, Beryl Howell, said of the Bush campaign to enhance the 2001 Patriot Act: "The best defense is a good offense, and this administration plays that strategy very well. Their attitude is, 'if you think the USA Patriot Act is so bad, wait and see what else we want.' They're marking their position" (quoted in Lichtblau, "Bush's Counter-Terror Proposals," 2003, 1). And as a Republican congressional aide said: "This is the President speaking, and not John Ashcroft, and the fact is that we have to be as supportive as we can of the president and his efforts to combat terrorism" (quoted in Lichtblau, "Bush's Counter-Terror Proposals," 2003, 17).

As already observed, the problem of excessive secrecy has always plagued the executive branch—especially when the nation is at war. In time of war and other national catastrophes, the American people look to the president for executive actions that will ultimately overcome the calamity. National security matters do demand a degree of confidentiality and secrecy. However, there needs to be some balance so that the public is informed about the actions of government at appropriate times—without jeopardizing the ongoing war against terrorists. In the end, history will judge whether the actions of the Bush administration jeopardized civil liberties and due process or whether the government used its authority properly in this era of asymmetrical warfare.

For Further Reading

Ashcroft, John. "Mobilization against Terrorist Actions Outlined." Statement, September 21, 2001. www.usdoj.gov/opa/pr/2001/Sept/.

———. Remarks, December 3, 2001, www.usdoj.gov/ag/remarks/2001.

———. "Terrorist Threat: Working Together to Protect America." Remarks before the U.S. Senate Committee on the Judiciary, March 4, 2003. www.usdoj.gov.

Edgar, Timothy H. "Section-by-Section Analysis of Justice Department Draft, 'Domestic Security Enhancement Act of 2003.'" American Civil Liberties Union Legislative Update, February 14, 2003.

Frum, David. "David Frum's Diary: The Hysteria of the Civil Libertarians." *National Review,* April 7, 2003.

Lichtblau, Eric. "Ashcroft's Tour Rallies Supporters and Detractors." *New York Times,* September 8, 2003.

———. "Bush Administration Plans Defense of Terror Law." *New York Times,* August 19, 2003.

———. "Bush's Counter-Terror Proposals Could Be a Hard Sell." *New York Times,* September 11, 2003.

Lowery, Rich. "Over the Top Over Patriot Act." *New York Post,* August 27, 2003.

MacDonald, Heather. "Straight Talk on Homeland Security." *City Journal,* Summer 2003.

"Patriot Act Limits Public's Right-to-Know." *OMB Watch* 3, February 20, 2003.

"Patriot Act, Part II." Editorial, *New York Times,* September 22, 2003, A18.

Ponnuru, Ramesh. "1984 in 2003?: Fears About the Patriot Act Are Misguided." *National Review,* June 2, 2003.

Rossiter, Clinton. *Constitutional Dictatorship: Crisis Government in the Modern Democracies.* New York: Transaction Publishers, 2002.

Sanger, David E. "President Urging Wider U.S. Powers in Terrorism Law." *New York Times,* September 11, 2003, A1.

Schlesinger, Arthur M., Jr. *The Imperial Presidency.* New York: Replica Books, 1998.

U.S. Department of Justice. "Domestic Security Enhancement Act of 2003: Section-By-Section Analysis." Draft ("Confidential—Not for Distribution"). January 9, 2003.

Wedgwood, Ruth. "The Rule of Law and the War on Terror." *New York Times,* December 23, 2003, 28.

Welch, Matt. "Get Ready for PATRIOT II." AlterNet.org, April 2, 2003. Available at: www.alternet.org.

Yepsen, David. "Ashcroft's Defense Is Simple: The Patriot Act Works." *Des Moines Register,* August 21, 2003.

5

Key Players, Organizations, and Governmental Responses: U.S. National Security and the 2001 Patriot Act

The Major Players

Umar Abd al-Rahman

Al-Rahman is a sixty-two-year-old cleric and Islamic scholar and the leader of an Islamic Jihad group living in New Jersey. Originally from Egypt, in 1990 he acquired a U.S. visitor visa. In 1993, he and several of his followers were indicted and charged with conspiracy in connection with the Islamic terrorist plot to assassinate prominent Americans and blow up buildings in New York City. The case went to trial in September 1993 and al-Rahman was sentenced to life in prison for his leadership of the group that bombed the World Trade Center in 1993.

Dick Armey

Armey was the first Republican House majority leader in forty years. He retired from public office at the end of 2002. Armey was an economics professor from Texas before his election to the House of Representatives. He spent nine terms in the House. His successes include membership in the base-closing congressional commission, which had the difficult task of deciding which military bases were no longer viable, and winning House approval of school choice for Washington, D.C., students. He led the fight against the first President Bush's 1990 tax increase, and his harsh economic condemnation of President Clinton's health-care scheme marked the beginning of its end. Shortly after that, he helped draft the Contract with America. He actively, and successfully, sought sunset provisions in the 2001 USA Patriot Act.

John Ashcroft

Ashcroft was Missouri's state auditor from 1973–75, and then became the state's assistant attorney general in 1975. The following year he moved up to the attorney-general job, where he stayed until 1984 when he was elected governor of Missouri, and won a second term in 1988. Ashcroft was elected to the Senate in 1995, and briefly considered running for the Republican presidential nomination in 2000. In the end he ran for Senate reelection, but lost his seat to a dead man, Mel Carnahan, whose widow, Jean, stepped in as the Democrat candidate when her husband died. In 2001, Ashcroft became George W. Bush's U.S. attorney-general. He has been the key actor in the passage and implementation of the 2001 USA Patriot Act.

Osama bin Laden

Bin Laden is the dynamic leader of al Qaeda ("the base"), the worldwide Islamic terrorist organization, and a hero to millions of Islamic fundamentalists around the globe. He was born in Saudi Arabia, the seventeenth of fifty-two children of an immigrant from neighboring Yemen, construction magnate Muhammad Awad bin Laden, who runs a construction company, the Saudi bin Laden Group. In 1979, Osama bin Laden went to Afghanistan to help Afghan resistance fighters, known as the *mujahedeen*, beat back the Soviet military forces that had occupied that nation since 1979. He transferred his business to Afghanistan—including several hundred loyal workmen and heavy construction tools—and set out to liberate the land. After the Soviets pulled out of Afghanistan, bin Laden returned to Saudi Arabia to work for the family construction firm. In 1990, the Saudi government allowed U.S. troops to be stationed in Saudi Arabia following the Iraqi invasion of Kuwait, which led to the Persian Gulf War. Outraged by the U.S. military presence in Saudi Arabia, bin Laden condemned the Saudi leaders for allowing western infidels into the holy lands. The Saudis expelled him and revoked his citizenship. He moved to the Sudan, a nation whose leadership was more respectful toward him and his ideas. However, under intense pressure from the Saudis and the Americans, Sudan expelled him in 1996. Bin Laden moved back to Afghanistan and declared a jihad, or holy war, against U.S. forces. The United States indicted bin Laden on charges of training the people involved in the 1993 attack that killed eighteen U.S. servicemen in Somalia. On August 7, 1998, a pair of truck bombs exploded outside the U.S. embassies in Nairobi, Kenya, and Dar es Salaam, Tanzania, killing 224 people. On August 20, U.S. president Clinton ordered cruise missile attacks against suspected terrorist training camps in Afghanistan and a pharmaceutical plant in Khartoum, Sudan. In November 1998, the United States indicted bin Laden on charges of masterminding the attacks on the U.S. embassies. Following the September 11, 2001, terrorism attacks in the United States, the U.S. government named bin Laden as the prime suspect. In 2002, the U.S.-led military operation in Afghanistan led to the fall of the Taliban government and the hunt for bin Laden picked up in intensity. By spring 2004, coalition forces led by the United States had more special forces in the mountainous territory between Afghanistan and Pakistan to further intensify the search for the elusive bin Laden.

L. Paul Bremer

U.S. president George W. Bush chose a longtime career diplomat as his top man in Baghdad on May 6, 2003. It was the Bush administration's effort to show that the rebuilding of Iraq was a civilian-led reconstruction effort and not a military occupation. L. Paul Bremer is a sixty-one-year-old U.S. State Department veteran whose foreign service career began in 1966 in Kabul, Afghanistan, and ended twenty-three years later when he was appointed President Ronald Reagan's chief counterterrorism adviser. In 1999, House Speaker Dennis Hastert named Bremer to head the National Commission on Terrorism. He presented an important, though forgotten, report about the terrorist threat to the United States in the twenty-first century. In 2001, Bush appointed Bremer to the Homeland Security Advisory Council. Since May 2003, he has been the point man for the United States' efforts to create a democratic Iraq.

George H. W. Bush

George Herbert Walker Bush was the forty-first president of the United States, from 1989 to 1993. Bush served two terms as a representative to Congress from Texas. Twice he ran unsuccessfully for the Senate. Then he was appointed to a series of high-level positions: ambassador to the United Nations, chairman of the Republican National Committee, chief of the U.S. Liaison Office in the People's Republic of China, and director of the Central Intelligence Agency. In 1980 Bush campaigned for the Republican nomination for president. He lost, but was chosen as Ronald Reagan's running mate. In 1988 Bush won the Republican nomination for president and, with Senator Dan Quayle of Indiana as his running mate, he defeated Massachusetts governor Michael Dukakis in the general election. The Bush presidency faced a major foreign policy challenge when Iraqi president Saddam Hussein invaded Kuwait, then threatened to move into Saudi Arabia. Bush rallied the United Nations, the U.S. people, and Congress and sent 425,000 American troops to drive Iraq from Kuwait. They were joined by 118,000 troops from dozens of coalition nations. After weeks of air and missile bombardment, the 100-hour land battle called Desert Storm routed Hussein's million-man army. Despite unprecedented popularity from this military and diplomatic action, Bush was unable to withstand discontent at home. In 1992 he lost his bid for reelection to Democrat William Clinton (www.whitehouse.gov/history/presidents/gb41.html; www.patriotacademy.com/patriots.html).

George W. Bush

George W. Bush is the son of the forty-first president and is the forty-third president of the United States. He was sworn into office on January 20, 2001, after a campaign in which he outlined sweeping proposals to reform America's public schools, transform the national defense, provide tax relief, modernize Social Security and Medicare, and encourage "faith-based" and community organizations to work with government to help Americans in need. He became governor of Texas in 1994, and in 1998 Bush became the first governor in Texas history to be elected to consecutive four-year terms when he was reelected on November 3, 1998, with 68.6 percent of the vote. Since taking office in

2001, President Bush has signed a tax relief bill that provided rebate checks and lower tax rates for most Americans. The attacks of September 11 changed America—and gave President Bush a mission. He declared war against terror and has made victory in the war on terrorism the major goal of his administration. As part of the war on terror, he and Attorney General John Ashcroft pushed for quick passage of the major domestic weapon against terrorism, the 2001 USA Patriot Act.

Dick Cheney

Vice President Richard B. Cheney has a career as a businessman and public servant, serving four presidents and, as a member of the House of Representatives, his Wyoming constitutents. As secretary of defense during the first Bush presidency, Cheney directed two military campaigns: Operation Just Cause in Panama and Operation Desert Storm in Kuwait. For his role in the Gulf War, Secretary Cheney was awarded the Presidential Medal of Freedom by President George Bush on July 3, 1991. Mr. Cheney married his high school sweetheart, Lynne Ann Vincent, in 1964; they have two grown daughters, Elizabeth and Mary. In the Spring of 2000, he was selected by George W. Bush to be Bush's running mate in the 2000 presidential election.

John Conyers

Representative John Conyers, Jr., a Detroit Democrat, was elected in November 2002 to his nineteenth term in the U.S. House of Representatives, winning 83 percent of the vote in Michigan's 14th Congressional District. First elected in 1964, Conyers is the second most senior member in the House of Representatives and was elected by his congressional colleagues to lead the Democratic side of the important House Committee on the Judiciary. Congressman Conyers was also a member of the Judiciary Committee in its 1974 hearings on the Watergate impeachment scandal and played a prominent role in the recent impeachment process of President Clinton, giving him the distinction as the only Judiciary Committee member to have served on both panels.

He was one of the legislators in the House to push for the inclusion of checks on the FBI and the CIA during the debates surrounding the passage of the USA Patriot Act.

Viet Dinh

Viet D. Dinh was sworn in as assistant attorney general for the Office of Legal Policy on May 31, 2001. In the two weeks following 9/11, Dinh worked hard, with the attorney general, to quickly pull together a draft of what was to become the USA Patriot Act. He left the DOJ in 2003 and subsequently expressed, in essays, reservations about the major powers granted to the DOJ, the FBI, and the intelligence community, including the CIA, in the 2001 USA Patriot Act.

Yaser Esam Hamdi

Hamdi, then age twenty-two, was captured in Afghanistan in November 2001 during the battles between the Taliban forces and the American military. He was brought to Guantanamo Bay Naval Base in Cuba but, after it was determined that he was born in Louisiana and moved with his family to Saudi Arabia as an infant, he was relocated to the American mainland and placed in a navy brig. Hamdi was flown to a detention facility in the United States where he has remained since 2001. He has been held incommunicado and was not allowed to speak to an attorney until March 2004. The U.S. Supreme Court will review the circumstances of his detention to determine whether Hamdi has been denied the due process all citizens have or whether the government can declare him to be an enemy combatant. Its decision was scheduled for late June 2004.

Orrin Hatch

Orrin Hatch was elected to the United States Senate in 1976. As chairman of the important Senate Judiciary Committee, Senator Hatch is a leader in the fight for tougher anticrime laws, civil justice reform to unclog the courts, and legislation to protect individual property rights. He has served on the Senate Intelligence Committee, the Committee on Indian Affairs, the Special Committee on Aging, and the Joint Economic Committee. As chair of the Senate Judiciary Committee in September 2001, he worked to support the antiterrorism proposal the Bush administration presented within weeks of 9/11. He remains a vigorous supporter of the 2001 USA Patriot Act and supported the actions of the Bush administration to enhance the federal government's powers in an amended Patriot Act.

Patrick Leahy

Patrick Leahy of Burlington, Vermont, was elected to the United States Senate in 1974 and remains the only Democrat from Vermont to have been elected to this office. Leahy is the ranking minority member of the Judiciary Committee and is a senior minority member of the Agriculture and Appropriations Committees. In the immediate aftermath of the terrorist attacks of September 11, Leahy headed the Senate's negotiations on the 2001 antiterrorism bill, the USA Patriot Act. He called for greater constraints on the powers of the federal government and supported the inclusion of sunset provisions in the act.

Jose Padilla

Padilla was seized, in December 2002, by FBI agents in Chicago's O'Hare International Airport, allegedly en route to contaminate a U.S. city with a radiological bomb. Padilla, however, is an American citizen arrested outside a "war zone." The issue presented by his incarceration is whether he lost his constitutional and legal rights. Like Yassar Esam Hamdi, he has been locked up without any constitutional rights, especially the right to speak with an attorney. In January 2004, the U.S. Supreme Court announced that it would hear oral arguments in both the Padilla and the Hamdi appeals. The essential question in these two cases is whether the two men, as American citizens, have the right to due process of law in a federal courtroom, rather than before a special military tribunal. The court's decision was made at the end of June 2004 (see Chronology, p. 224).

Colin L. Powell

Colin L. Powell was nominated by President Bush on December 16, 2000, as Secretary of State. After being unanimously confirmed by the U.S. Senate, he was sworn in as the sixty-fifth Secretary of State on January 20, 2001. Secretary Powell was a professional soldier for thirty-five years, during which time he held myriad command and staff positions and rose to the rank of four-star General. He was assistant to the president for National Security Affairs from December 1987 to January 1989. His last assignment, from October 1, 1989, to September 30, 1993, was as the twelfth chairman of the Joint Chiefs of Staff, the highest military position in the Department of Defense (www.state.gov/r/pa/ei/biog/1349.htm).

Tom Ridge

Ridge is the secretary of the Department of Homeland Security (HS). Ridge leads more than 180,000 employees from almost two dozen combined agencies in HS. According to the language of the law creating the department, its focused mission is to (1) strengthen America's borders, (2) provide for intelligence analysis and infrastructure protection, (3) improve the use of science and technology to counter weapons of mass destruction, and (4) create a comprehensive response and recovery division. Tom Ridge was sworn in as the first director of the Office of Homeland Security in October 2001, following the events of September 11. He is a strong advocate of an enhanced USA Patriot Act and has worked closely with Attorney General Ashcroft to push for such a change.

Donald Rumsfeld

Donald H. Rumsfeld was sworn in as the twenty-first secretary of defense on January 20, 2001. Before assuming his present post, he served as the thirteenth secretary of defense, White House chief of staff, U.S. ambassador to NATO, U.S. congressman, and chief executive officer of two Fortune 500 companies. Rumsfeld is responsible for directing the actions of the Defense Department in response to the terrorist attacks on September 11, 2001.

James Sensenbrenner

"Sensenbrenner is a Republican member of Congress representing the Fifth Congressional District of Wisconsin. He won his race to become a member of Congress in November of 1978, after serving ten years in the Wisconsin State Legislature. Congressman Sensenbrenner assumed the chairmanship of the House Committee on the Judiciary beginning in the 107th Congress. He has established a strong record on crime, constitutional, and intellectual property issues as a long-serving member of the Judiciary Committee. Previously, Congressman Sensenbrenner also served as chairman of the House Committee on Science, where he solidified his reputation as an independent leader on science issues" (http://www.house.gov/sensenbrenner/bio.htm). As one of the major figures in the drafting of the 2001 USA Patriot Act, he called for constraints, in the form of sunset provisions, in the legislation.

Ramzi Yousef

"Yousef is the convicted mastermind of the 1993 World Trade Center bombing. . . . According to the presiding judge in his 1998 trial, the bombing of New York's World Trade Center on February 26, 1993, was meant to topple the city's tallest tower onto its twin." Had the attack gone as planned, tens of thousands of Americans would have died. However, one tower did not fall on the other, and only six people died. He fled the country after the failed bombing and took up residence in Pakistan. Pakistani police arrested Yousef on February 7, 1995, in an Islamabad hotel room. U.S. district court judge Kevin Duffy sentenced Yousef to life in prison on January 8, 1998, for the trade center bombings (www.terrorismfiles.org/individuals/ramzi_yousef.html).

Foreign Terrorist Organizations/Governments

Al Qaeda

Al Qaeda, "the base" in Arabic, is a multinational support group that funds and orchestrates the activities of Islamic militants worldwide. It grew out of the Afghan war against the Soviets, and its core members are Afghan war veterans from all over the Muslim world. Al Qaeda was established in 1988 by the Saudi militant Osama bin Laden. Based in Afghanistan, bin Laden used an extensive international network to maintain a loose connection among Muslim extremists in diverse countries. The train bombings in Madrid, Spain, in March 2004, are the latest example of al Qaeda working with Islamic extremists to wreak havoc on Western nations at war against Islam (in Iraq and Afghanistan). The organization's primary goal is the overthrow of what it sees as the corrupt and heretical governments of Muslim states, and their replacement with the rule of *sharia* (Islamic law). Al Qaeda is intensely anti-Western, and views the United States in particular as the prime enemy of Islam (www.fsuwap.org/documents/2002_rtc/RTC%20Spring%202002,%20DISEC.pdf).

Islamic Jihad

Islamic Jihad originated among militant Palestinians in the Gaza Strip during the 1970s. Committed to the creation of an Islamic Palestinian state and the destruction of Israel through holy war, Islamic Jihad also opposes moderate Arab governments that it believes have been tainted by Western secularism. Its activists have conducted many attacks including large-scale suicide bombings against Israeli civilian and military targets. The group increased its operational activity in 2002, claiming responsibility for numerous attacks against Israeli interests. The group has not yet targeted U.S. interests and continues to confine its attacks to Israelis inside Israel and the territories, although U.S. citizens have died in attacks mounted by the organization.

Taliban

In 1994, in the chaos and anarchy that followed Russian dominance of Afghanistan, the Taliban—a large group of fundamentalist Islamic militants and priests—began to control territory in Afghanistan. After capturing the city of Kandahar, their forces began a lightening-like advance, which led to their capture of the capital, Kabul, in September 1996. The Taliban's popularity with many Afghans was because of their successes in stamping out corruption, restoring peace, and allowing commerce to flourish again. The Taliban said their aim was to set up the world's pure Islamic state. In this effort, frivolities like television, music, and movies were banned. Regulations forbidding girls from going to school and women from working quickly brought them into conflict with the international community. After 9/11, President Bush declared war on terrorism and led a coalition of nations in a military attack on the Taliban, quickly routing the Taliban from Kabul. The coalition forces, in 2004, still patrolled the streets of cities and the mountains of Afghanistan in an effort to locate

Osama bin Laden and to prevent Taliban leaders and military from entering Afghanistan.

Governmental Actions in Response to Threats, War, and Terrorism

Alien and Sedition Act, 1798.
Taken from United States Code (USC)

These pieces of legislation were introduced by the Federalist President John Adams, and passed by the Federalist-controlled Congress. They were efforts to curtail and to punish those who supported French interests vis-à-vis American policy as well as to punish those who were critical of Adams's foreign policy. In part, the Act stated:

"An Act respecting Alien Enemies. July 6, 1798 SECTION I. Be it enacted . . . That whenever there shall be a declared war between the United States and any foreign nation or government, or any invasion or predatory incursion shall be perpetrated, attempted, or threatened against the territory of the United States, by any foreign nation or government, and the President of the United States shall make public proclamation of the event, all natives, citizens, denizens, or subjects of the hostile nation or government, being males of the age of fourteen years and upwards, who shall be within the United States, and not actually naturalized, shall be liable to be apprehended, restrained, secured and removed, as alien enemies. And the President of the United States shall be, and he is hereby authorized, in any event, as aforesaid, by his proclamation thereof, or other public act, to direct the conduct to be observed, on the part of the United States, towards the aliens who shall become liable, as aforesaid; the manner and degree of the restraint to which they shall be subject, and in what cases, and upon what security their residence shall be permitted, and to provide for the removal of those, who, not being permitted to reside within the United States, shall refuse or neglect to depart therefrom; and to establish any other regulations which shall be found necessary in the premises and for the public safety: Provided, that aliens resident within the United States, who shall become liable as enemies, in the manner aforesaid, and who shall not be chargeable with actual hostility, or other crime against the public safety, shall be allowed, for the recovery, disposal, and removal of their goods and effects, and for their departure, the full time which is, or shall be stipulated by any treaty, where any shall have been between the United States, and the hostile nation or government, of which they shall be natives, citizens, denizens or subjects: and when no such treaty shall have existed, the President of the United States may ascertain and declare such reasonable time as may be consistent with the public safety, and according to the dictates of humanity and national hospitality."

Alien Registration Act, 1940 (Smith Act)

The Alien Registration Act of 1940, usually called the Smith Act because the antisedition section was authored by Representative Howard W. Smith of Virginia, was passed and signed by President Franklin Roosevelt in 1940. The Act has been amended several times and can now be found at 18 U.S. Code § 2385 (2000), Advocating Overthrow of Government:

"Anyone who teaches the duty, necessity, desirability, or propriety of overthrowing or destroying the government of the United States or the government of any State, Territory, District or Possession thereof, or the government of any political subdivision therein, by force or violence, or by the assassination of any officer of any such government; or Whoever, with intent to cause the overthrow or destruction of any such government, prints, publishes, edits, issues, circulates, sells, distributes, or publicly displays any written or printed matter advocating, advising, or teaching the duty, necessity, desirability, or propriety of overthrowing or destroying any government in the United States by force or violence, or attempts to do so; or Whoever organizes or helps or attempts to organize any society, group, or assembly of persons who teach, advocate, or encourage the overthrow or destruction of any such government by force or violence; or becomes or is a member of, or affiliates with, any such society, group, or assembly of persons, knowing the purposes thereof— Shall be fined under this title or imprisoned not more than twenty years, or both, and shall be ineligible for employment by the United States or any department or agency thereof, for the five years next following his conviction. If two or more persons conspire to commit any offense named in this section, each shall be fined under this title or imprisoned not more than twenty years, or both, and shall be ineligible for employment by the United States or any department or agency thereof, for the five years next following his conviction. As used in this section, the terms "organizes" and "organize," with respect to any society, group, or assembly of persons, include the recruiting of new members, the forming of new units, and the regrouping or expansion of existing clubs, classes, and other units of such society, group, or assembly of persons."

Antiterrorism and Effective Death Act, 1996

The Oklahoma City and World Trade Center bombings led to the passage of the first Anti-Terrorism Act. At the signing of the Anti-Terrorism Act, President Clinton remarked: "From now on, we can quickly expel foreigners who dare to come to America and support terrorist activities. From now on, American prosecutors can wield new tools and expanded penalties against those who terrorize Americans at home and abroad. From now on, we can stop terrorists from raising money in the United States to pay for their horrible crimes. From now on, criminals sentenced to death for their vicious crimes will no longer be able to use endless appeals to delay their sentences, and families of victims will no longer have to endure years of anguish and suffering for many people and nations around the world" (Public Papers of President William J. Clinton). The Anti-Terrorism Act allows the government to activate "alien terrorist removal procedures" without having to give even a nod to due process—a clear violation of the Fifth Amendment. Under the act, noncitizens can be accused, tried, and deported without ever appearing in court. The Anti-Terrorism Act allows the government to avoid informing the accused that an investigation or "trial" took place. The Anti-Terrorism Act also relaxes electronic surveillance laws, expanding the government's ability to investigate groups or organizations the government "suspects" of terrorism. Moreover, the bill granted the president sweeping new powers to selectively target unpopular domestic groups, as well as arbitrarily criminalize activities he or she determines a threat to national security. Under the Crime Bill, sixty new offenses are punishable by death, including terrorist homicides, murder of a federal law enforcement official, and large-scale drug trafficking, drive-by shootings, and carjackings that result in death (quoted from USC). The

Patriot Act of 2001 is, in one sense, a continuation of this 1996 effort to protect the public through harsh actions against suspected terrorists.

Camp X-Ray, Guantanamo Bay, Cuba

U.S. Naval Base Guantanamo Bay is the oldest U.S. base overseas and the only one in a Communist country. Located on the southeast corner of Cuba, in the Oriente Province, the base is about four hundred air miles from Miami, Florida. In December 1903, the United States leased the forty-five square miles of land and water for use as a coaling station. A treaty reaffirmed the lease in 1934 granting Cuba and her trading partners free access through the bay, payment of $2,000 in gold per year, equating to $4,085 today, and a requirement that both the U.S. and Cuba must mutually consent to terminate the lease. Diplomatic relations with Cuba were cut in 1961 by President Dwight Eisenhower. Today, U.S. Marines and Cuba's "Frontier Brigade" still man fence-line posts twenty-four hours a day (www.globalsecurity.org/military/facility/guantanamo-bay.htm).

In May 2004, there were more than six hundred Afghan and Iraqi detainees still held by the Americans in this facility.

Espionage Act, 1917

The Espionage Act was passed by Congress in 1917 after the United States entered World War I. It prescribed a $10,000 fine and twenty years' imprisonment for interfering with the recruiting of troops or the disclosure of information dealing with national defense. Additional penalties were included for the refusal to perform military duty. Over the next few months around nine hundred people went to prison under the Espionage Act. Criticized as unconstitutional, the act resulted in the imprisonment of many members of the antiwar movement. This included the arrest of left-wing political figures such as Eugene V. Debs, Bill Haywood, Philip Randolph, Victor Berger, John Reed, Max Eastman, and Emma Goldman. Debs was sentenced to ten years for a speech in Canton, Ohio, on June 16, 1918, attacking the Espionage Act. On August 23, six members of the *Frayhayt*, a group of Jewish anarchists based in New York, were arrested. Charged under the Espionage Act, the group was accused of publishing articles in the *Der Shturm* that undermined the American war effort. This included criticizing the United States government for invading Russia after the Bolshevik government signed the Brest-Litovsk Treaty (www.museumstuff.com/articles/art155981058703841.html; www.spartacus.schoolnet.co.uk/FWWespionage.htm).

Japanese-American Internment, 1942–1946

Franklin D. Roosevelt issued an Executive Order that led to the internment of more than 120,000 persons of Japanese ancestry, including over 70,000 Japanese-American citizens.

"Executive Order No. 9066 AUTHORIZING THE SECRETARY OF WAR TO PRESCRIBE MILITARY AREAS Executive Order No. 9066 WHEREAS the successful prosecution of the war requires every possible protection against espionage and against sabotage to national-defense material, national-defense premises, and national-defense utilities as defined in section 4, Act of April 20, 1918, 40 Stat. 533, as amended by the act of November 30, 1940, 54 Stat. 1220, and the Act of August 21, 1941, 55 Stat. 655 (U. S. C.,Title 50, Sec. 104): NOW, THEREFORE, by virtue of the authority vested in me as President of the United States, and Commander in Chief of the Army and Navy, I hereby authorize and direct the Secretary of War, and the Military Commanders whom he may from time to time designate, whenever he or any designated Commander deems such actions necessary or desirable, to prescribe military areas in such places and of such extent as he or the appropriate Military Commanders may determine, from which any or all persons may be excluded, and with such respect to which, the right of any person to enter, remain in, or leave shall be subject to whatever restrictions the Secretary of War or the appropriate Military Commander may impose in his discretion. The Secretary of War is hereby authorized to provide for residents of any such area who are excluded therefrom, such transportation, food, shelter, and other accommodations as may be necessary, in the judgement of the Secretary of War or the said Military Commander, and until other arrangements are made, to accomplish the purpose of this order. The designation of military areas in any region or locality shall supersede designations of prohibited and restricted areas by the Attorney General under the Proclamations of December 7 and 8, 1941, and shall supersede the responsibility and authority of the Attorney General under the said Proclamations in respect of such prohibited and restricted areas. I hereby further authorize and direct the Secretary of War and the said Military Commanders to take such other steps as he or the appropriate Military Commander may deem advisable to enforce compliance with the restrictions applicable to each Military area hereinabove authorized to be designated, including the use of Federal troops and other Federal Agencies, with authority to accept assistance of state and local agencies. I hereby further authorize establishments and other Federal Agencies, to assist the Secretary of War or the said Military Commanders in carrying out this Executive Order, including the furnishing of medical aid, hospitalization, food, clothing, transportation, use of land, shelter, and other supplies, equipment, utilities, facilities and services. This order shall not be construed as modifying or limiting in any way the authority heretofore granted under Executive Order No. 8972, dated December 12, 1941, nor shall it be construed as limiting or modifying the duty and responsibility of the Federal Bureau of Investigation, with respect to the investigation of alleged acts of sabotage or the duty and responsibility of the Attorney General and the Department of Justice under the Proclamations of December 7 and 8, 1941, prescribing regulations for the conduct and control of alien enemies, except as such duty and responsibility is superseded by the designation of military areas hereunder. FRANKLIN D. ROOSEVELT February 19, 1942" (quoted from USC).

Sedition Act, 1918

"Whoever, when the United States is at war, shall willfully make or convey false reports or false statements with intent to interfere with the operation or success of the military or naval forces of the United States, or to promote the success of its enemies, or shall willfully make or convey false reports, or false statements, . . . or incite insubordination, disloyalty, mutiny, or refusal of duty, in the military or naval forces of the United States, or shall willfully obstruct . . . the recruiting or enlistment service of the United States, or . . . shall willfully utter, print, write, or publish any disloyal, profane, scurrilous, or abusive language about the form of government of the United States, or the Constitution of the United States, or the military or naval forces of the United States . . . or shall willfully display the flag of any foreign enemy, or shall willfully . . . urge, incite, or advocate any curtailment of production . . . or advocate, teach, defend, or suggest the doing of any of the acts or things in this section enumerated and whoever shall by word or act support or favor the cause of any country with which the United States is at war or by word or act oppose the cause of the United States therein, shall be punished by a fine of not more than $10,000 or imprisonment for not more than twenty years, or both" (quoted from USC).

6

Documents

USA Patriot Act of 2001 (Excerpts)

HR 3162 RDS, 107th CONGRESS, 1st Session
H. R. 3162, IN THE SENATE OF THE UNITED STATES
October 24, 2001
AN ACT
* * *

TITLE II

(1) IN GENERAL—Notwithstanding any other provision of law, it shall be lawful for foreign intelligence or counterintelligence (as defined in section 3 of the National Security Act of 1947 (50 U.S.C. 401a)) or foreign intelligence information obtained as part of a criminal investigation to be disclosed to any Federal law enforcement, intelligence, protective, immigration, national defense, or national security official in order to assist the official receiving that information in the performance of his official duties. Any Federal official who receives information pursuant to this provision may use that information only as necessary in the conduct of that person's official duties subject to any limitations on the unauthorized disclosure of such information.

(2) DEFINITION—In this subsection, the term 'foreign intelligence information' means—

(A) information, whether or not concerning a United States person, that relates to the ability of the United States to protect against—(i) actual or potential attack or other grave hostile acts of a foreign power or an agent of a foreign power; (ii) sabotage or international terrorism by a foreign power or an agent of a foreign power; or (iii) clandestine intelligence activities by an intelligence service or network of a foreign power or by an agent of a foreign power; or

(B) information, whether or not concerning a United States person, with respect to a foreign power or foreign territory that relates to—(i) the national defense or the security of the United States; or (ii) the conduct of the foreign affairs of the United States.

SEC. 206. ROVING SURVEILLANCE AUTHORITY UNDER THE FOREIGN INTELLIGENCE SURVEILLANCE ACT OF 1978.

Section 105(c)(2)(B) of the Foreign Intelligence Surveillance Act of 1978 (50 U.S.C. 1805(c)(2)(B)) is amended by inserting ', or in circumstances where the Court finds that the actions of the target of the application may have the effect of thwarting the identification of a specified person, such other persons,' after 'specified person'.

    *   *   *

SEC. 209. SEIZURE OF VOICE-MAIL MESSAGES PURSUANT TO WARRANTS.

Title 18, United States Code, is amended—(1) in section 2510—

(A) in paragraph (1), by striking beginning with 'and such' and all that follows through 'communication'; and (B) in paragraph (14), by inserting 'wire or' after 'transmission of'; and (2) in subsections (a) and (b) of section 2703—(A) by striking 'CONTENTS OF ELECTRONIC' and inserting 'CONTENTS OF WIRE OR ELECTRONIC' each place it appears; (B) by striking 'contents of an electronic' and inserting 'contents of a wire or electronic' each place it appears; and (C) by striking 'any electronic' and inserting 'any wire or electronic' each place it appears.

SEC. 210. SCOPE OF SUBPOENAS FOR RECORDS OF ELECTRONIC COMMUNICATIONS.

Section 2703(c)(2) of title 18, United States Code, as redesignated by section 212, is amended—(1) by striking 'entity the name, address, local and long distance telephone toll billing records, telephone number or other subscriber number or identity, and length of service of a subscriber' and inserting the following: 'entity the—'(A) name; '(B) address; '(C) local and long distance telephone connection records, or records of session times and durations; '(D) length of service (including start date) and types of service utilized; '(E) telephone or instrument number or other subscriber number or identity, including any temporarily assigned network address; and '(F) means and source of payment for such service (including any credit card or bank account number), of a subscriber'; and (2) by striking 'and the types of services the subscriber or customer utilized,' (ii) in paragraph (2)(B), by striking the period and inserting '; and'; and (iii) by inserting after paragraph (2) the following: '(3) a provider of remote computing service or electronic communication service to the public shall not knowingly divulge a record or other information pertaining to a subscriber to or customer of such service (not including the contents of communications covered by paragraph (1) or (2)) to any governmental entity.';

* * *

SEC. 213. AUTHORITY FOR DELAYING NOTICE OF THE EXECUTION OF A WARRANT.

Section 3103a of title 18, United States Code, is amended—(1) by inserting '(a) IN GENERAL- ' before 'In addition'; and (2) by adding at the end the following:

'(b) DELAY- With respect to the issuance of any warrant or court order under this section, or any other rule of law, to search for and seize any property or material that constitutes evidence of a criminal offense in violation of the laws of the United States, any notice required, or that may be required, to be given may be delayed if—

'(1) the court finds reasonable cause to believe that providing immediate notification of the execution of the warrant may have an adverse result (as defined in section 2705); '(2) the warrant prohibits the seizure of any tangible property, any wire or electronic communication (as defined in section 2510), or, except as expressly provided in chapter 121, any stored wire or electronic information, except where the court finds reasonable necessity for the seizure; and '(3) the warrant provides for the

154 Documents

giving of such notice within a reasonable period of its execution, which period may thereafter be extended by the court for good cause shown.'

SEC. 214. PEN REGISTER AND TRAP AND TRACE AUTHORITY UNDER FISA.

(a) APPLICATIONS AND ORDERS- Section 402 of the Foreign Intelligence Surveillance Act of 1978 (50 U.S.C. 1842) is amended—

(1) in subsection (a)(1), by striking 'for any investigation to gather foreign intelligence information or information concerning international terrorism' and inserting 'for any investigation to obtain foreign intelligence information not concerning a United States person or to protect against international terrorism or clandestine intelligence activities, provided that such investigation of a United States person is not conducted solely upon the basis of activities protected by the first amendment to the Constitution'; (2) by amending subsection (c)(2) to read as follows: '(2) a certification by the applicant that the information likely to be obtained is foreign intelligence information not concerning a United States person or is relevant to an ongoing investigation to protect against international terrorism or clandestine intelligence activities, provided that such investigation of a United States person is not conducted solely upon the basis of activities protected by the first amendment to the Constitution.'; . . . (4) by amending subsection (d)(2)(A) to read as follows: '(A) shall specify—'(i) the identity, if known, of the person who is the subject of the investigation; '(ii) the identity, if known, of the person to whom is leased or in whose name is listed the telephone line or other facility to which the pen register or trap and trace device is to be attached or applied; '(iii) the attributes of the communications to which the order applies, such as the number or other identifier, and, if known, the location of the telephone line or other facility to which the pen register or trap and trace device is to be attached or applied and, in the case of a trap and trace device, the geographic limits of the trap and trace order'.

* * *

SEC. 215. ACCESS TO RECORDS AND OTHER ITEMS UNDER THE FOREIGN INTELLIGENCE SURVEILLANCE ACT.

Title V of the Foreign Intelligence Surveillance Act of 1978 (50 U.S.C. 1861 et seq.) is amended by striking sections 501 through 503 and inserting the following:

SEC. 501. ACCESS TO CERTAIN BUSINESS RECORDS FOR FOREIGN INTELLIGENCE AND INTERNATIONAL TERRORISM INVESTIGATIONS.

'(a)(1) The Director of the Federal Bureau of Investigation or a designee of the Director (whose rank shall be no lower than Assistant Special Agent in Charge) may make an application for an order requiring the production of any tangible things (including books, records, papers, documents, and other items) for an investigation to protect against international terrorism or clandestine intelligence activities, provided that such investigation of a United States person is not conducted solely upon the basis of activities protected by the first amendment to the Constitution.

'(2) An investigation conducted under this section shall— '(A) be conducted under guidelines approved by the Attorney General under Executive Order 12333 (or a successor order); and '(B) not be conducted of a United States person solely upon the basis of activities protected by the first amendment to the Constitution of the United States. '(b) Each application under this section—'(1) shall be made to—'(A) a judge of the court established by section 103(a); or '(B) a United States Magistrate Judge under chapter 43 of title 28, United States Code, who is publicly designated by the Chief Justice of the United States to have the power to hear applications and grant orders for the production of tangible things under this section on behalf of a judge of that court; and '(2) shall specify that the records concerned are sought for an authorized investigation conducted in accordance with subsection (a)(2) to protect against international terrorism or clandestine intelligence activities. '(c)(1) Upon an application made pursuant to this section, the judge shall enter an ex parte order as requested, or as modified, approving the release of records if the judge finds that the application meets the requirements of this section. '(2) An order under this subsection shall not disclose that it is issued for purposes of an investigation described in subsection (a). '(d) No person shall disclose to any other person (other than those persons necessary to produce the tangible things under this section) that the Federal Bureau of Investigation has sought or obtained tangible things under this section. '(e) A person who, in good faith, produces tangible things under an order pursuant to this section shall not be liable to any other person for such production. Such production shall not be deemed to constitute a waiver of any privilege in any other proceeding or context'.

* * *

SEC. 216. MODIFICATION OF AUTHORITIES RELATING TO USE OF PEN REGISTERS AND TRAP AND TRACE DEVICES.

... (b) ISSUANCE OF ORDERS- (1) IN GENERAL- Section 3123(a) of title 18, United States Code, is amended to read as follows: '(a) IN GENERAL- '(1) ATTORNEY FOR THE GOVERNMENT- Upon an application made under section 3122(a)(1), the court shall enter an ex parte order authorizing the installation and use of a pen register or trap and trace device anywhere within the United States, if the court finds that the attorney for the Government has certified to the court that the information likely to be obtained by such installation and use is relevant to an ongoing criminal investigation. The order, upon service of that order, shall apply to any person or entity providing wire or electronic communication service in the United States whose assistance may facilitate the execution of the order. Whenever such an order is served on any person or entity not specifically named in the order, upon request of such person or entity, the attorney for the Government or law enforcement or investigative officer that is serving the order shall provide written or electronic certification that the order applies to the person or entity being served.

'(2) STATE INVESTIGATIVE OR LAW ENFORCEMENT OFFICER- Upon an application made under section 3122(a)(2), the court shall enter an ex parte order authorizing the installation and use of a pen register or trap and trace device within the jurisdiction of the court, if the court finds that the State law enforcement or investigative officer has certified to the court that the information likely to be obtained by such installation and use is relevant to an ongoing criminal investigation. '(3)(A) Where the law enforcement agency implementing an ex parte order under this subsection seeks to do so by installing and using its own pen register or trap and trace device on a packet-switched data network of a provider of electronic communication service to the public, the agency shall ensure that a record will be maintained which will identify—'(i) any officer or officers who installed the device and any officer or officers who accessed the device to obtain information from the network; '(ii) the date and time the device was installed, the date and time the device was uninstalled, and the date, time, and duration of each time the device is accessed to obtain information; '(iii) the configuration of the device at the time of its installation and any subsequent modification thereof; and

'(iv) any information which has been collected by the device. To the extent that the pen register or trap and trace device can be set automatically to record this information electronically, the record shall be maintained electronically throughout the installation and use of such device. '(B) The record maintained under subparagraph (A) shall be provided ex parte and under seal to the court which entered the ex parte order authorizing the installation and use of the device within 30 days after termination of the order (including any extensions thereof).'.

(2) PEN REGISTER- Section 3127(3) of title 18, United States Code, is amended—

(A) by striking 'electronic or other impulses' and all that follows through 'is attached' and inserting 'dialing, routing, addressing, or signaling information transmitted by an instrument or facility from which a wire or electronic communication is transmitted, provided, however, that such information shall not include the contents of any communication'; . . . (3) TRAP AND TRACE DEVICE- Section 3127(4) of title 18, United States Code, is amended—(A) by striking 'of an instrument' and all that follows through the semicolon and inserting 'or other dialing, routing, addressing, and signaling information reasonably likely to identify the source of a wire or electronic communication, provided, however, that such information shall not include the contents of any communication'; and (B) by inserting 'or process' after 'a device'.

* * *

SEC. 218. FOREIGN INTELLIGENCE INFORMATION.

Sections 104(a)(7)(B) and section 303(a)(7)(B) (50 U.S.C. 1804(a)(7)(B) and 1823(a)(7)(B)) of the Foreign Intelligence Surveillance Act of 1978 are each amended by striking 'the purpose' and inserting 'a significant purpose'.

SEC. 219. SINGLE-JURISDICTION SEARCH WARRANTS FOR TERRORISM.

Rule 41(a) of the Federal Rules of Criminal Procedure is amended by inserting after 'executed' the following: 'and (3) in an investigation of domestic terrorism or international terrorism (as defined in section 2331 of title 18, United States Code), by a Federal magistrate judge in any district in which activities related to the terrorism may have occurred, for a search of property or for a person within or outside the district'.

* * *

SEC. 220. NATIONWIDE SERVICE OF SEARCH WARRANTS FOR ELECTRONIC EVIDENCE.

(a) IN GENERAL- Chapter 121 of title 18, United States Code, is amended—

(1) in section 2703, by striking 'under the Federal Rules of Criminal Procedure' every place it appears and inserting 'using the procedures described in the Federal Rules of Criminal Procedure by a court with jurisdiction over the offense under investigation'; and . . . (C) by inserting at the end the following: '(3) the term 'court of competent jurisdiction' has the meaning assigned by section 3127, and includes any Federal court within that definition, without geographic limitation'.

* * *

SEC. 222. ASSISTANCE TO LAW ENFORCEMENT AGENCIES.

Nothing in this Act shall impose any additional technical obligation or requirement on a provider of a wire or electronic communication service or other person to furnish facilities or technical assistance. A provider of a wire or electronic communication service, landlord, custodian, or other person who furnishes facilities or technical assistance pursuant to section 216 shall be reasonably compensated for such reasonable expenditures incurred in providing such facilities or assistance.

*   *   *

SEC. 303. 4-YEAR CONGRESSIONAL REVIEW; EXPEDITED CONSIDERATION.

(a) IN GENERAL- Effective on and after the first day of fiscal year 2005, the provisions of this title and the amendments made by this title shall terminate if the Congress enacts a joint resolution, the text after the resolving clause of which is as follows: 'That provisions of the International Money Laundering Abatement and Anti-Terrorist Financing Act of 2001, and the amendments made thereby, shall no longer have the force of law'.

*   *   *

SEC. 403. ACCESS BY THE DEPARTMENT OF STATE AND THE INS TO CERTAIN IDENTIFYING INFORMATION IN THE CRIMINAL HISTORY RECORDS OF VISA APPLICANTS AND APPLICANTS FOR ADMISSION TO THE UNITED STATES.

(a) AMENDMENT OF THE IMMIGRATION AND NATIONALITY ACT- Section 105 of the Immigration and Nationality Act (1) in the section heading, by inserting '; DATA EXCHANGE' after 'SECURITY OFFICERS'; (2) by inserting '(a)' after 'SEC. 105.'; (3) in subsection (a), by inserting 'and border' after 'internal' the second place it appears; and (4) by adding at the end the following: '(b)(1) The Attorney General and the Director of the Federal Bureau of Investigation shall provide the Department of State and the Secret Service access to the criminal history record information contained in the National Crime Information Center's Interstate Identification Index (NCIC-III), Wanted Persons File, and to any other files maintained by the National Crime Information Center that may be mutually agreed upon by the Attorney General and the agency receiving the access, for the purpose of determining whether or not a visa applicant or applicant for admission has a criminal history record indexed in any such file.

* * *

(a) GROUNDS OF INADMISSIBILITY- Section 212(a)(3) of the Immigration and Nationality Act (8 U.S.C. 1182(a)(3)) is amended—(1) in subparagraph (B)—(A) in clause (i)—(i) by amending subclause (IV) to read as follows: '(IV) is a representative (as defined in clause (v)) of—'(aa) a foreign terrorist organization, as designated by the Secretary of State under section 219, or '(bb) a political, social or other similar group whose public endorsement of acts of terrorist activity the Secretary of State has determined undermines United States efforts to reduce or eliminate terrorist activities,'; (ii) in subclause (V), by inserting 'or' after 'section 219,'; and (iii) by adding at the end the following new subclauses: '(VI) has used the alien's position of prominence within any country to endorse or espouse terrorist activity, or to persuade others to support terrorist activity or a terrorist organization, in a way that the Secretary of State has determined undermines United States efforts to reduce or eliminate terrorist activities . . . (F) by amending clause (iv) (as redesignated by subparagraph (B)) to read as follows: '(iv) ENGAGE IN TERRORIST ACTIVITY

DEFINED - As used in this chapter, the term 'engage in terrorist activity' means, in an individual capacity or as a member of an organization—'(I) to commit or to incite to commit, under circumstances indicating an intention to cause death or serious bodily injury, a terrorist activity; '(II) to prepare or plan a terrorist activity; '(III) to gather information on potential targets for terrorist activity; '(IV) to solicit funds or other things of value for—'(aa) a terrorist activity; '(bb) a terrorist organization described in clause (vi)(I) or (vi)(II); or '(cc) a terrorist organization described in clause (vi)(III), unless the solicitor can demonstrate that he did not know, and should not reasonably have known, that the solicitation would further the organization's terrorist activity; '(V) to solicit any individual—'(aa) to engage in conduct otherwise described in this clause; '(bb) for membership in a terrorist organization . . . '(cc) for membership in a terrorist organization described in clause (vi)(III), unless the solicitor can demonstrate that he did not know, and should not reasonably have known, that the solicitation would further the organization's terrorist activity; or '(VI) to commit an act that the actor knows, or reasonably should know, affords material support, including a safe house, transportation, communications, funds, transfer of funds or other material financial benefit, false documentation or identification, weapons (including chemical, biological, or radiological weapons), explosives, or training—'(aa) for the commission of a terrorist activity; '(bb) to any individual who the actor knows, or reasonably should know, has committed or plans to commit a terrorist activity; '(cc) to a terrorist organization described in clause (vi)(I) or (vi)(II); or '(dd) to a terrorist organization described in clause (vi)(III), unless the actor can demonstrate that he did not know, and should not reasonably have known, that the act would further the organization's terrorist activity. . . . '(vi) TERRORIST ORGANIZATION DEFINED- As used in clause (i)(VI) and clause (iv), the term 'terrorist organization' means an organization—'(I) designated under section 219; '(II) otherwise designated, upon publication in the Federal Register, by the Secretary of State in consultation with or upon the request of the Attorney General, as a terrorist organization, after finding that the organization engages in the activities described in subclause (I), (II), or (III) of clause (iv), or that the organization provides material support to further terrorist activity; or '(III) that is a group of two or more individuals, whether organized or not, which engages in the activities described in subclause (I), (II), or (III) of clause (iv).'; and

(2) by adding at the end the following new subparagraph: '(F) ASSOCIATION WITH TERRORIST ORGANIZATIONS- Any alien who the Secretary of State, after consultation with the Attorney General, or the Attorney General, after consultation with the Secretary of State, determines has been associated with a terrorist organization and intends while in the United States to engage solely, principally, or incidentally in activities that could endanger the welfare, safety, or security of the United States is inadmissible'

*   *   *

SEC. 412. MANDATORY DETENTION OF SUSPECTED TERRORISTS; HABEAS CORPUS; JUDICIAL REVIEW. (a) IN GENERAL- The Immigration and Nationality Act (8 U.S.C. 1101 et seq.) is amended by inserting after section 236 the following:

'MANDATORY DETENTION OF SUSPECTED TERRORISTS; HABEAS CORPUS; JUDICIAL REVIEW 'SEC. 236A. (a) DETENTION OF TERRORIST ALIENS-

'(1) CUSTODY- The Attorney General shall take into custody any alien who is certified under paragraph (3). '(2) RELEASE- Except as provided in paragraphs (5) and (6), the Attorney General shall maintain custody of such an alien until the alien is removed from the United States. Except as provided in paragraph (6), such custody shall be maintained irrespective of any relief from removal for which the alien may be eligible, or any relief from removal granted the alien, until the Attorney General determines that the alien is no longer an alien who may be certified under paragraph (3). If the alien is finally determined not to be removable, detention pursuant to this subsection shall terminate. '(3) CERTIFICATION- The Attorney General may certify an alien under this paragraph if the Attorney General has reasonable grounds to believe that the alien—'(B) is engaged in any other activity that endangers the national security of the United States. . . . '(5) COMMENCEMENT OF PROCEEDINGS- The Attorney General shall place an alien detained under paragraph (1) in removal proceedings, or shall charge the alien with a criminal offense, not later than 7 days after the commencement of such detention. If the requirement of the preceding sentence is not satisfied, the Attorney General shall release the alien. '(6) LIMITATION ON INDEFINITE DETENTION- An alien detained solely under paragraph (1) who has not been removed under section 241(a)(1)(A), and whose removal is unlikely in the reasonably foreseeable future, may be detained for additional periods of up to six months only if the release of the alien will threaten the national security of the United States or the safety of the community or any person. '(7) REVIEW OF CERTIFICATION- The Attorney General shall review the certification made under paragraph (3) every 6 months. If the Attorney General determines, in the Attorney General's discretion, that the certification should be revoked, the alien may be released on such conditions as the Attorney General deems appropriate, unless such release is otherwise prohibited by law. The alien may request each 6 months in writing that the Attorney General reconsider the certification and may submit documents or other evidence in support of that request.

'(b) HABEAS CORPUS AND JUDICIAL REVIEW- '(1) IN GENERAL- Judicial review of any action or decision relating to this section (including judicial review of the merits of a determination made under subsection (a)(3) or (a)(6)) is available exclusively in habeas corpus proceedings consistent with this subsection. Except as provided in the preceding sentence, no court shall have jurisdiction to review, by habeas corpus petition or otherwise, any such action or decision. '(2) APPLICATION- '(A) IN GENERAL- Notwithstanding any other provision of law, including section 2241(a) of title 28, United States Code, habeas corpus proceedings described in paragraph (1) may be initiated only by an application filed with—'(i) the Supreme Court; '(ii) any justice of the Supreme Court; '(iii) any circuit judge of the United States Court of Appeals for the District of Columbia Circuit; or '(iv) any district court otherwise having jurisdiction to entertain it.

      *   *   *

SEC. 503. DNA IDENTIFICATION OF TERRORISTS AND OTHER VIOLENT OFFENDERS.

Section 3(d)(2) of the DNA Analysis Backlog Elimination Act of 2000 (42 U.S.C. 14135a(d)(2)) is amended to read as follows: '(2) In addition to the offenses described in paragraph (1), the following offenses shall be treated for purposes of this section as qualifying Federal offenses, as determined by the Attorney General:

    '(A) Any offense listed in section 2332b(g)(5)(B) of title 18, United States Code. '(B) Any crime of violence (as defined in section 16 of title 18, United States Code). '(C) Any attempt or conspiracy to commit any of the above offenses.'.

      *   *   *

SEC. 802. DEFINITION OF DOMESTIC TERRORISM.

(a) DOMESTIC TERRORISM DEFINED- Section 2331 of title 18, United States Code, is amended—(1) in paragraph (1)(B)(iii), by striking 'by assassination or kidnapping' and inserting 'by mass destruction, assassination, or kidnapping'; (2) in paragraph (3), by striking 'and'; (3) in paragraph (4), by striking the period at the end and inserting '; and'; and (4) by adding at the end the following: '(5) the term 'domestic terrorism' means activities that— '(A) involve acts dangerous to human life that are a violation of the criminal laws of the United States or of any State; '(B) appear to be intended—'(i) to intimidate or coerce a civilian population; '(ii) to influence the policy of a government by intimidation or coercion; or '(iii) to affect the conduct of a government by mass destruction, assassination, or kidnapping; and '(C) occur primarily within the territorial jurisdiction of the United States'.

SEC. 803. PROHIBITION AGAINST HARBORING TERRORISTS.

. . . Sec. 2339. Harboring or concealing terrorists

'(a) Whoever harbors or conceals any person who he knows, or has reasonable grounds to believe, has committed, or is about to commit, an offense under section 32 (relating to destruction of aircraft or aircraft facilities), section 175 (relating to biological weapons), section 229 (relating to chemical weapons), section 831 (relating to nuclear materials), paragraph (2) or (3) of section 844(f) (relating to arson and bombing of government property risking or causing injury or death), section 1366(a) (relating to the destruction of an energy facility), section 2280 (relating to violence against maritime navigation), section 2332a (relating to weapons of mass destruction), or section 2332b (relating to acts of terrorism transcending national boundaries) of this title, section 236(a) (relating to sabotage of nuclear facilities or fuel) of the Atomic Energy Act of 1954 (42 U.S.C. 2284(a)), or section 46502 (relating to aircraft piracy) of title 49, shall be fined under this title or imprisoned not more than ten years, or both'. '(b) A violation of this section may be prosecuted in any Federal judicial district in which the underlying offense was committed, or in any other Federal judicial district as provided by law'.

SEC. 804. JURISDICTION OVER CRIMES COMMITTED AT U.S. FACILITIES ABROAD.

. . . (9) With respect to offenses committed by or against a national of the United States as that term is used in section 101 of the Immigration and Nationality Act—'(A) the premises of United States diplomatic, consular, military or other United States Government missions or entities in foreign States, including the buildings, parts of buildings, and land appurtenant or ancillary thereto or used for purposes of those missions or entities, irrespective of ownership; and '(B) residences in foreign States and the land appurtenant or ancillary thereto, irrespective of ownership, used for purposes of those missions or entities or used by United States personnel assigned to those missions or entities.

* * *

SEC. 814. DETERRENCE AND PREVENTION OF CYBERTERRORISM.

(a) CLARIFICATION OF PROTECTION OF PROTECTED COMPUTERS- Section 1030(a)(5) of title 18, United States Code, is amended— . . . (4) by adding at the end the following: '(B) (1) by inserting '(i)' after '(A)'; by conduct described in clause (i), (ii), or (iii) of subparagraph (A), caused (or, in the case of an attempted offense, would, if completed, have caused)—'(i) loss to 1 or more persons during any 1-year period (and, for purposes of an investigation, prosecution, or other proceeding brought by the United States only, loss resulting from a related course of conduct affecting 1 or more other protected computers) aggregating at least $5,000 in value;' (ii) the modification or impairment, or potential modification or impairment, of the medical examination, diagnosis, treatment, or care of 1 or more individuals; '(iii) physical injury to any person; '(iv) a threat to public health or safety; or '(v) damage affecting a computer system used by or for a government entity in furtherance of the administration of justice, national defense, or national security;'. (c) PENALTIES- Section 1030(c) of title 18, United States Code, is amended— . . . a fine under this title, imprisonment for not more than 10 years, or both, in the case of an offense under subsection (a)(5)(A)(i), or an attempt to commit an offense punishable under that subsection; '(B) a fine under this title, imprisonment for not more than 5 years, or both, in the case of an offense under subsection (a)(5)(A)(ii), or an attempt to commit an offense punishable under that subsection; '(C) a fine under this title, imprisonment for not more than 20 years, or both, in the case of an offense under subsection (a)(5)(A)(i) or (a)(5)(A)(ii), or an attempt to commit an offense punishable under either subsection, that occurs after a conviction for another offense under this section.'. . . . (f) AMENDMENT OF SENTENCING GUIDELINES RELATING TO CERTAIN COMPUTER FRAUD AND ABUSE- Pursuant to its authority under section 994(p) of title 28, United States Code, the United States Sentencing Commission shall amend the Federal sentencing guidelines to ensure that any individual convicted of a violation of section 1030 of title 18, United States Code, can be subjected to appropriate penalties, without regard to any mandatory minimum term of imprisonment.

* * *

SEC. 816. DEVELOPMENT AND SUPPORT OF CYBERSECURITY FORENSIC CAPABILITIES.

(a) IN GENERAL- The Attorney General shall establish such regional computer forensic laboratories as the Attorney General considers appropriate, and provide support to existing computer forensic laboratories, in order that all such computer forensic laboratories have the capability—(1) to provide forensic examinations with respect to seized or intercepted computer evidence relating to criminal activity (including cyberterrorism); (2) to provide training and education for Federal, State, and local law enforcement personnel and prosecutors regarding investigations, forensic analyses, and prosecutions of computer-related crime (including cyberterrorism). . . .

* * *

SEC. 901. RESPONSIBILITIES OF DIRECTOR OF CENTRAL INTELLIGENCE REGARDING FOREIGN INTELLIGENCE COLLECTED UNDER FOREIGN INTELLIGENCE SURVEILLANCE ACT OF 1978.

Section 103(c) of the National Security Act of 1947 (50 U.S.C. 403–3(c)) is amended— . . . (2) by inserting after paragraph (5) the following new paragraph (6):

'(6) establish requirements and priorities for foreign intelligence information to be collected under the Foreign Intelligence Surveillance Act of 1978 (50 U.S.C. 1801 et seq.), and provide assistance to the Attorney General to ensure that information derived from electronic surveillance or physical searches under that Act is disseminated so it may be used efficiently and effectively for foreign intelligence purposes, except that the Director shall have no authority to direct, manage, or undertake electronic surveillance or physical search operations pursuant to that Act unless otherwise authorized by statute or executive order;'.

* * *

SEC. 1008. FEASIBILITY STUDY ON USE OF BIOMETRIC IDENTIFIER SCANNING SYSTEM WITH ACCESS TO THE FBI INTEGRATED AUTOMATED FINGERPRINT IDENTIFICATION SYSTEM AT OVERSEAS CONSULAR POSTS AND POINTS OF ENTRY TO THE UNITED STATES.

(1) IN GENERAL- The Attorney General, in consultation with the Secretary of State and the Secretary of Transportation, shall conduct a study on the feasibility of utilizing a biometric identifier (fingerprint scanning system, with access to the database of the Federal Bureau of Investigation Integrated Automated Fingerprint Identification System, at consular offices abroad and at points of entry into the United States to enhance the ability of State Department and immigration officials to identify aliens who may be wanted in connection with criminal or terrorist investigations in the United States or abroad prior to the issuance of visas or entry into the United States.

* * *

2001 Report on Foreign Terrorist Organizations Released by the Office of the Coordinator for Counterterrorism, U.S. Department of State, October 5, 2001

Background

The Secretary of State designates Foreign Terrorist Organizations (FTO's), in consultation with the Attorney General and the Secretary of the Treasury. These designations are undertaken pursuant to the Immigration and Nationality Act, as amended by the Antiterrorism and Effective Death Penalty Act of 1996. FTO designations are valid for two years, after which they must be redesignated or they automatically expire. Redesignation after two years is a positive act and represents a determination by the Secretary of State that the organization has continued to engage in terrorist activity and still meets the criteria specified in law. In

October 1997, former Secretary of State Madeleine K. Albright approved the designation of the first 30 groups as Foreign Terrorist Organizations.

In October 1999, Secretary Albright re-certified 27 of these groups' designations but allowed three organizations to drop from the list because their involvement in terrorist activity had ended and they no longer met the criteria for designation.

Secretary Albright designated one new FTO in 1999 (al Qa'ida) and another in 2000 (Islamic Movement of Uzbekistan). Secretary of State Colin L. Powell has designated two new FTO's (Real IRA and AUC) in 2001. In October 2001, Secretary Powell re-certified the designation of 26 of the 28 FTO's whose designation was due to expire, and combined two previously designated groups (Kahane Chai and Kach) into one. Current List of Designated Foreign Terrorist Organizations (as of October 5, 2001):

1. Abu Nidal Organization (ANO)
2. Abu Sayyaf Group
3. Armed Islamic Group (GIA)
4. Aum Shinrikyo
5. Basque Fatherland and Liberty (ETA)
6. Gama'a al-Islamiyya (Islamic Group)
7. HAMAS (Islamic Resistance Movement)
8. Harakat ul-Mujahidin (HUM)
9. Hizballah (Party of God)
10. Islamic Movement of Uzbekistan (IMU)
11. al-Jihad (Egyptian Islamic Jihad)
12. Kahane Chai (Kach)
13. Kurdistan Workers' Party (PKK)
14. Liberation Tigers of Tamil Eelam (LTTE)
15. Mujahedin-e Khalq Organization (MEK)
16. National Liberation Army (ELN)
17. Palestinian Islamic Jihad (PIJ)
18. Palestine Liberation Front (PLF)
19. Popular Front for the Liberation of Palestine (PFLP)
20. PFLP-General Command (PFLP-GC)
21. al-Qa'ida
22. Real IRA
23. Revolutionary Armed Forces of Colombia (FARC)
24. Revolutionary Nuclei (formerly ELA)
25. Revolutionary Organization 17 November

26. Revolutionary People's Liberation Army/Front (DHKP/C)
27. Shining Path (Sendero Luminoso, SL)
28. United Self-Defense Forces of Colombia (AUC)

Legal Criteria for Designation

1. The organization must be foreign.
2. The organization must engage in terrorist activity as defined in Section 212 (a)(3)(B) of the Immigration and Nationality Act. (** - see below)
3. The organization's activities must threaten the security of U.S. nationals or the national security (national defense, foreign relations, or the economic interests) of the United States.

Effects of Designation

Legal.

1. It is unlawful for a person in the United States or subject to the jurisdiction of the United States to provide funds or other material support to a designated FTO.
2. Representatives and certain members of a designated FTO, if they are aliens, can be denied visas or excluded from the United States.
3. U.S. financial institutions must block funds of designated FTO's and their agents and report the blockage to the Office of Foreign Assets Control, U.S. Department of the Treasury.

Other Effects.

1. Deters donations or contributions to named organizations
2. Heightens public awareness and knowledge of terrorist organizations
3. Signals to other governments our concern about named organizations

4. Stigmatizes and isolates designated terrorist organizations internationally

The Process

The Secretary of State makes decisions concerning the designation and redesignation of FTO's following an exhaustive interagency review process in which all evidence of a group's activity, from both classified and open sources, is scrutinized. The State Department, working closely with the Justice and Treasury Departments and the intelligence community, prepares a detailed "administrative record" which documents the terrorist activity of the designated FTO. Seven days before publishing an FTO designation in the Federal Register, the Department of State provides classified notification to Congress.

Under the statute, designations are subject to judicial review. In the event of a challenge to a group's FTO designation in federal court, the U.S. government relies upon the administrative record to defend the Secretary's decision. These administrative records contain intelligence information and are therefore classified.

FTO designations expire in two years unless renewed. The law allows groups to be added at any time following a decision by the Secretary, in consultation with the Attorney General and the Secretary of the Treasury. The Secretary may also revoke designations after determining that there are grounds for doing so and notifying Congress.

The Immigration and Nationality Act defines terrorist activity to mean: any activity which is unlawful under the laws of the place where it is committed (or which, if committed in the United States, would be . . . unlawful under the laws of the United States or any State) and which involves any of the following:

(I) The highjacking or sabotage of any conveyance (including an aircraft, vessel, or vehicle).

(II) The seizing or detaining, and threatening to kill, injure, or continue to detain, another individual in order to compel a third person (including a governmental organization) to do or abstain from doing any act as an explicit or implicit condition for the release of the individual seized or detained.

(III) A violent attack upon an internationally protected person (as defined in section 1116(b)(4) of title 18, United States Code) or upon the liberty of such a person.

(IV) An assassination.

(V) The use of any-

    (a) biological agent, chemical agent, or nuclear weapon or device, or

    (b) explosive or firearm (other than for mere personal monetary gain), with intent to endanger, directly or indirectly, the safety of one or more individuals or to cause substantial damage to property.

(VI) A threat, attempt, or conspiracy to do any of the foregoing.

(iii) The term "engage in terrorist activity" means to commit, in an individual capacity or as a member of an organization, an act of terrorist activity or an act which the actor knows, or reasonably should know, affords material support to any individual, organization, or government in conducting a terrorist activity at any time, including any of the following acts:

(I) The preparation or planning of a terrorist activity.

(II) The gathering of information on potential targets for terrorist activity.

(III) The providing of any type of material support, including a safe house, transportation, communications, funds, false documentation or identification, weapons, explosives, or training, to any individual the actor knows or has reason to believe has committed or plans to commit a terrorist activity.

(IV) The soliciting of funds or other things of value for terrorist activity or for any terrorist organization.

(V) The solicitation of any individual for membership in a terrorist organization, terrorist government, or to engage in a terrorist activity.

Office of Counter-terrorism
U.S. Department of State
Washington, DC
January 30, 2003

Foreign Terrorist Organizations List (Updated)

1. Abu Nidal Organization (ANO)
2. Abu Sayyaf Group
3. Al-Aqsa Martyrs Brigades
4. Armed Islamic Group
5. 'Asbat al-Ansar
6. Aum Shinrikyo
7. Basque Fatherland and Liberty (ETA)
8. Gama'a al-Islamiyya (Islamic Group)
9. Hamas (Islamic Resistance Movement)
10. Harakat ul-Mujahidin (HUM)
11. Hizballah (Party of God)
12. Islamic Movement of Uzbekistan (IMU)
13. Jaish-e-Mohammed (JEM) (Army of Mohammed)
14. Al-Jihad (Egyptian Islamic Jihad)
15. Kahane Chai (Kach)
16. Kurdistan Workers' Party (PKK)
17. Lashkar-e-Tayyiba (LT) (Army of the Righteous)
18. Lahskar-i-Jhangvi
19. Liberation Tigers of Tamil Eelam (LTTE)
20. Mujahedin-e Khalq Organization (MEK)
21. National Liberation Army (ELN)
22. Palestinian Islamic Jihad (PIJ)
23. Palestine Liberation Front (PLF)
24. Popular Front for the Liberation of Palestine (PFLP)
25. PFLP–General Command (PFLP-GC)
26. Al-Qaida
27. Real IRA
28. Revolutionary Armed Forces of Colombia (FARC)
29. Revolutionary Nuclei (formerly ELA)
30. Revolutionary Organization 17 November
31. Revolutionary People's Liberation Army/Front (DHKP/C)
32. Salafist Group for Call and Combat (GSPC)
33. Shining Path (Sendero Luminoso, SL)
34. United Self-Defense Forces of Colombia (AUC)
35. Communist Party of the Philippines/New People's Army (CPP/NPA)
36. Jemaah Islamiya organization (JI)

Domestic Security Enhancement Act of 2003—DOJ Section-by-Section Analysis (Excerpts)

*   *   *

Section 101: Individual Terrorists as Foreign Powers

Under 50 U.S.C. § 1801(a)(4), the definition of "foreign power" includes groups that engage in international terrorism, but does not reach unaffiliated individuals who do so. As a result, investigations of "lone wolf" terrorists or "sleeper cells" may not be authorized under FISA. Such investigations therefore must proceed under the stricter standards and shorter time periods set forth in Title III, potentially resulting in unnecessary and dangerous delays and greater administrative burden. This provision would expand FISA's definition of "foreign power" to include all persons, regardless of whether they are affiliated with an international terrorist group, who engage in international terrorism.

Section 102: Clandestine Intelligence Activities by Agent of a Foreign Power

FISA currently defines "agent of a foreign power" to include a person who knowingly engages in clandestine intelligence gathering activities on behalf of a foreign power—but only if those activities "involve or may involve a violation of" federal criminal law. Requiring the additional showing that the intelligence gathering violates the laws of the United States is both unnecessary and counterproductive, as such activities threaten the national security regardless of whether they are illegal.

This provision would expand the definitions contained in 50 U.S.C. § 1801(b)(2)(A) & (B). Any person who engages in clandestine intelligence gathering activities for a foreign power would qualify as an "agent of a foreign power," regardless of whether those activities are federal crimes.

Section 103: Strengthening Wartime Authorities Under FISA

Under 50 U.S.C. §§ 1811, 1829 & 1844, the Attorney General may authorize, without the prior approval of the FISA Court, electronic surveillance, physical searches, or the use of pen registers for a period of 15 days following a congressional declaration of war. This wartime exception is unnecessarily narrow; it may be invoked only when Congress formally has declared war, a rare event in the nation's history and something that has not occurred in more than sixty years. This provision would expand FISA's wartime exception by allowing the wartime exception to be invoked after Congress authorizes the use of military force, or after the United States has suffered an attack creating a national emergency.

Section 104: Strengthening FISA's Presidential Authorization Exception

50 U.S.C. § 1802 allows the Attorney General to authorize electronic surveillance for up to a year, without the FISA Court's prior approval, in two narrow circumstances: (1) if the surveillance is directed solely at communications between foreign powers; or (2) if the surveillance is directed solely at the acquisition of technical intelligence, other than spoken communications, from property under the exclusive control of a foreign power. In addition, the Attorney General must certify that there is no substantial likelihood that such surveillance will acquire the communications of U.S. persons. (In essence, § 1802 authorizes the surveillance of communications between foreign governments, and between a foreign government and its embassy.) Section 1802 is of limited use, however, because it explicitly prohibits efforts to acquire spoken communications. (No such limitation exists in the parallel exception for physical searches, 50 U.S.C. § 1822(a), under which agents presumably could infiltrate a foreign power's property for the purpose of overhearing conversations.) This provision would enhance the presidential authorization exception by eliminating the requirement that electronic surveillance cannot be directed at the spoken communications of foreign powers.

Section 105: Law Enforcement Use of FISA Information

50 U.S.C. § 1806(b) currently prohibits the disclosure of information "for law enforcement purposes" unless the disclosure includes a statement that the information cannot be used in a criminal proceeding without the Attorney General's advance authorization. This provision would amend § 1806(b) to give federal investigators and prosecutors greater flexibility to use FISA-obtained information. Specifically, it would eliminate the requirement that the Attorney General personally approve the use of such information in the criminal context, and would substitute a requirement that such use be approved by the Attorney General, the Deputy Attorney General, the Associate Attorney General, or an Assistant Attorney General designated by the Attorney General.

Section 106: Defense of Reliance on Authorization

50 U.S.C. § 1809(b) and 1827(b) create a defense for agents who engage in unauthorized surveillance or searches, or who disclose information without authorization, if they were relying on an order issued by the FISA Court. However, there does not appear to be a statutory defense for agents who engage in surveillance or searches pursuant to FISA authorities under which no prior court approval is required—e.g., pursuant to FISA's wartime exception (50 U. S.C. §§1811, 1829 & 1844), or FISA's presidential authorization exception (50 U.S.C. § 1802 & 1822(a)). This provision would clarify that the "good faith reliance" defense is available, not just when agents are acting pursuant to a FISA Court order, but also when they are acting pursuant to a lawful authorization from the President or the Attorney General.

Section 107: Pen Registers in FISA Investigations

50 U.S.C. § 1842(a)(1) makes FISA pen registers available in investigations of non-U.S. persons to "obtain foreign intelligence information." But for U.S. persons, the standard is much higher:

in cases involving U.S. persons, pen registers are only available "to protect against international terrorism or clandestine intelligence activities." Perversely, this appears to be stricter than the standard for pen registers under Title III, which requires only that it be shown that the information "is relevant to an ongoing criminal investigation." 18 U.S.C. § 3123(a)(1). This provision would amend § 1842(a)(1) by eliminating the stricter standard for U.S. persons. Specifically, FISA pen registers would be available in investigations of both U.S. persons and non-U.S. persons whenever they could be used "to obtain foreign intelligence information."

* * *

Section 109: Enforcement of Foreign Intelligence Surveillance Court Orders

The Foreign Intelligence Surveillance Act does not specify the means for enforcement of orders issued by the Foreign Intelligence Surveillance Court. Thus, for example, if a person refuses to comply with an order of the court to cooperate in the installation of a pen register or trap and trace device under 50 U.S.C. § 1842(d), or an order to produce records under 50 U.S.C. § 1861, existing law provides no clearly defined recourse to secure compliance with the court's order. This section remedies this omission by providing that the Foreign Intelligence Surveillance Court has the same authority as a United States district court to enforce its orders, including the authority to impose contempt sanctions in case of disobedience. . . .

Section 121: Definition of Terrorist Activities

This section adds a definition of "terrorist activities" to the definitional section for the chapter of the criminal code governing electronic surveillance (chapter 119). The definition encompasses criminal acts of domestic and international terrorism as defined in 18 U.S.C. § 2331, together with related preparatory, material support, and criminal activities. The same definition of terrorist activities would also apply through cross-referencing provisions, see 18 U.S.C. § 2711(1) and 3127(1) (as amended), in the chapters of the criminal code that govern accessing stored communications and the use of pen registers and trap and trace devices (chapters

121 and 206). The surveillance chapters of the criminal code contain many provisions which state that the authorized surveillance activities may be carried out as part of "criminal investigations." Section 121 also adds a provision to 18 U.S.C. § 2510 which specifies that "criminal investigations" include all investigations of criminal terrorist activities, to make it clear that the full range of authorized surveillance techniques are available in investigations of "terrorist activities" under the new definition.

Section 122: Inclusion of Terrorist Activities as Surveillance Predicates

This section adds terrorist activities, as defined under the amendment of section 121, and four specific offenses that are likely to be committed by terrorists (the offenses defined by 18 U.S.C. § 37, 930(c), 956, and 1993), as explicit predicates for electronic surveillance and monitoring. It further adds an explicit reference to terrorist activities to the provision authorizing electronic surveillance without a court order in emergency situations—18 U.S.C. § 2518(7)—and makes conforming changes in the corresponding provision (18 U.S.C. § 3125) for using pen registers and trap and trace devices without a court order in emergency situations.

The final subsection of this section modifies the definition of "court of competent jurisdiction" in 18 U.S.C. § 3127(2), to correct an unintended effect of amendments in sections 216(c)(1) and 220 of the USA PATRIOT Act. The purpose of the amendments was to authorize courts having jurisdiction over an offense to issue orders for pen registers and trap and trace devices, and search warrants for the disclosure of e-mails, which could be executed outside of their districts.

However, the language utilized inadvertently created a lack of clarity concerning the continued validity of the pre-existing authority of the courts to issue such orders and warrants for execution within their own districts (regardless of whether they have "jurisdiction over the offense"). This threatens to be a serious practical problem when information gathering in the United States is needed in response to requests by foreign law enforcement agencies to assist in foreign terrorism (or other criminal investigations) and to fulfill the United States' obligations under mutual legal assistance treaties, and in the context of investigations relating to crimes committed on U.S. military bases abroad, because in those cases the U.S. courts generally do not have jurisdiction over the offense. This section corrects the problem in relation to pen register and trap and trace orders through definitional language that explicitly includes both a court with jurisdiction over the offense or activities being investigated, and a court in the district in which the order will be executed. A parallel correction for the problem relating to search warrants for e-mails appears in section 125(b) of this bill.

Section 123: Extension of Authorized Periods Relating to Surveillance and Searches in Investigations of Terrorist Activities

In Katz v. United States, 389 U.S. 347 (1967), the Supreme Court held for the first time that government wiretapping was subject to the Fourth Amendment. In response, Congress enacted Title III of the 1968 Omnibus Crime Control and Safe Streets Act, 28 U.S.C. §§ 2510–2522, which governs electronic surveillance for all federal criminal offenses. Congress also subsequently enacted the Electronic Communications Privacy Act (ECPA), 18 U.S.C. §§ 2701–2712, which addresses government access to stored communications, and established statutory standards and procedures for the use of pen registers and trap and trace devices, 18 U.S.C. §§ 3121–3127. Further, because Katz and progeny specifically stated that the Court did not hold that the same Fourth Amendment restrictions applied with respect to the activities of foreign powers and their agents, in 1978 Congress enacted the Foreign Intelligence Surveillance Act, 50 U.S.C. §§ 1801–1862, which establishes standards applicable to surveillance of foreign powers and agents of foreign powers—including electronic surveillance, physical searches, and use of pen registers and trap and trace devices—in relation to the investigation of such matters as international terrorism and espionage. Congress has not provided separate statutory standards governing investigations of wholly domestic threats to the national security, particularly domestic terrorism. Thus, such investigations are subject to the time limits set forth in Title III. However, the Supreme Court in United States v. United States District Court ("Keith"), 407 U.S. 297 (1972), explicitly recognized that domestic security investigations would require different standards than those set forth in Title III:

"We recognize that domestic security surveillance may involve different policy and practical considerations from the surveillance of 'ordinary crime.' The gathering of security intelligence is often long range and involves the interrelation of various sources and types of information. The exact targets of such surveillance may be more difficult to identify than in surveillance operations against many types of crime specified in Title III. Often, too, the emphasis of domestic intelligence gathering is on the prevention of unlawful activity or the enhancement of the Government's preparedness for some possible future crisis or emergency. Thus, the focus of domestic surveillance may be less precise than that directed against more conventional types of crime." Id. at 322. Because domestic security investigations were subject to Title III, despite these considerations, the Court invited Congress to legislate new and different standards for such investigations: "Given [the] potential distinctions between Title III criminal surveillances and those involving the domestic security, Congress may wish to consider protective standards for the latter which differ from those already prescribed for specified crimes in Title III. Different standards may be compatible with the Fourth Amendment if they are reasonable both in relation to the legitimate need of Government for intelligence information and the protected rights of our citizens." Id. In Keith, the court noted that, with respect to surveillance in domestic security cases, "the time and reporting requirements need not be so strict as those in § 2518." Id. at 323. This section accepts the Court's invitation and extends, in investigations of terrorist activities, a number of statutory time limits or periods relating to electronic surveillance or monitoring and searches. The specific changes are (1) Amend 18 U.S.C. § 2518(5) to extend the normal duration of electronic surveillance orders in investigations of terrorist activities from 30 days to 90 days. (2) Amend 18 U.S.C. § 2518(6), which provides that an electronic surveillance order may require periodic progress reports to the judge who issued the order "at such intervals as the judge may require." As amended, the provision would not allow reports to be required at shorter intervals than 30 days in investigations of terrorist activities. (3) Amend 18 U.S.C. § 2705, which permits delaying notification concerning the accessing of a person's stored electronic communications where specified "adverse results" would result from the notification. As amended, the provision would include endangerment of the national security as a specified adverse result that permits delaying notification. (4) Amend 18 U.S.C. § 3123 to extend the normal authorization periods for pen registers and trap and trace devices in investigations of terrorist activities from 60 days to 120 days.

Section 124: Multi-function Devices

Electronic manufacturers increasingly are producing devices that are capable of performing multiple functions—e.g., cell phones that also can send e-mail like a Blackberry, and that include a calendar like a Palm Pilot. Multiple functions are also illustrated by ordinary home computers, which may, for example, be used to send and receive e-mail messages, to engage in oral communications through an Internet phone service, to store sent and received messages, and to store other information. Current law does not make it clear that the authorization (e.g., under an electronic surveillance order) to monitor one of a device's functions also entails the authority to monitor other functions. This section accordingly amends 18 U.S.C. § 2518(4) to make it clear that authorization of electronic surveillance with respect to a device, unless otherwise specified, may be relied on to intercept and access communications through any of the device's functions. The section also effectively allows a search warrant for other information retrievable from the device (whether or not related to the intercepted communications) to be combined with the electronic surveillance order, and makes conforming changes in the chapters relating to accessing stored communications and pen registers and trap and trace devices. The section further incorporates a correction for an unintended consequence of amendments in section 220 of the USA Patriot Act. As discussed in relation to section 122 of the bill above, amendments designed to authorize courts having jurisdiction over an offense to issue search warrants for the disclosure of e-mails outside of their districts have inadvertently clouded the pre-existing authority of the courts to issue such orders and warrants for execution within their own districts. This section corrects the problem by amending the pertinent language in 18 U.S.C. § 2703(b)(1)(A) and (c)(1)(A) to refer to a court in a district in which a provider of electronic communications service is located, as well as a court having jurisdiction over the offense or activities under investigation.

Section 125: Nationwide Search Warrants in Terrorism Investigations

Federal Rule of Criminal Procedure 41(a)(3) currently authorizes judges in one district to issue search warrants that are valid in another district, if the crime being investigated is "domestic terrorism or international terrorism" as defined in 18 U.S.C. § 2331. But § 2331 sets forth an extremely narrow definition of terrorism, as it is limited to "violent acts or acts dangerous to human life." Thus section 2331 arguably does not include investigations into terrorist financing, or other crimes that terrorists are likely to commit. As a result, a federal judge sitting in New York would be able to issue a search warrant that is valid in California in an investigation of a plot to bomb a building, but arguably could not issue the same warrant if the investigation concerned the raising of money to support terrorist operations. This provision would expand the types of terrorism crimes for which judges may issue search warrants that are valid nationwide. Specifically, it would authorize nationwide search warrants in investigations of the offenses listed in 18 U.S.C. § 2332b(g)(5)(B), including computer crimes, attacks on communications infrastructure, and providing material support to terrorists or terrorist organizations.

Section 126: Equal Access to Consumer Credit Reports

In recent years, it has become increasingly apparent that law enforcement investigators need access to suspected terrorists' banking information to determine their connections to terrorist organizations, including financial ties. The current version of 15 U.S.C. § 1681b(a)(1) allows investigators to obtain a suspect's credit report—the first step in locating his banking records only in response to a court order or a federal grand jury subpoena. As a result, law enforcement cannot obtain a suspect's banking information without issuing multiple time consuming subpoenas. In some cases, it can take a series of three subpoenas—first to the credit reporting agency, then to the suspect's creditors, then to the suspect's banks—and a period of nine to 12 weeks to learn where a suspected terrorist keeps his accounts. Perversely, the law makes it far easier for private entities to obtain an individual's credit reports; under 15 U.S.C. § 1681b(a)(3)(F), a private entity can obtain—usually within minutes—a credit report on anyone in the United States so long as it has a "legitimate business need" for the information. This provision would enable the government to obtain credit reports on virtually the same terms that private entities may. Specifically, it would amend § 1681b(a)(1) to allow law enforcement officers to obtain credit reports upon their certification that they will use the information only in connection with their duties to enforce federal law. This certification parallels the existing requirement that a private entity must have a "legitimate business need" before obtaining a credit report. . . .

* * *

Section 128: Administrative Subpoenas in Terrorism Investigations

The Department of Justice currently has the authority to issue administrative subpoenas in investigations of a wide variety of federal offenses, including health-care fraud, see 18 U.S.C. § 3486(a)(1)(A), immigration violations, see 8 U.S.C. § 1225(a), and false claims against the United States, see 31 U.S.C. § 3733. But administrative subpoenas are not available in investigations of terrorism, even though the consequences of a terrorist attack are far more dire than committing simple fraud against the United States government. As a result, law enforcement personnel are required to seek grand jury subpoenas before individuals who may have information relevant to a terrorism investigation can be compelled to testify or provide documents. This provision would extend the existing administrative-subpoena authorities into investigations involving domestic or international terrorism. It also would prohibit a subpoena recipient from disclosing to any other person (except to a lawyer in order to obtain legal advice) the fact that he has received a subpoena. This proposal would not give the Justice Department a unilateral, unreviewable authority to compel production of documents relevant to a terrorism investigation. If recipients refuse to comply with subpoenas, the Justice Department would have to ask a court to enforce them. And subpoena recipients would retain the ability, as they do in other contexts, to ask a court to quash the subpoena. See, e.g., In re Administrative Subpoena, John Doe, D.P.M., 253 F.3d 256 (6th Cir. 2001).

Section 129: Strengthening Access to and Use of Information in National Security Investigations

This section is primarily concerned with correcting problems and weaknesses in provisions authorizing the use of "national security letters." In substance, national security letters are administrative subpoenas that may be issued by FBI officials—or in some instances, other authorized government officials—to obtain specified types of records or information for use in national security investigations. The existing national security letter provisions include the following: (1) 18 U.S.C. § 2709—Providing FBI access, in connection with investigations of international terrorism or espionage, to certain electronic communication transactional records maintained by communication service providers. (2) Section 625(a)-(b) of the Fair Credit Reporting Act (15 U.S.C. § 168 Iu(a)(b))—Providing FBI access, in connection with investigations of international terrorism or espionage, to certain consumer information maintained by consumer reporting agencies. (3) Section 626 of the Fair Credit Reporting Act (15 U.S.C. § 1681v)—Providing access to consumer reports and other consumer information maintained by consumer reporting agencies, where needed by government agencies authorized to investigate or carry out intelligence or analysis activities related to international terrorism. (4) Section 1114(a)(5) of the Right to Financial Privacy Act (12 U.S.C. § 3414(a)(5))—Providing FBI access, in connection with investigations of international terrorism or espionage, to financial records maintained by financial institutions. (5) Section 802(a) of the National Security Act of 1947 (50 U.S.C. § 436(a))—Providing access by authorized investigative agencies to financial records and information, consumer reports, and travel records in relation to a person having access to classified information, based on indications that the person has disclosed or may disclose classified information to a foreign power. Problems under these provisions include the following: (1) The statutes in which the national security letter provisions appear generally prohibit persons from disclosing that they have received these requests for information, to safeguard the integrity of the terrorism and espionage investigations in which national security letters are used. However, they specify no penalty for persons who make such unlawful disclosures. (2)

While these statutes create a legal obligation for the recipient to provide the requested information, they do not specify any procedures for judicial enforcement in case the recipient refuses to comply with the request. (3) The scope of the national security letter provisions on the terrorism side is generally limited to international terrorism; however, the distinction between international and domestic terrorism is increasingly elusive in contemporary circumstances. (4) These provisions are restrictive regarding the sharing of information among federal agencies with relevant responsibilities. This is in conflict with current needs and with the broad principles favoring the sharing of intelligence among federal agencies under the USA PATRIOT Act. Subsection (a) of this section provides appropriate penalties for violations of the nondisclosure provisions of the national security letter provisions. Currently, 18 U.S.C. § 1510(b) makes it an offense for an officer of a financial institution to notify other persons about a grand jury subpoena or an administrative subpoena issued by the Department of Justice for records of the financial institution. The offense is punishable by up to a year of imprisonment, or up to five years of imprisonment if the disclosure was made with the intent to obstruct a judicial proceeding. Similarly, 18 U.S.C. § 1510(d) makes it an offense, punishable by up to five years of imprisonment, for an insurance company employee to notify other persons about a grand jury subpoena for records with intent to obstruct a judicial proceeding. Subsection (a) of this section adds a parallel offense (proposed 18 U.S.C. § 1510(e)) covering violations of the non-disclosure requirements of the national security letter provisions described above. As with current 18 U.S.C. § 1510(b), the offense would be a misdemeanor punishable by up to a year of imprisonment, but would be punishable by up to five years of imprisonment if the unlawful disclosure was committed with the intent to obstruct the terrorism or espionage investigation. In addition to providing appropriate penalties for unlawful disclosure of national security letter requests, the same penalties would apply to: (i) violation of the non-disclosure requirement under 50 U.S.C. § 1861(d) for orders of the Foreign Intelligence Surveillance Court requiring the production of records, documents, and other tangible things in connection with investigations to obtain foreign intelligence information about non–United States persons or to protect against international terrorism or espionage, and (ii) violation of the non-disclosure provision of proposed 18 U.S.C. § 2332f(d) in section

129 of this bill, relating to administrative subpoenas in terrorism investigations. The national security letter provisions make compliance with the request for information mandatory. See 12 U.S.C. § 3414(a)(5)(A); 15 U.S.C. § 1681u(a)-(b), 1681v(a); 18 U.S.C. § 2709(a); 50 U.S.C. § 436(c). However, they make no provision for judicial enforcement in case this legal obligation is not met. Subsection (b) of this section authorizes the Attorney General to seek judicial enforcement in such cases. This is similar, for example, to the existing judicial enforcement provision in 18 U.S.C. § 3486(c) for administrative subpoenas under that section. Subsection (c) of this section amends the national security letter provisions relating to electronic communication transactional records, consumer credit information, and financial institution records, so that they apply in investigations of all types of terrorist activities. The specific amendments involve substituting, for current references in these provisions to investigations relating to "international terrorism," references to investigations relating to "terrorist activities." The latter notion is defined in proposed 18 U.S.C. § 2510(20) in section 121 of this bill so as to include domestic, as well as international, terrorism. The limitation to international terrorism in existing law is an impediment to the effective use of national security letters because it may not be apparent in the early stages of a terrorism investigation—or even after it has continued for some time—whether domestic or international terrorism is involved. The Oklahoma City bombing and the anthrax letter incidents illustrate this point. Moreover, in the current circumstances, domestic terrorists who attempt to ally with or are inspired to emulate international terrorists are an increasing concern. The dangers posed to the national security by such persons may be comparable to those posed by international terrorists, and national security letters should likewise be an available tool in the investigation of their criminal activities.

Subsection (d) of this section deletes or modifies language in the national security letter provisions which unduly limits information sharing among federal agencies. For example, 18 U.S.C. § 2709 is the national security letter provision for electronic communication transactional records. Subsection (d) of § 2709 states that the FBI may disseminate information and records obtained pursuant to that section only as provided in guidelines approved by the Attorney General "for foreign intelligence collection and foreign counterintelligence investigations conducted by the Federal Bureau of Investigation, and, with respect to dissemination to an agency of the United States, only if such information is clearly relevant to the authorized responsibilities of such agency." The reference to guidelines that relate to "foreign intelligence collection and foreign counterintelligence investigations" is inconsistent with the amendment proposed in subsection (c) of this section to extend the scope of 18 U.S.C. § 2709 to include investigations of domestic terrorism, as well as international terrorism. The restrictive language regarding information sharing with other federal agencies is in conflict with the principles favoring broad sharing of intelligence among federal agencies under section 203 of the USA PATRIOT Act (Pub. L. 107–56).

Subsection (c) of this section accordingly deletes the restrictive language quoted above in 18 U.S.C. § 2709(d), so that it states simply that the FBI may disseminate information and records obtained under § 2709 only as provided in guidelines approved by the Attorney General. Subsection (c) also makes similar changes in the other national security letter provisions. The general effect of the amendments is to remove existing impediments to the sharing of information obtained by means of national security letters in terrorism and espionage investigations with other federal agencies having relevant responsibilities.

* * *

Section 201: Prohibition of Disclosure of Terrorism Investigation Detainee Information

In certain instances, the release of information about persons detained in connection with terrorism investigations could have a substantial adverse impact on the United States' security interests, as well as the detainee's privacy. Cf. North Jersey Media Group, Inc. v. Ashcroft, 308 F.3d 198, 217–19 (3d Cir. 2002). Publicizing the fact that a particular alien has been detained could alert his coconspirators about the extent of the federal investigation and the imminence of their own detention, thus provoking them to flee to avoid detention and prosecution or to accelerate their terrorist plans before they can be disrupted.

Although existing Freedom of Information Act (FOIA) exemptions 7(A), 7(C), and 7(F) (5 U.S.C. § 552(b)(7)) permit the government to protect information relating to detainees, defending this interpretation through litigation requires extensive

Department of Justice resources, which would be better spent detecting and incapacitating terrorists. This provision thus establishes a specific authority under Exemption 3 of the FOIA to clarify what is already implicit in various FOIA exemptions: the government need not disclose information about individuals detained in investigations of terrorism until disclosure occurs routinely upon the initiation of criminal charges.

Section 202: Distribution of "Worst Case Scenario" Information

Section 112(r) of the Clean Air Act, 42 U.S.C. § 7412(r), requires private companies that use potentially dangerous chemicals to submit to the Environmental Protection Agency a "worst case scenario" report detailing what would be the impact on the surrounding community of release of the specified chemicals. Such reports are a roadmap for terrorists, who could use the information to plan attacks on the facilities. This provision would revise section 112(r)(7)(H) of the Clean Air Act to better manage access to information contained in "worst case scenario" reports. This revised section would continue to allow such information to be shared with federal and state officials who are responsible for preventing or responding to accidental or criminal releases. However, the revised section will require that public access be limited to "read-only" methods, and only to those persons who live or work in the geographical area likely to be affected by a worst-case release from a facility.

*   *   *

Section 204: Ex Parte Authorizations Under Classified Information Procedures Act

Under the current version of the Classified Information Procedures Act, 18 U.S.C. App. 3 § 116, courts have discretion over whether to approve the government's request for a CIPA authorization—which enables the submission of sensitive evidence ex parte and in camera. See 18 U.S.C. App. 3 § 4 ("The court may permit the United States to make a request for such authorization [for a protective order] in the form of a written statement to be inspected by the court alone."). As a result, the government is forced to divert valuable resources to litigating this question.

And even worse, a request for confidentiality itself can be a security breach: the government risks disclosing sensitive national-security information simply by explaining in open court why the information should be redacted. See, e.g., United States v. Rezaq, 899 F. Supp. 697, 707 (D.D.C. 1995) (government's CIPA pleadings must be served "on the defendant and then litigated in an adversarial hearing").

This provision would amend CIPA to provide that courts shall allow the United States to make a request for a CIPA authorization ex parte and in camera. This amendment would not affect the showing that the United States is required to make in order to obtain a protective order, but by replacing "may" with "shall," the United States will be able to obtain the court's guidance in every case in which classified information may potentially be discoverable, without risking disclosure of the very secrets that it seeks to protect. See United States v. Klimavicius-Viloria, 144 F.3d 1249, 1261 (9th Cir. 1998) (upholding the use under CIPA of ex parte, in camera hearings and written submissions by the government when the court is required to make discovery determinations).

* * *

Section 303: Establishment of Database to Facilitate Investigation and Prevention of Terrorist Activities

This provision would allow the Attorney General to establish databases of DNA records pertaining to the terrorists or suspected terrorists from whom DNA samples or other identification information have been collected. All federal agencies, including the Department of Defense and probation offices, would be required to give the Attorney General, for inclusion in the databases, any DNA records, fingerprints, or other identification information that can be collected under this Subtitle. This provision also allows the Attorney General to use the information to detect, investigate, prosecute, prevent, or respond to terrorist activities, or other unlawful activities by suspected terrorists. In addition, the Attorney General would be able to share the information with other federal, state, local, or foreign agencies for the same purposes.

* * *

Section 322: Extradition Without Treaties and for Offenses Not Covered by an Existing Treaty

Many of the United States' older extradition treaties contain "lists" or "schedules" of extraditable offenses that reflect only those serious crimes in existence at the time the treaties were negotiated. (For example, our treaty with Egypt dates from 1874, and our treaty with Great Britain which includes Pakistan dates from the 1930s.) As a result, these older treaties often fail to include more modern offenses, such as money laundering, computer crimes, and certain crimes against children. While some old treaties are supplemented by newer multilateral terrorism treaties, extradition is possible under these newer treaties only if the other country is also a party to the multinational treaty, leaving gaps in coverage. Additionally, absent a few narrow exceptions, U.S. law permits the extradition of offenders to a foreign nation only when there is a treaty or convention in force with that country or a statute conferring such authority upon the executive branch. See Valentine v. United States, 299 U.S. 5, 8 (1936). At present, there are close to seventy countries in the world with which the U.S. has no extradition treaty at all. This means that the U.S. can become a "safe haven" for some foreign criminals, and that we cannot take advantage of some countries' willingness to surrender fugitives to us in the absence of an extradition treaty these nations usually require at least the possibility of reciprocity. This provision would amend current extradition law to. (1) authorize the U.S. to extradite offenders to treaty partners for modern crimes that may not be included in our older list treaties with those countries; and (2) provide for on a case by case basis and with the approval of the Attorney General and the Secretary of State extradition from the United States for serious crimes even in the absence of an extradition treaty.

*   *   *

Section 401: Terrorism Hoaxes

In the wake of the anthrax attacks in the fall of 2001, a number of individuals chose to perpetrate terrorism hoaxes (e.g., sending unidentified white powder in a letter with the intent that the recipient believe it to be anthrax). Such hoaxes divert law-enforcement and emergency services resources, and thus impede our ability to respond to actual terrorist events. Current federal law does not adequately address the problem of hoaxes relating to various weapons of mass destruction. At present, the primary way to prosecute terrorism hoaxes is to use "threat" statutes— e.g., 18 U.S.C. § 2332a, which criminalizes certain threats to use a weapon of mass destruction, and 18 U.S.C. § 876, which criminalizes the use of the mails to threaten injury to a person. But some terrorism hoaxes are simply false reports that cannot easily be characterized as outright threats.

This section would amend federal law to create a new prohibition on terrorism hoaxes. In particular, it would (1) make it unlawful to knowingly convey false or misleading information, where the information reasonably may be believed, and concerns criminal activity relating to weapons of mass destruction; (2) require criminal defendants to reimburse any person, including the United States, State and local first responders who incur expenses incident to an emergency or investigative response to the terrorism hoax; and (3) authorize a civil action for such expenses.

Section 402: Providing Material Support to Terrorism

18 U.S.C. § 2339A's prohibition on providing material support to terrorists is unnecessarily narrow; it currently does not reach all situations where material support or resources are provided to facilitate the commission of "international terrorism." Rather, § 2339A only encompasses those acts of international terrorism which are prohibited by some other federal statute. Because, unlike the existing underlying offenses in § 2339A(a), "international terrorism" per se is not an offense under Title 18, it is prudent to establish unassailable constitutional bases for prohibiting such support. The first basis is if the material support is in or affects interstate or foreign commerce. The second basis is the regulation and control over the activities of U.S. nationals and U.S. legal entities who are outside the United States. Such control is based on, among others, the United States' constitutional foreign affairs power. In addition, this section amends the definition of "international terrorism" to make it clear that it covers acts which by their nature appear to be intended for the stated purposes. Hence, there would be no requirement to show that the

defendants actually had such an intent. (There is a conforming amendment to the definition of "domestic terrorism" to maintain the existing parallel between the two definitions.)

Second, one court of appeals recently has questioned whether the current prohibition in 18 U.S.C. § 2339B on providing "training" or "personnel" to terrorist organizations designated under section 219 of the Immigration and Nationality Act are unconstitutionally vague. See Humanitarian Law Project v. Reno, 205 F.3d 1130 (9th Cir. 2000), cert. denied, 121 S. Ct. 1226 (2001). But see United States v. Lindh, ___ F. Supp. 2d (E.D. Va. 2002) (rejecting the holding of Humanitarian Law Project). Subsection (b) would amend the pertinent statutes to remove any possible doubts about the scope of the prohibition. In particular, "training" would now be defined as "instruction or teaching designed to impart a specific skill." And criminal liability for "personnel" would apply to "knowingly provid[ing], attempt[ing] to provide, or conspir[ing] to provide a terrorist organization with one or more individuals (including himself) to work in concert with it or under its direction or control."

Section 403: Weapons of Mass Destruction

At present, the federal weapons of mass destruction statute, 18 U.S.C. § 2332a, contains only one of the several constitutional bases for asserting federal jurisdiction over a terrorist attack involving weapons of mass destruction in certain circumstances: if the attack is against a person or property and "affect[s] interstate commerce." Id. § 2332a(a)(2). This provision would amend the statute to specifically cover property and persons in three other circumstances where federal jurisdiction constitutionally can be asserted: (1) if the mail or any facility of interstate or foreign commerce is used in furtherance of the offense; (2) if the attacked property is used in interstate or foreign commerce, or in an activity that affects interstate or foreign commerce; or (3) if any perpetrator travels in or causes another to travel in interstate or foreign commerce in furtherance of the offense.

Second, with respect to attacks on government buildings, the WMD statute only applies to attacks on property owned by the United States. It currently does not directly criminalize attacks on foreign governments' property in the United States.

This section therefore amends the statute, in new Subsection 2332a(a)(4), to provide for jurisdiction where the property against which the weapon of mass destruction is directed is property within the United States that is owned, leased, or used by a foreign government. (The term "foreign government" is defined in 18 U.S.C. § 11.) Third, the current version of the WMD statute does not prohibit the use of chemical weapons; in fact, it expressly states that it does not apply to attacks carried out with "a chemical weapon as that term is defined in section 229F." 18 U.S.C. § 2332a(a), (b). This restriction was added in the implementing legislation for the Chemical Weapons Convention on October 22, 1998. Removing "chemical weapons" from the ambit of the WMD statute has proven improvident, as it has created needless factual confusion in situations where the WMD contains explosive materials but no toxic chemicals, and where it contains toxic chemicals in addition to the explosive material. Since most chemical weapons will always contain some explosive material in order to cause the dispersal of the toxic chemical, it makes little sense to arbitrarily limit the scope of the use of WMD statute since the damage resulting from its use can be caused by either the explosive material, or the toxic chemicals, or a combination of both. Restoring "chemical weapons" to the scope of the WMD statute eliminates a defendant's ability to make technical arguments that the prosecutor has charged under the wrong statute. In addition to making the foregoing changes in the WMD statute, this section includes a technical amendment to 18 U.S.C. 175b (relating to biological agents and toxins), to correct a cross-reference to a related regulation which has been modified.

* * *

Section 405: Presumption for Pretrial Detention in Cases Involving Terrorism

Defendants in federal cases who are accused of certain crimes are presumptively denied pretrial release. 18 U.S.C. § 3142(e). Specifically, for these crimes, there is a rebuttable presumption that "no condition or combination of conditions will reasonably assure the appearance of the person as required and the safety of the community." The list of crimes currently includes drug offenses carrying maximum prison terms of 10 years or more, but it does not include most terrorism offenses. Thus, persons accused of many drug offenses are presumptively to be detained before trial, but no comparable presumption exists for persons accused of most terrorist crimes. This section would amend 18 U.S.C. § 3142(e) to presumptively deny release to persons charged with crimes listed in 18 U.S.C. § 2332b(g)(5)(B), which contains a standard list of offenses that are likely to be committed by terrorists. This presumption is warranted because of the unparalleled magnitude of the danger to the United States and its people posed by acts of terrorism, and because terrorism is typically engaged in by groups—many with international connections—that are often in a position to help their members flee or go into hiding. In addition to adding terrorism offenses to those creating a presumption in favor of detention, this section makes conforming changes in a provision describing offenses for which pretrial detention may be considered (§ 3142(f)(1)) and in a provision identifying factors to be considered by the judicial officer in determining whether the defendant's appearance and public safety can reasonably be assured through release conditions (§ 3142(g)(1)).

*   *   *

Section 410: No Statute of Limitations for Terrorism Crimes

This section broadens the class of offenses that may be prosecuted without limitation of time under 18 U.S.C. § 3286(b) by deleting a limitation to offenses which result in, or create a foreseeable risk of, death or serious injury. With this amendment, the provision includes all offenses in the standard list of crimes likely to be committed by terrorists and supporters of terrorism (see 18 U.S.C. § 2332b(g)(5)(B)). The existing limitation could complicate or prevent the prosecution of persons convicted of non-violent terrorist offenses—such as a cyberterrorism attack on the United States that results in tens of billions of dollars of economic damage—and of persons who provide the essential financial or other material support for the apparatus of terrorism, but do not directly engage themselves in violent terrorist acts. The continuing danger posed to the national security by such persons may be no less than that posed by the direct perpetrators of terrorist violence, and they should not be entitled to permanent immunity from prosecution merely because they have succeeded in avoiding identification and apprehension for some period of time.

Section 411: Penalties for Terrorist Murders

Existing law does not consistently provide adequate maximum penalties for fatal acts of terrorism. For example, in a case in which a terrorist caused massive loss of life by sabotaging a national defense installation in violation of 18 U.S.C. § 2155, sabotaging a nuclear facility in violation of 42 U.S.C. § 2284, or destroying an energy facility in violation of 18 U.S.C. § 1366, there would be no possibility of imposing the death penalty under the statutes defining these offenses because they contain no death penalty authorizations. In contrast, dozens of other federal violent crime provisions authorize up to life imprisonment or the death penalty in cases where victims are killed. There are also cross-cutting provisions which authorize these sanctions for specified classes of offenses whenever death results, such as 18 U.S.C. § 2245, which provides that a person who, in the course of a sexual abuse offense, "engages in conduct that results in the death of a person, shall be punished by death or imprisoned for any term of years or for life." This section similarly authorizes uniformly up to life imprisonment or the death penalty for conduct resulting in death that occurs in the course of the offenses likely to be committed by terrorists that are listed in 18 U.S.C. § 2232b(g)(5)(B) or in the course of terrorist activities as defined in 18 U.S.C. § 2510 under the amendment in section 121 of this bill. This section also adds the new provision covering terrorist offenses resulting in death (proposed 18 U.S.C. § 2339D) to the list of offenses in 18 U.S.C. § 3592(c)(1) whose commission permits the jury to consider imposition of the death penalty. This will make the option of capital punishment available more consistently in cases involving fatal terrorist crimes. The imposition of capital punishment in such cases will continue to be subject to the requirement under 18 U.S.C. § 3591 that the offender have a high degree of culpability with respect to the death of the victim or victims, and to the requirement that the jury conclude that the death penalty is warranted under the standards and procedures of 18 U.S.C. § 3593.

* * *

Section 421: Increased Penalties for Terrorism Financing

At present, the maximum civil penalty for violations of the International Emergency Economic Powers Act, 50 U.S.C. § 1701 et seq., is only $10,000 per violation; see 50 U.S.C. § 1705. This is a relatively mild maximum fine; the civil penalty for violations of the Clean Water Act, for example, is . . . $25,000 for each day the violation persists. See 33 U.S.C. § 1319(d). IEEPA's modest civil penalty may not adequately deter individuals who are considering engaging in economic transactions that finance terrorist organizations, or otherwise trading with prohibited persons. And given the severity of terrorist threats, and the consequences of a successful terrorist attack, the United States should be able to punish those who finance terrorism at least as severely as it can punish polluters. This proposal therefore would amend IEEPA to increase the maximum civil penalty amount from $10,000 per violation to $50,000 per violation.

Section 422: Money Laundering Through Hawalas

Under federal law, a financial transaction constitutes a money laundering offense only if the funds involved in the transaction represent the proceeds of some criminal offense. See 18 U.S.C. § 1956(a)(1) ("represents the proceeds of some form of unlawful activity"); 18 U.S.C. § 1957(f)(2) ("property constituting, or derived from, proceeds obtained from a criminal offense"). There is some uncertainty, however, as to whether the "proceeds element" is satisfied as to all aspects of a money laundering scheme when two or more transactions are conducted in parallel. For example, consider the following transaction: A sends drug proceeds to B, who deposits the money in Bank Account 1. Simultaneously or subsequently, B takes an equal amount of money from Bank Account 2 and sends it to A, or to a person designated by A. The first transaction from A to B clearly satisfies the proceeds element of the money laundering statute, but there is some question as to whether second transaction—the one that involves only funds withdrawn from Bank Account 2—does so. The question has become increasingly important because such parallel transactions are the technique used to launder money through hawalas and the Black Market Peso Exchange. Several courts have addressed related issues, holding that both parts of the parallel or later transaction (sometimes called a "dependent" transaction because it would not have occurred but for the first transaction) involve criminal proceeds for purposes of the money laundering statute. See United States v. Covey, 232 F.3d 641 (8th Cir. 2000) (where defendant receives cash from drug dealer, and gives drug dealer checks drawn on own funds in return, transfer of checks is a money laundering offense involving SUA proceeds); United States v. Mankarious, 151 F.3d 694 (7th Cir. 1998) (if check constituting SUA proceeds is deposited in bank account, and second check is written on that account, second check constitutes proceeds, even if first check has not yet cleared); United States v. Farrington, 2000 WL 1751996 (D.V.I. 2000) (if check constituting SUA proceeds is deposited into bank account, and second check is drawn on same account on same day, second check is SUA proceeds, even though first check has not yet cleared). This proposal is intended to remove all uncertainty on this point by providing that all constitute parts of a set of parallel or dependent transactions involve criminal proceeds if one such transaction does so.

*   *   *

Section 503: Inadmissibility and Removability of National Security Aliens or Criminally Charged Aliens

The Attorney General does not have sufficient authority to bar an alien from the United States, or to remove an alien from the United States, on the basis of national security. The direct authority for barring admission or removing an alien does not provide sufficient authority for action based strictly on national security grounds. This provision would give the Attorney General sufficient authority to deny admission to the United States, or to remove from the United States, those individuals whom the Attorney General has reason to believe would pose a danger to the national security of the United States, based on the statutory definition of "national security" under the Act in connection with the designation of foreign terrorist organizations. The new ground of admissibility, and the new ground of removal, would parallel the authority currently granted to the Secretary of State in INA § 212(a)(3)(C)(i) . . . the Secretary has reasonable grounds to believe would have potentially serious adverse foreign policy consequences for the United States, thereby making the alien excludable. In this case, the Attorney General must have reason to believe that the alien poses a danger to the national security of the United States and may deny admission. In addition, this provision would give the Attorney General the authority to bar from the United States aliens who have been convicted of, or charged with, serious crimes in other countries.

* * *

U.S. Secretary of Defense Donald Rumsfeld's War-on-Terror Memo, October 16, 2003

October 16, 2003
TO: Gen. Dick Myers
Paul Wolfowitz
Gen. Pete Pace
Doug Feith
FROM: Donald Rumsfeld
SUBJECT: Global War on Terrorism

The questions I posed to combatant commanders this week were:

Are we winning or losing the Global War on Terror? Is DoD changing fast enough to deal with the new 21st century security environment? Can a big institution change fast enough? Is the USG changing fast enough?

DoD has been organized, trained and equipped to fight big armies, navies and air forces. It is not possible to change DoD fast enough to successfully fight the global war on terror; an alternative might be to try to fashion a new institution, either within DoD or elsewhere, one that seamlessly focuses the capabilities of several departments and agencies on this key problem. With respect to global terrorism, the record since September 11 seems to be: We are having mixed results with Al Qaida; although we have put considerable pressure on them, nonetheless, a great many remain at large. USG has made reasonable progress in capturing or killing the top 55 Iraqis. USG has made somewhat slower progress tracking down the Taliban, Omar, Hekmatyar, etc. With respect to the Ansar Al-Islam, we are just getting started. Have we fashioned the right mix of rewards, amnesty, protection and confidence in the US?

Does DoD need to think through new ways to organize, train, equip and focus to deal with the global war on terror?

Are the changes we have and are making too modest and incremental? My impression is that we have not yet made truly bold moves, although we have made many sensible, logical moves in the right direction, but are they enough?

Today, we lack metrics to know if we are winning or losing the global war on terror. Are we capturing, killing or deterring and dissuading more terrorists every day than the madrassas and the radical clerics are recruiting, training and deploying against us?

Does the US need to fashion a broad, integrated plan to stop the next generation of terrorists? The US is putting relatively little effort into a long-range plan, but we are putting a great deal of effort into trying to stop terrorists. The cost-benefit ratio is against us! Our cost is billions against the terrorists' costs of millions.

Do we need a new organization?

How do we stop those who are financing the radical madrassa schools?

Is our current situation such that "the harder we work, the behinder we get"?

It is pretty clear that the coalition can win in Afghanistan and Iraq in one way or another, but it will be a long, hard slog.

Does CIA need a new finding?

Should we create a private foundation to entice radical madrassas to a more moderate course?

What else should we be considering?

Please be prepared to discuss this at our meeting on Saturday or Monday.

Thanks.

dr

7

Directory of Major Organizations Involved with the USA Patriot Act of 2001

The groups in this chapter are some of the major organizations—governmental and nongovernmental; pro- and con- USA Patriot Act of 2001. All the information in this chapter is taken from the Websites of the various groups listed herein.

Nongovernmental Websites

American Civil Liberties Union

"The American Civil Liberties Union (ACLU) is our nation's guardian of liberty, working daily in courts, legislatures and communities to defend and preserve the individual rights and liberties guaranteed to all people in this country by the Constitution and laws of the United States. In 1920, when the ACLU was founded by Roger Baldwin, Crystal Eastman, Albert DeSilver and others, civil liberties were in a sorry state. Activists were languishing in jail for distributing anti-war literature. Foreign-born people suspected of political radicalism were subject to summary deportation. Racial segregation was the law of the land and state sanctioned violence against African Americans was routine. Constitutional rights for lesbians and gay men, the poor and many other groups were virtually unthinkable. Moreover, the U.S. Supreme Court had yet to uphold a single free speech claim under the First Amendment. Since our founding in 1920, the non-profit, nonpartisan ACLU has grown from a roomful of civil liberties activists to an organization of nearly 400,000 members and supporters, with offices in almost every state. The ACLU has also maintained, since its founding, the position that civil liberties must be respected, even in times of national emergency. In support of that position, the ACLU has appeared before the Supreme Court and other federal courts on numerous occasions, both as direct counsel and by filing amicus briefs. The ACLU's mission is to fight civil liberties violations wherever and whenever they occur. Most of our clients are ordinary people who have experienced an injustice and have decided to fight back. The ACLU is also active in our national and state capitals, fighting to ensure that the Bill of Rights will always be more than a "parchment barrier" against government oppression and the tyranny of the majority. The ACLU is supported by annual dues and contributions from its members, plus grants from private foundations and individuals. We do not receive any government funding" (www.aclu.org).

AMERICAN CIVIL LIBERTIES UNION
125 Broad Street, 18th Floor, New York, NY 10004
1-888-567-ACLU
www.aclu.org

American Conservative Union

"The American Conservative Union is the nation's oldest conservative lobbying organization. ACU's purpose is to effectively communicate and advance the goals and principles of conservatism through one multi-issue, umbrella organization. The Statement of Principles makes clear ACU's support of capitalism, belief in the doctrine of original intent of the framers of the Constitution, confidence in traditional moral values, and commitment to a strong national defense. Over the years, ACU has been on the cutting edge of major public policy battles. Among ACU's significant efforts, past and present, are fighting to keep OSHA off the back of small businesses, opposing the Panama Canal giveaway, opposing the SALT treaties, supporting aid to freedom fighters in Marxist countries, promoting the confirmation of conservative Justices to the Supreme Court, battling against higher taxes, and advocating the need for near-term deployment of strategic defenses. In 1994, through its Citizens Against Rationing Health coalition, sponsorship of national "town meetings," and a "Health Care Truth Tour," ACU spearheaded the conservative response on the health reform issue. Whether fighting for lower taxes and less government spending, more effective and efficient military protection, or the cause of freedom world-wide, by speaking for the entire conservative movement the American Conservative Union is always 'Your Conservative Voice in Washington'" (acu@conservative.org).

AMERICAN CONSERVATIVE UNION
1007 Cameron Street, Alexandria, VA 22314
703-836-8602
Fax: 703-836-8606
acu@conservative.org

Cato Institute

"The Cato Institute was founded in 1977 by Edward H. Crane. It is a non-profit public policy research foundation headquartered in Washington, D.C. The Institute is named for Cato's Letters, a series of libertarian pamphlets that helped lay the philosophical foundation for the American Revolution. The Cato Institute seeks to broaden the parameters of public policy debate to allow consideration of the traditional American principles of limited government, individual liberty, free markets and peace. Toward that goal, the Institute strives to achieve greater involvement of the intelligent, concerned lay public in questions of policy and the proper role of government. Today, those who subscribe to the principles of the American Revolution—individual liberty, limited government, the free market, and the rule of law—call themselves by a variety of terms, including conservative, libertarian, classical liberal, and liberal. We see problems with all of those terms. 'Conservative' smacks of an unwillingness to change, of a desire to preserve the status quo. Only in America do people seem to refer to free-market capitalism—the most progressive, dynamic, and ever-changing system the world has ever known— as conservative. Additionally, many contemporary American conservatives favor state intervention in some areas, most notably in trade and into our private lives.

"'Classical liberal' is a bit closer to the mark, but the word 'classical' connotes a backward-looking philosophy. Finally, 'liberal' may well be the perfect word in most of the world—the liberals in societies from China to Iran to South Africa to Argentina are supporters of human rights and free markets—but its meaning has clearly been corrupted by contemporary American liberals. The Jeffersonian philosophy that animates Cato's work has increasingly come to be called 'libertarianism' or 'market liberalism.' It combines an appreciation for entrepreneurship, the market process, and lower taxes with strict respect for civil liberties and skepticism about the benefits of both the welfare state and foreign military adventurism" (www.cato.org).

CATO INSTITUTE
1000 Massachusetts Avenue, NW, Washington, DC 20001-5403
202-842-0200
Fax: 202-842-3490
www.cato.org

Center for Constitutional Rights

"The Center for Constitutional Rights (CCR) is a non-profit legal and educational organization dedicated to protecting and advancing the rights guaranteed by the U.S. Constitution and the Universal Declaration of Human Rights. CCR uses litigation proactively to advance the law in a positive direction, to empower poor communities and communities of color, to guarantee the rights of those with the fewest protections and least access to legal resources, to train the next generation of constitutional and human rights attorneys, and to strengthen the broader movement for constitutional and human rights.

"Since 1966, the Center for Constitutional Rights has remained dedicated to defending and advancing the rights guaranteed by the United States Constitution and the Universal Declaration of Human Rights. Our work began on behalf of civil rights activists in the Jim Crow South and the racist North, and over the last four decades CCR has played an important role in many popular movements for social justice. During the seventies CCR brought and won *Monell v. Department of Social Services*, which enabled private individuals and civil rights groups to enforce the Constitution in court. Throughout the seventies and eighties, we won groundbreaking victories for women's rights, including *NOW v. Terry*, the first case to establish a 'buffer zone' around abortion clinics besieged by Operation Rescue.

"In 1980, our *Filártiga v. Peña-Irala* created a right to sue for human rights violations occurring anywhere in the world under the then-obscure Alien Tort Claims Act. For 35 years, CCR has served as an incubator for progressive lawyering, producing numerous important precedents and innovative legal strategies that have become an established part of law and the legal culture. As we look to the future, CCR will continue to be at the forefront of legal thinking, using the law creatively in the service of justice, and serving as a model to other progressive legal organizations both here and abroad. Using *Filártiga* and the precedent set by *Doe v. Unocal*, which allowed suits against corporations for complicity in human rights abuses, we will fight to ensure that globalization does not mean rampant exploitation of the world's people. Through organizing efforts and through cases such as *Daniels et al. v. New York,* we will work to complete the unfinished civil rights movement, targeting racial profiling and other modern-day manifestations of racial intolerance.

"Through efforts such as our Supermax Litigation Project and Immigrant Workers' Rights Project, we are vigilant in defense of the rights of those in our society who have the fewest resources and the least access to justice. As society changes, new social problems are constantly arising, even as old ones are solved. CCR will continue to evolve with these changes, seeking out new threats to the rights and well-being of citizens and devising new strategies in their defense" (www.ccr.org).

CENTER FOR CONSTITUTIONAL RIGHTS
666 Broadway, 7th Floor, New York, NY 10012
212-614-6464
Fax: 212-614-6499
Email. info@ccr-ny.org
www.ccr.org

Center for Democracy and Technology

"The Center for Democracy and Technology (CDT) is a 501(c)(3) non-profit public policy organization dedicated to promoting the democratic potential of today's open, decentralized global Internet. Our mission is to conceptualize, develop, and implement public policies to preserve and enhance free expression, privacy, open access, and other democratic values in the new and increasingly integrated communications medium.

"CDT pursues its mission through research and public policy development in a consensus-building process based on convening and operating broad-based working groups composed of public interest and commercial representatives of divergent views to explore solutions to critical policy issues. In addition, CDT promotes its own policy positions in the United States and globally through public policy advocacy, online grassroots organizing with the Internet user community and public education campaigns, and litigation, as well as through the development of technology standards and online information resources.

"Work on our mission is guided by the following principles:

"1. Unique Nature of the Internet: We believe that the open, decentralized, user-controlled, and shared resource nature of the Internet creates unprecedented opportunities for enhancing democracy and civil liberties. A fundamental goal of our work is seeking public policy solutions that preserve these unique qualities and thereby maximize the democratizing potential of the Internet.

"2. Freedom of Expression: The Center for Democracy and Technology champions the right of individuals to communicate, publish and obtain an unprecedented array of information on the Internet. We oppose governmental censorship and other threats to the free flow of information. As an effective alternative to government controls, we believe that a diversity of technology tools can empower families and individuals on the Internet to communicate freely and make choices about the information they receive.

"3. Privacy: CDT is working for individual privacy on the Internet. We believe that maintaining privacy and freedom of association on the Internet requires the development of public policies and technology tools that give people the ability to take control of their personal information online and make informed, meaningful choices about the collection, use and disclosure of personal information.

"4. Surveillance: CDT challenges invasive government policies. CDT is working for strong privacy protections against surveillance on the Internet. We believe that the content of communications, stored information, and transactional data deserve strong legal protection against unreasonable government search and seizure. Protections against government searches should extend to the network, as well as to the home. CDT advocates for stronger legal standards controlling government surveillance to keep pace with the growing exposure of personal information in communications media.

"5. Access: CDT is working to foster widely-available, affordable access to the Internet. We believe that broad access to and use of the Internet enables greater citizen participation in democracy, promotes a diversity of views, and enhances civil society. We work for public policy solutions that maximize, in a just and equitable fashion, the unique openness and accessibility of the Internet and preserve its vision as it evolves with ever more powerful broadband technologies.

"6. Democratic Participation: CDT is pioneering the use of the Internet to enhance citizen participation in the democratic process, and to ensure the voice of Internet users is heard in critical public policy debates about the Internet. CDT believes that the Internet provides unique and effective means of promoting democracy and of facilitating grassroots organizing and public education. We support using the Internet to afford citizens the immediate, broad access to government information necessary to the full practice of democracy" (www.cdt.org).

CENTER FOR DEMOCRACY AND TECHNOLOGY
1634 Eye Street NW, Suite 1100, Washington, DC 20006
202-637-9800
Fax: 202-637-0968
www.cdt.org

Center for National Security Studies

"The Center for National Security Studies, a non-governmental advocacy and research organization, was founded in 1974 to work for control of the FBI and CIA and to prevent violations of civil liberties in the United States. A central challenge for democratic societies is to maintain national security while enhancing individual freedoms. Defense of civil liberties and constitutional procedures in the face of claims of national security is a never-ending task that requires constant vigilance and public awareness. The Center for National Security Studies plays that role as the only institution devoted solely to this constitutional watchdog function. The Center works to develop a consensus on policies that facilitate the exercise of government responsibilities in ways that do not interfere with civil liberties and constitutional government.

"The Center works to strengthen the public right of access to government information, combat excessive government secrecy, assure effective oversight of intelligence agencies, protect the right of political dissent, prevent illegal government surveillance, ensure congressional authority in war powers, and protect the free exchange of ideas and information across international borders.

"Since 1993, the Center has also worked internationally to assist human rights organizations and government officials in establishing oversight and accountability of intelligence agencies in emerging democracies throughout the world" (cnss@gwu.edu).

CENTER FOR NATIONAL SECURITY STUDIES
1120 19th Street, NW, 8th Floor, Washington, DC 20036
202-721-5650
Fax: 202-530-0128
Email: cnss@gwu.edu

Center for Public Integrity

"The mission of the Center for Public Integrity is to provide the American people with the findings of our investigations and analyses of public service, government accountability and ethics related issues. The Center's books, studies and newsletters combine political science and investigative reporting, unfettered by the usual time and space constraints. Through its hard-earned reputation for "public service journalism," the Center aims to produce high-quality, well-documented, investigative research resulting in a better-informed citizenry that demands a higher level of accountability from its government and elected leaders. The Center also extends globally its style of watchdog journalism in the public interest through the International Consortium of Investigative Journalists (ICIJ). Created in 1997, ICIJ includes more than 80 leading investigative reporters and editors in over 40 countries. Since opening its doors in downtown Washington, D.C. in 1990, the Center has released more than 100 investigative studies including 10 books. Four of them were finalists in the best investigative book category for the prestigious Investigative Reporters and Editors (IRE) award. In 1999, *Animal Underworld* won that prize. Another book, *Citizen Muckraking* provides ordinary Americans a step-by-step guide on how professionals, such as journalists and lawyers, gather information on ethical lapses of corporate and government groups. The March 2001 book, *The Cheating of America,* documents how wealthy individuals and corporations avoid paying their fair share of taxes. The Center's report, 'Our Private Legislatures: Public Service, Personal Gain,' was the winner of the 2000 IRE Award for outstanding investigative reporting in the online category. In two of the last three years, ICIJ reports have been IRE finalists" (www.publicintegrity. org).

THE CENTER FOR PUBLIC INTEGRITY
910 17th Street, NW, Seventh Floor, Washington, DC 20006
202-466-1300
Fax: 202-466-1101
www.publicintegrity.org

Center for Strategic and International Studies

"For four decades, the Center for Strategic and International Studies (CSIS) has been dedicated to providing world leaders with strategic insights on—and policy solutions to—current and emerging global issues. First, CSIS addresses the full spectrum of new challenges to national and international security. Second, we maintain resident experts on all of the world's major geographical regions. Third, we are committed to helping to develop new methods of governance for the global age; to this end, CSIS has programs on technology and public policy, international trade and finance, and energy. Our gateway to Asia is Pacific Forum CSIS. Based in Honolulu, Pacific Forum CSIS collaborates with a network of more than 30 research institutes around the Pacific Rim. Forum programs encompass current and emerging political, security, economic, and business issues. Brent Scowcroft chairs the board of governors of Pacific Forum CSIS, and Ralph Cossa serves as its president" (www.csis.org).

CENTER FOR STRATEGIC AND INTERNATIONAL STUDIES
1800 K Street, NW, Washington, DC 20006
202-775-3167
Fax: 202-463-7217
www.csis.org

Federalist Society

"The Federalist Society for Law and Public Policy Studies is a group of conservatives and libertarians interested in the current state of the legal order. It is founded on the principles that the state exists to preserve freedom, that the separation of governmental powers is central to our Constitution, and that it is emphatically the province and duty of the judiciary to say what the law is, not what it should be. The Society seeks both to promote an awareness of these principles and to further their application through its activities. This entails reordering priorities within the legal system to place a premium on individual liberty, traditional values, and the rule of law. It also requires restoring the recognition of the importance of these norms among lawyers, judges, law students, and professors. In working to achieve these goals, the Society has created a conservative intellectual network that extends to all levels of the legal community" (www.fed-soc. org).

THE FEDERALIST SOCIETY FOR LAW AND
PUBLIC POLICY STUDIES
Washington, D.C.
www.fed-soc.org

Friends Committee on National Legislation

"The Friends Committee on National Legislation (FCNL) is a public interest lobby founded in 1943 by members of the Religious Society of Friends. FCNL seeks to bring the concerns, experiences and testimonies of Friends (called Quakers) to bear on policy decisions in the nation's capital. People of many religious backgrounds participate in this work. FCNL's staff and volunteers work with a nationwide network of thousands of people to advocate social and economic justice, peace, and good government. FCNL is a 501(c)4 public interest lobby, not a political action committee (PAC) nor a special interest lobby. FCNL's multi-issue advocacy connects historic Quaker testimonies on peace, equality, simplicity and truth with peace and social justice issues which the United States government is or should be addressing. FCNL seeks to follow the leadings of the Spirit as it speaks for itself and for like-minded people. Our offices are strategically located on Capitol Hill, across the street from the

Hart Senate Office Building and provide ready access to the offices of government. As FCNL works with many groups that share similar concerns, our Wilson conference room is frequently the venue of coalition meetings and meetings of organizations other than FCNL. In all its work, FCNL seeks to promote dialog and cooperation among those with varied viewpoints. FCNL is governed by a General Committee of 240 Friends, the majority of whom have been appointed by 26 Yearly Meetings and seven national Friends' organizations. The General Committee meets each November to conduct business. This includes establishing legislative policy and priorities. An Executive Committee and several other subcommittees oversee the program and administration of FCNL between Annual Meetings. The FCNL Education Fund is governed by a board appointed by the General Committee of FCNL. It is a 501(c)3 organization that exists in parallel with FCNL to support the research, analysis and education for which FCNL is known and respected.

FRIENDS COMMITTEE ON NATIONAL LEGISLATION
245 Second Street, NE, Washington, DC, 20002-5795
202-547-6000
800-630-1330
Fax: 202-547-6019
Email: fcnl@fcnl.org

The Heritage Foundation

"The Heritage Foundation is a unique institution—a public policy research organization, or "think tank." We draw solutions to contemporary problems from the ideas, principles and traditions that make America great. We are not afraid to begin our sentences with the words "We believe," because we do believe: in individual liberty, free enterprise, limited government, a strong national defense, and traditional American values. We want an America that is safe and secure; where choices (in education, health care and retirement) abound; where taxes are fair, flat, and comprehensible; where everybody has the opportunity to go as far as their talents will take them; where government concentrates on its core functions, recognizes its limits and shows favor to none. And the policies we propose would accomplish these things.

"Our expert staff—with years of experience in business, government and on Capitol Hill—don't just produce research.

We generate solutions consistent with our beliefs and market them to the Congress, the Executive Branch, the news media and others. These solutions build on our country's economic, political and social heritage to produce a safer, stronger, freer, more prosperous America. And a safer, more prosperous, freer world. As conservatives, we believe the values and ideas that motivated our Founding Fathers are worth conserving. And as policy entrepreneurs, we believe the most effective solutions are consistent with those ideas and values.

"We believe that ideas have consequences, but that those ideas must be promoted aggressively. So, we constantly try innovative ways to market our ideas. We are proud of our broad base of support among the American people and we accept no government funds. Our vision is to build an America where freedom, opportunity, prosperity and civil society flourish" (www. heritage.org).

THE HERITAGE FOUNDATION
214 Massachusetts Ave, NE, Washington, DC 20002-4999
202-546-4400
Fax: 202-546-8328
www.heritage.org

National Association for the Advancement of Colored People

"Formed in 1909, by a multiracial group of progressive thinkers, the National Association for the Advancement of Colored People (NAACP) is a non-profit organization established with the objective of insuring the political, educational, social and economic equality of minority groups. The NAACP has as its mission the goal of eliminating race prejudice and removing all barriers of racial discrimination through democratic processes. Since its inception the NAACP was poised for a long, tumultuous and rewarding history.... The history of the NAACP, is one of blood sweat and tears. From bold investigations of mob brutality, protests of mass murders, segregation and discrimination, to testimony before congressional committees on the vicious tactics used to bar African Americans from the ballot box, it was the talent and tenacity of NAACP members that saved lives and changed many negative aspects of American society. While much of its history is chronicled in books, articles, pamphlets and magazines, the true movement lies in the faces—black, white, yellow, red, and brown—united to awaken the conscientiousness of a people, and a nation. This is the legacy of the NAACP!" (www.naacp.org).

NAACP
4805 Mt. Hope Drive, Baltimore, MD 21215
877-NAACP-98
410-521-4939
www.naacp.org

Governmental Websites

U.S. Department of Defense

"The Secretary of Defense is the principal defense policy adviser to the President and is responsible for the formulation of general defense policy and policy related to all matters of direct concern to the Department of Defense, and for the execution of approved policy. Under the direction of the President, the Secretary exercises authority, direction and control over the Department of Defense. The Secretary of Defense is a member of the President's Cabinet and of the National Security Council" (www.defenselink.mil).

Honorable Donald H. Rumsfeld, Secretary of Defense
1000 Defense Pentagon, Washington, DC 20301
703-545-6700
www.defenselink.mil

U.S. Department of Homeland Security

"The new Department of Homeland Security (DHS) has three primary missions: Prevent terrorist attacks within the United States, reduce America's vulnerability to terrorism, and minimize the damage from potential attacks and natural disasters. An essential part of homeland security is working with the local stakeholders around the country. As Secretary Ridge has said, 'When our hometowns are secure, our nation will be secure.' As we finalize the structure of the Department of Homeland Security, we will establish regional offices to which our citizens can turn. It is a critical function of homeland security to ensure that our state and local governments, police, fire departments, paramedics, and concerned citizens are able to connect with local people representing the department. Where and how these regions will be drawn is an issue upon which we are still working" (www.dhs.gov).

U.S. DEPARTMENT OF HOMELAND SECURITY
Washington, DC 20528
www.dhs.gov

U.S. Department of Justice

"The Attorney General, as head of the Department of Justice and chief law enforcement officer of the Federal Government, represents the United States in legal matters generally and gives advice and opinions to the President and to the heads of the executive departments of the Government when so requested. The Attorney General appears in person to represent the Government before the U.S. Supreme Court in cases of exceptional gravity or importance" (usdoj.gov).

U.S. DEPARTMENT OF JUSTICE
950 Pennsylvania Avenue, NW, Washington, DC 20530-0001
usdoj.gov
202-353-1555
DOJ's new Website launched to educate Americans about the USA Patriot Act: www.lifeandliberty.gov

U.S. Department of State

"As the lead foreign affairs agency, the Department of State has the primary role in: Leading interagency coordination in developing and implementing foreign policy; Managing the foreign affairs budget and other foreign affairs resources; Leading and coordinating U.S. representation abroad, conveying U.S. foreign policy to foreign governments and international organizations through U.S. embassies and consulates in foreign countries and diplomatic missions to international organizations; Conducting negotiations and concluding agreements and treaties on issues ranging from trade to nuclear weapons; Coordinating and sup-

porting international activities of other U.S. agencies and officials. The services the Department provides include: Protecting
and assisting U.S. citizens living or traveling abroad; Assisting
U.S. businesses in the international marketplace; Coordinating
and providing support for international activities of other U.S.
agencies (local, state, or federal government), official visits overseas and at home, and other diplomatic efforts. Keeping the public informed about U.S. foreign policy and relations with other
countries and providing feedback from the public to administration officials" (www.state.gov).

U.S. DEPARTMENT OF STATE
2201 C Street, NW, Washington, DC 20520
202-647-4000
www.state.gov

U.S. General Accounting Office

"The General Accounting Office is the audit, evaluation, and
investigative arm of Congress. GAO exists to support the Congress in meeting its Constitutional responsibilities and to help
improve the performance and ensure the accountability of the
federal government for the American people. GAO examines the
use of public funds, evaluates federal programs and activities,
and provides analyses, options, recommendations, and other
assistance to help the Congress make effective oversight, policy,
and funding decisions. In this context, GAO works to continuously improve the economy, efficiency, and effectiveness of the
federal government through financial audits, program reviews
and evaluations, analyses, legal opinions, investigations, and
other services. GAO's activities are designed to ensure the executive branch's accountability to the Congress under the Constitution and the government's accountability to the American people.
GAO is dedicated to good government through its commitment
to the core values of accountability, integrity, and reliability"
(www.gao.gov).

GAO
441 G Street, NW, Washington, DC 20548
202-512-4800
www.gao.gov

The White House

The White House
1600 Pennsylvania Avenue, NW, Washington, DC 20500
Comments: 202-456-1111, 202-456-6213
Switchboard: 202-456-1414
Visitors Office: 202-456-2121
Fax: 202-456-2461
Email: President George W. Bush: president@whitehouse.gov
Vice President Richard Cheney: vice.president@whitehouse.gov
Executive and other Orders issued by the President:
www.archives.gov/federalregister/executiveorders

8

Bibliography

Books, Journal Articles, Reports

Beale, Jon, and Felman, Eric. "The Consequences of Enlisting Federal Grand Juries in the War on Terrorism: Assessing the USA Patriot Act's Changes to Grand Jury Secrecy." 25 *Harvard Journal of Law and Public Pol icy*, 699, Fall 2002.

Best, D. *Intelligence and Law Enforcement: Countering Transnational Threats to the U.S.* U.S. Congressional Research Service Report No. RL 30252, December 5, 2001. Washington, DC: GPO, 2001.

Bill, Steven. *After: How America Confronted the September 12 Era.* New York: Simon and Schuster, 2003.

Brown, Cynthia, ed. *Lost Liberties: Ashcroft and the Assault on Personal Freedom.* New York: New Press, 2003. An excellent collection of essays critical of the Bush administration's responses to the events of 9/11.

Carr, Caleb. *The Lessons of Terror: A History of Warfare Against Civilians.* New York: Random House, 2003. A provocative essay about the ubiquitous presence of terror throughout history.

Chang, Nancy, and Howard Zinn. *Silencing Political Dissent: How Post-September 11 Anti-Terrorism Measures Threaten Our Civil Liberties.* New York: Seven Stories Press, 2002. A collection of essays critical of the Bush administration's war on terrorism.

Churchill, Ward, Jim Vander Wall, and John Trudell, eds. *The COINTEL-PRO Papers: Documents from the FBI's Secret Wars Against Dissent in the United States.* 2nd ed. Boston: South End Press, 2002. This book contains many documents that illustrate the nature of the FBI's "disinformation" campaigns.

Clancy, Tom. *The Teeth of the Tiger.* New York: G. Putnam and Sons, 2003.

Cole, David. "The Course of Least Resistance: Repeating History in the War on Terrorism." In Cynthia Brown, ed., *Lost Liberties: Ashcroft and the Assault on Personal Freedom.* New York: New Press, 2003. Cole, a law professor, is one of the foremost critics of the Patriot Act and other efforts by the Bush administration to counter the international terrorist threat to the United States.

———. "Enemy Aliens." 54 *Stanford Law Review* 953, 2002.

———. *Enemy Aliens.* New York: New Press, 2003.

Cole, David, James X. Dempsey, and Carole E. Goldberg. *Terrorism and the Constitution: Sacrificing Civil Liberties in the Name of National Security.* New York: New Press, 2002.

Cooper, Mary H. "Combating Terrorism." *CQ Researcher,* July 21, 1995.

Edgar, Timothy H. "The Color Line: Watch Out America, the White House Is Seeking to Expand the Patriot Act." *The Crisis,* November-December 2003.

———. "Section-by-Section Analysis of Justice Department Draft, 'Domestic Security Enhancement Act of 2003.'" *American Civil Liberties Union: Legislative Update,* February 14, 2003.

Ewing, Alphonse B. *The USA Patriot Act.* Huntington, NY: Nova Science Publishers, 2003.

Fisher, Louis. *Presidential War Power.* 2nd ed. Lawrence: University Press of Kansas, 2004. An excellent historical-political examination of the expansion of the chief executive's power to send forces into battle at the expense of the legislative powers, with the resultant adverse impact on the separation of powers.

Foerstel, Herbert N. *Refuge of a Scoundrel: The Patriot Act in Libraries.* New York: Libraries Unlimited, 2003.

Frum, David. "David Frum's Diary: The Hysteria of the Civil Libertarians." *National Review,* April 7, 2003. A literate defense of the Patriot Act by a neoconservative essayist.

Greenstein, Fred I., ed. *The George W. Bush Presidency: An Early Assessment.* Baltimore: Johns Hopkins University Press, 2003.

Griset, Pamela L., and Sue Mahan. *Terrorism in Perspective.* Thousand Oaks, CA: Sage Publications, 2003.

Gutman, Roy, and David Rieff, eds. *Crimes of War.* New York: W. W. Norton, 1999. An excellent reference work that provides the reader with an overview of the laws of war in contemporary times.

Harth, Erica, ed. *Last Witnesses: Reflections on the Wartime Internment of Japanese Americans.* New York: Palgrave Macmillan, 2003. One of a number of excellent books that recount the internment in the United States of more than 120,000 people of Japanese ancestry.

Herman, Susan. "The U.S.A. Patriot Act and the U.S. Department of Justice: Losing Our Balance?" *Jurist,* December 2001.

House of Representatives, Committee on the Judiciary. *Bush Administration Draft Anti-Terrorism Act of 2001.* Hearings Before the House of Representatives, Committee on the Judiciary, 107th Congress, first session, September 20, 2001. The hearings were the first open discussion of the Bush administration's Anti-Terror Act (ATA), with Attorney General Ashcroft and his chief deputies testifying before legislators. This led to the development of the Leahy alternative plan; ultimately, however, the ATA was transformed—with few changes—into the USA Patriot Act of 2001.

Hudson, Rex A., and staff of the Federal Research Division of the Library of Congress. *Who Becomes a Terrorist and Why: The 1999 Government Report on Profiling Terrorists.* Guilford, CT: Lyons Press, 2002.

Joo, Thomas. "Presumed Disloyal: Executive Power, Judicial Deference, and the Construction of Race Before and After September 11." 34 *Columbia University Human Rights Law Journal,* 1, 2002.

Journal of Supreme Court History, 28, no. 3, 2003. Special issue: "Civil Liberties in Wartime."

Kerr, Orrin S. "Internet Surveillance Law After the Patriot Act: The Big Brother That Isn't." 97 *Northwestern University Law Review,* 1, 2003. A fine law review essay on the impact of the Patriot Act on Internet privacy.

Kushner, Harvey W. *Encyclopedia of Terrorism,* Thousand Oaks, CA: Sage Publications, 2003. A basic compendium of facts about persons and organizations engaged in either terrorism or the effort to eliminate it as well as laws used to combat it.

Leone, Richard C., and Greg Anrig Jr., eds. *The War on Our Freedoms: Civil Liberties in an Age of Terrorism.* New York: Public Affairs Press, 2003.

Mooney, Chris. "A Short History of Sunsets." *Legal Affairs,* January-February 2004.

Neier, Aryeh. "The Military Tribunals on Trial." 49 *New York Review of Books,* no. 2, February 14, 2002.

Podesta, John. "Bush's Secret Government." *American Prospect,* September 2003.

Posner, Gerald. *Why America Slept: The Failure to Prevent 9/11.* New York: Random House, 2003.

Rehnquist, William H. *All the Laws but One.* New York: Random House, 2003. Written by the chief justice of the Supreme Court, a book that focuses on the impact war has on the functioning of the federal courts as guardians of civil liberties and civil rights.

Rossiter, Clinton. *Constitutional Dictatorship: Crisis Government in the Modern Democracies.* New York: Transaction Publishers, 2002. A classic that examines the nature of a federal system's change during time of war or other national dangers or catastrophes.

Scheidegger, Kent, Charles Hobson, and Maritza Meskan. *Federalist Society White Paper on the USA PATRIOT Act of 2001, Criminal Procedure Sections.* Washington, DC: Federalist Society, 2001.

Schlesinger, Arthur M., Jr. *The Imperial Presidency.* New York: Replica Books, 1998.

Stern, Jessica. *The Ultimate Terrorists.* Cambridge, MA: Harvard, 1999.

Strossen, Nadine. "It's a War on Terrorism, not a War on Immigrants." *Civil Liberties,* Fall 2003.

Tomasky, Michael. "Strange Bedfellows: Conservative Civil Libertarians Join the Fight." *American Prospect,* September 2003.

Uniting and Strengthening America by Providing Appropriate Tools Required to Intercept and Obstruct Terrorism (USA PATRIOT) Act of 2001 (SuDoc AE 2.110:107–56) by U.S. National Archives and Records Administration.

U.S. Department of Justice. Office of the Inspector General. *A Review of the Treatment of Aliens Held on Immigration Charges in Connection with the Investigation of the September 11 Attacks.* Washington, DC: 2003.

White, Jonathan R. *Terrorism: An Introduction.* 4th edition. Belmont, CA: Wadsworth/Thomson Learning, 2003.

Zelizer, Barbie, and Stuart Allan, eds. *Journalism after September 11 (Communication and Society).* New York: Routledge, 2003.

Internet Resources

American Civil Liberties Union (ACLU). "Legislative Analysis of the USA PATRIOT Act." October 2001. Available at: www.aclu.org.

American Library Association (ALA). "Libraries and the Patriot Legislation." Available at: www.ala.org.

Association of Research Libraries (ARL). "The Search and Seizure of Electronic Information: The Law Before and After the USA Patriot Act." January 18, 2002. Available at: www.arl.org.

Bill of Rights Defense Committee (BORDC). "Tools and Tips for Organizing Resolutions in Defense of the Bill of Rights." Available at: www.bordc.org.

Center for Constitutional Rights (CCR). "The USA PATRIOT Act—What's So Patriotic about Trampling on the Bill of Rights?" November 2001. Available at: www.ccr-ny.org.

Center for Democracy and Technology (CDT). "Response to September 11th, 2001 Terrorist Attacks." Available at: www.cdt.org/terrorism.

Center for National Security Studies (CNSS). "Memorandum to Interested Persons, Re: Material Witnesses Detained since September 11." April 12, 2002. Available at: www.cnss.org.

———. "Memorandum to Interested Persons, Re: Secret Arrests and Closed Immigration Hearings." July 19, 2002. Available at: www.cnss.org.

———. "USA-Patriot Act." Available at: www.cnss.org/patriot.

Center for Public Integrity (CPI). "Justice Dept. Drafts Sweeping Expansion of Anti-Terrorism Act." January 29, 2004. Available at: www.publicintegrity.org/dtaweb/report.asp?ReportID=502&L1=10&L2=10&L3=0&L4=0&L5=0.

Congressional Research Service (CRS). "Domestic Security Enhancement Act of 2003: DOJ Section-by-Section Analysis." January 9, 2003. Available at: www.crs.gov.

———. "The Internet and the USA PATRIOT Act: Potential Implications for Electronic Privacy, Security, Commerce, and Government." CRS Report for Congress RL-31289, updated March 4, 2002. Available at: www.crs.gov.

———. "Personal Privacy Protection: The Legislative Response." CRS Report for Congress RL-30671, updated May 24, 2001. Available at: www.crs.gov.

———. "Privacy: An Overview of Federal Statutes Governing Wiretapping and Electronic Eavesdropping." CRS Report for Congress 98-326, updated January 13, 2003. Available at: www.crs.gov.

———. "Terrorism: Section by Section Analysis of the USA PATRIOT Act." CRS Report for Congress RL-31200, updated December 10, 2001. Available at: www.crs.gov.

———. "The USA PATRIOT Act: A Legal Analysis." CRS Report for Congress RL-31377, April 15, 2002. Available at: www.crs.gov.

Department of Justice. "Field Guidance on New Authorities Enacted in the 2001 Anti-Terrorism Legislation." Available at: www.doj.gov.

Electronic Frontier Foundation (EFF). "Analysis of the Provisions of the USA PATRIOT Act That Relate to Online Activities." October 31, 2001. Available at: www.eff.org.

Electronic Privacy Information Center (EPIC). "DOJ Inspector General Criticizes DOJ for Treatment of Immigrant Detainees." EPIC Alert 10.10, June 17, 2003. Available at: www.epic.org.

————. "EPIC's Analysis of the Anti-Terrorism Act of 2001." Special EPIC Alert, September 24, 2001. Available at: www.epic.org/terrorism.

Investigative Reporters and Editors, Inc. (IRE). "Security vs. Open Records." Available at: www.ire.org.

OMB Watch. "Access to Government Information Post September 11th." February 2, 2002. Available at: www.ombwatch.org.

Welch, Matt. "Get Ready for PATRIOT II." April 2, 2003. Available at: www.alternet.org.

Chronology: Events Leading to the USA Patriot Act, 1983–2004

April 18, 1983

ω πʳ 50atʳ

U.S. embassy in Beirut, Lebanon, is bombed by Islamic Jihad. Sixty-three persons are killed and 120 injured in the blast.

October 23, 1983

Terrorist attack on U.S. Marine Corps headquarters in Beirut, Lebanon, kills 241 marines.

December 21, 1988

Pan American Flight 103 is destroyed by bomb over Lockerbie, Scotland. All 259 on board are killed, as well as eleven persons on the ground. Two Libyan nationals are convicted of the crime.

January 17, 1991

Operation Desert Storm to remove Saddam Hussein's forces from Kuwait commences. President George Bush's coalition of more than thirty nations quickly drives the Iraqi forces from Kuwait.

April 14, 1992

Iraqi attempt to assassinate former president George Bush, visiting Kuwait, fails.

February 26, 1993

Explosion at the World Trade Center, New York City, kills six and injures thousands. *This is the initial attack on America's homeland by Islamic fundamentalists.* Followers of Omar Abdel Rahman are convicted of the terrorist act.

April 19, 1995	Domestic terrorist Timothy McVeigh sets off a massive bomb that destroys the Murrah Federal Building in Oklahoma City, Oklahoma, killing 169 persons, including nineteen children. McVeigh is quickly apprehended, charged, tried, and convicted; he was executed on June 11, 2001.
June 26, 1996	Al Qaeda bombing of Khobar Towers, a U.S. military compound in Dharan, Saudi Arabia, kills nineteen U.S. military personnel and injures another 500 people.
July 27, 1996	Bomb blast at the Olympic Games, held in Atlanta, Georgia, kills two and injures over 100 others. A domestic terrorist, Eric Robert Rudolph, awaits trial for the bombing.
August 7, 1998	Simultaneous Al Qaeda bombings of two U.S. embassies kill twelve Americans, thirty-two foreign service nationals, and over 200 Kenyans in Kenya and kill twelve people and injure 100 others in Dar es Salaam.
August 20, 1998	In retaliation for the U.S. embassy bombings, President Bill Clinton orders missile strikes against Osama bin Laden's Al Qaeda training bases in Afghanistan.
October 12, 2000	Osama bin Laden's Al Qaeda cell in Yemen blasts the U.S.S. *Cole,* a U.S. naval vessel docked in Aden, Yemen. Seventeen sailors are killed and thirty-nine others injured.
September 11, 2001	Nineteen men of an Al Qaeda cell operating in the United States hijack four commercial airliners and, using the planes as missiles, ram two into the World Trade Center in New York City and another into the Pentagon. The fourth airliner is forced to crash in Pennsylvania, thereby preventing its attack on either the Capitol Building or the White House. All told, almost 3,000 civilians and military personnel are killed by these catastrophic attacks on symbols of U.S. financial and military prowess.

September 18, 2001   Congress passes PL 107–40, "Authorization for Use of Military Force," which notes that President George W. Bush "has constitutional authority . . . to take action to deter and prevent acts of international terrorism against the United States."

September 19, 2001   Attorney General John Ashcroft gives the Congress the draft of the new antiterrorism act, soon to be called the USA Patriot Act of 2001.

October 8, 2001   President Bush issues Executive Order 13228, establishing the Office of Homeland Security and the Homeland Security Council. Tom Ridge, former governor of Pennsylvania, is appointed to head the new office.

October 24, 2001   The Congress passes legislation entitled the "Uniting and Strengthening America by Providing Appropriate Tools Required to Intercept and Obstruct Terrorism Act of 2001"— the USA PATRIOT Act of 2001.

October 26, 2001   President Bush signs the Patriot Act, PL 107–56.

November 13, 2001   President Bush issues a military order creating secret detentions and secret military tribunals for noncitizens engaged in terrorist activities.

November 15, 2002   The Office of Homeland Security is converted to the cabinet-level Department of Homeland Security (DHS); Tom Ridge is appointed initial secretary of homeland security.

February 7, 2003   Draft proposal of the Domestic Security Enhancement Act of 2003 is circulated. This Patriot Act II, as it is referred to by the media and critics of the Patriot Act, leads to a firestorm of protest.

September 10, 2003   President Bush gives a speech proposing three major changes in the existing Patriot Act of 2001.

October 24, 2003   Senators Richard Durbin (D–IL) and Larry Craig (R–ID) introduce the SAFE Act of 2003 in an effort

October 24, 2002, cont.	to reduce the roving wiretap and other search powers given to the government in the Patriot Act.
January 20, 2004	In his State of the Union speech to the nation, President Bush calls upon the Congress to make the Patriot Act of 2001 a permanent piece of legislation by dropping all the sunset provisions in the law.
January 22, 2004	U.S. district court judge Audrey B. Collins, Central District, California, in *Humanitarian Law Project, et al. vs. John Ashcroft, et al.* CV 03–6107 ABC (MCx), 2004, issues an order striking down Sections 805 and 810 of the USA Patriot Act of 2001 as "void for vagueness," thus in conflict with the First Amendment. "The term 'expert advice or assistance' is not sufficiently clear so as to allow persons of 'ordinary intelligence a reasonable opportunity to know what is prohibited."
January 30, 2004	President Bush announces that he will veto the SAFE Act introduced by Senators Durbin and Craig should it ever get to his desk.
March–April 2004	U.S. Supreme Court hears oral arguments in litigation involving (1) due process rights of detainees at Guantanamo Bay (*Rasul, et al. v. Bush; Al Doah, et al. v. U.S.*) and (2) whether U.S. citizens can be detained in military brigs as "enemy combatants" without procedural protections found in the Bill of Rights (*Hamdi v. Rumsfeld; Rumsfeld v. Padilla*).
June 28, 2004	The Supreme Court hands down decisions on three Patriot Act–related cases. In *Rasul, et al. v. Bush,* the Court held that prisoners held at Guantanamo Bay have the right to petition the courts for due process rights. The Court vacated judgment in *Hamdi v. Rumsfeld,* remanding the case for a new hearing based on their determination that U.S. citizens held as enemy combatants have the right to contest their detention. In *Rumsfeld v. Padilla,* the Court did not reach the substantive question of whether the president can detain Padilla, a U.S. citizen, militarily. They ruled that his suit against Rumsfeld was outside of the correct jurisdiction and therefore not proper.

Glossary

Administrative Search Warrant A piece of paper signed by an FBI agent that requires any recipient to disclose documents or other tangible things. Such a warrant is issued with no prior judicial, prosecutorial, or grand jury approval. Under the Patriot Act, failure to comply with an administrative subpoena could result in civil and criminal penalties, and the subpoenas would be executed in complete secrecy. Anyone who disclosed the existence of an administrative subpoena could be subject to up to five years in prison.

Anarchism The political doctrine that teaches that government is evil and unnecessary and that society should be recognized on the basis of voluntary mutual aid associations. Anarchism is thus a political theory that aims to create a society without political, economic, or social hierarchies. Anarchists maintain that anarchy, the absence of rulers, is a viable form of social system and so work for the maximization of individual liberty and social equality. They see the goals of liberty and equality as mutually self-supporting. The history of human society proves this point. Liberty without equality is only liberty for the powerful, and equality without liberty is impossible and a justification for slavery. Although there are many different types of anarchism, from individualist anarchism to communist anarchism, there have always been two common positions at their core: opposition to government and opposition to capitalism. All anarchists view profit, interest, and rent as usury (i.e., as exploitation) and therefore oppose them and the conditions that create them just as much as they oppose government and the state. For anarchists, no person subject to state or capitalist authority can be free.

Asymmetrical Warfare In the modern age of global terrorism, wars can be fought not just between nation-states but also between a nation-state and terrorist groups or cells, individuals who are not agents or combatants of a nation-state. The U.S. war against terrorism, for example, pits a major nation against a very small number of Islamic fundamentalists led by an individual, Osama bin Laden, who does not act on behalf of a nation-state. Hence the asymmetry in this type of war:

225

millions of military personnel with the latest military hardware versus small bands of zealots who do not have the weapons to match their mightier foe.

Black Panthers A black revolutionary party; founded in 1966 in Oakland, California, by Huey Newton and Bobby Seale. The party's original purpose was to patrol black ghettoes to protect residents from acts of police brutality. The Panthers eventually developed into a Marxist revolutionary group that called for the arming of all blacks, the exemption of blacks from the draft and from all sanctions of so-called white America, the release of all blacks from jail, and the payment of compensation to blacks for centuries of exploitation by white Americans. At its peak in the late 1960s, Panther membership exceeded 2,000, and the organization operated chapters in several major cities. Conflicts between Black Panthers and police in the late 1960s and early 1970s led to shoot-outs in California, New York, and Chicago, one of which resulted in Newton's going to prison for the murder of a patrolman. While some members of the party were guilty of criminal acts, the group was subjected to police harassment that sometimes took the form of violent attacks, prompting congressional investigations. By the mid-1970s, having lost many members and having fallen out of favor with many American black leaders who objected to the party's methods, the Panthers turned from violence to concentrate on conventional politics and providing social services in black neighborhoods. The party was effectively disbanded by the early 1980s.

Certiorari A method of review by a superior court of the action of an inferior court of record. If granted by the superior court, that court will review the lower court record and proceedings in order to revise and correct the record, if necessary, in matters of law. The U.S. Supreme Court's primary work is the review of many thousands of petitions requesting the Court to grant certiorari. Less than 1 percent of the requests are granted.

COINTELPRO In the early 1950s, the Communist Party was illegal in the United States. The U.S. Senate and House of Representatives each set up investigating committees to prosecute communists and publicly expose them (the House Committee on Un-American Activities and the Senate Internal Security Subcommittee, led by Senator Joseph McCarthy). When a series of Supreme Court rulings in 1956 and 1957 challenged these committees and questioned the constitutionality of Smith Act prosecutions and Subversive Activities Control Board hearings, the FBI's response was COINTELPRO, short for Counterintelligence Program, designed to "neutralize" the activities of those who could no longer be prosecuted. Over the years, similar programs were created to "neutralize" civil rights, antiwar, and many other groups said to be "communist front organizations" (www.icdc.com/~paulwolf/cointelpro/cointel.htm). The FBI's covert action programs were aimed at five perceived threats to domestic tranquility: the Communist Party, USA, program (1956–1971); the Socialist Workers Party program (1961–1969) ; the White Hate Group program (1964–1971) ; the Black Nationalist-Hate Group program (1967–1971) ; and the New Left program (1968–1971). The breadth of targeting and lack of substantive content in the descriptive titles of the programs reflect the range of motivations for COINTELPRO activity: protecting national security, preventing violence, and maintaining the existing social and political order by "disrupting" and "neutralizing" certain groups and individuals. "Counterintelligence" was something of a misnomer for the FBI programs, since the targets were American political dissidents, not foreign spies. However, it is an accurate term in that the goal was not to collect evidence to use in criminal prosecutions, but to cause chaos and discord within the targeted groups. The FBI conducted more than 2000 COINTELPRO operations before they were officially discontinued in April 1971.

Cold War The Western democracies and the Soviet Union discussed the progress of World War II and the nature of the postwar settlement at conferences in Tehran (1943), Yalta (February 1945), and Potsdam (July–August 1945). After the war, disputes between the Soviet Union and the Western democracies, particularly over the Soviet takeover of East European states, led Winston Churchill to warn in 1946 that an "iron curtain" was descending through the middle of Europe. For his part, Joseph Stalin deepened the estrangement between the United States and the Soviet Union when he asserted in 1946 that World War II was an unavoidable and inevitable consequence of "capitalist imperialism" and implied that such a war might reoccur. The Cold War was a period of East-West competition, tension, and conflict short of full-scale war, characterized by mutual perceptions of hostile intention between military-political alliances. "Proxy wars" were fought by Soviet allies rather than the USSR itself, and the two superpowers competed for influence in the Third World and engaged in an arms race. After Stalin's death, East-West relations went through phases of alternating relaxation and confrontation, including a cooperative phase during the 1960s and another, termed détente, during the 1970s. A final phase during the late 1980s and early 1990s was hailed by President Mikhail Gorbachev, and especially by the president of the new post-Communist Russian republic, Boris Yeltsin, as well as by President George Bush, as beginning a partnership between the two states that could address many global problems. In 1989, the end of the Union of Soviet Socialist Republics (USSR) began when the Berlin Wall, erected in 1961 to separate East from West Berlin, was shattered by Germans on both sides of the wall. Within two years, the USSR no longer existed.

Commander-in-Chief Clause Section 2, clause 1 of Article Two of the Constitution provides: "The President shall be Commander in Chief of the Army and Navy of the United States." During periods of national emergency and times of war, presidents have created presidential "war powers" by joining the commander-in-chief clause with the presidential oath to maintain and protect the sovereignty of the United States.

Communism A social and political movement for the direct and communal control of a classless society composed entirely of workers. According to Lenin's approach, the first step of the long-term process of developing such a society is a revolutionary seizure of political power; in Marxist terms, the domination of the bourgeoisie is to be replaced by the domination of the working class. In Marxist literature this political stage is called the dictatorship of the proletariat. Lenin argued that the revolution would occur first in less-developed nations, such as Russia, and would require a vanguard of the proletariat made up of a relatively small, tightly organized communist party. This theoretically temporary stage has never had that desired effect in any "communist" state but rather remains a form of totalitarian dictatorship or has transitioned into some form of democracy or capitalism.

Domestic Terrorism Section 802 of the USA Patriot Act of 2001 contains what critics consider an overbroad definition of domestic terrorism: "Any action that endangers human life that is a violation of any Federal or State law. " Subsection 5 of the act states: "The term 'domestic terrorism' means activities that—(A) involve acts dangerous to human life that are a violation of the criminal laws of the United States or of any State; (B) appear to be intended—(i) to intimidate or coerce a civilian population; (ii) to influence the policy of a government by intimidation or coercion; or (iii) to affect the conduct of a government by mass destruction, assassination, or kidnapping; and (C) occur primarily within the territorial jurisdiction of the United States."

Domestic Terrorists Long predating religious Islamic fundamentalists, another kind of terrorist has existed throughout U.S. history: the American terrorist. From the first decades of the new republic to the present, there have been men and women, U.S. citizens, who have developed a deep hatred of the American social, political, or economic system and who have struck against the system with the tools of the terrorist: guns, bombs, and assassination. America has had, before Al Qaeda and Osama bin Laden, "enemies at home," such as John Brown and Timothy McVeigh. In a December 2003 op-ed piece in the *New York Times*, Daniel Levitas noted: "In April [2003], as Baghdad fell and American soldiers began searching for weapons of mass destruction in Iraq, federal officials uncovered a cache of deadly chemicals much closer to home—in the eastern Texas town of Noonday. The stockpile included a fully functional sodium cyanide bomb capable of killing hundreds, as well as neo-Nazi and anti-governmental literature, illegal weapons, half a million rounds of ammunition, and more than 100 explosives, including bombs disguised as suitcases" ("Our Enemies at Home," *New York Times*,

December 13, 2003, p. 25). The materials were located in a storage shed rented by William Krar, a member of the right-wing extremist New Jersey Militia. More than 150 subpoenas have been served by federal law enforcement authorities in this one incident alone. Examples of such extremist antigovernment group activities regularly appear in the courts and in the press. The Army of God, the Christian Identity Movement, the World Church of the Creator, and dozens of other neo-Nazi and right-wing antigovernment organizations are bent on seeing the federal government destroyed, replaced by the "Aryan Revolution." Levitas concluded that these groups "remain ready, willing and able to kill for their causes. As we saw in Oklahoma City and 9/11, it takes only a handful of committed zealots to wreak havoc. Given the violent track record of America's hate groups, the FBI and the public would do well to pay closer attention to our homegrown version of Al Qaeda."

Due Process of Law   Implies the fair administration of rules and laws equally applicable to all that do not violate fundamental principles of privacy. In *Dartmouth College v. Woodward* (1819), Daniel Webster's argument included the following definition of due process: "the law which hears before it condemns; which proceeds upon inquiry, and renders judgment only after trial." Procedural rules that reflect the principle are found in the Bill of Rights in the U.S. Constitution, especially those found in the Fourth, Fifth, Sixth, Seventh, and Eighth Amendments.

Enemy Combatant   The concept of the "enemy combatant" classification came out of the Supreme Court ruling in *Ex Parte Quirin*, 317 U.S. 1, 63 S.Ct. 2 (1942). The Court held that eight German-born U.S. residents who were captured by the United States as they tried to enter the country during wartime for the purpose of sabotage, espionage, and other hostile and warlike acts or violations under the law of war, having been designated as "enemy combatants," did not have a constitutional right to a criminal trial before a civilian jury. Instead, the president of the United States could try the petitioners in a military tribunal. The Court stated that a case involving "an enemy combatant who without uniform comes secretly through the lines for the purpose of waging war by destruction of life or property, are familiar examples of belligerents who are generally deemed not to be entitled to the status of prisoners of war, but to be offenders against the law of war subject to trial and punishment by military tribunals." The Court also affirmed the president's authority to try petitioners before a military tribunal without a jury. Those designated as enemy combatants are denied the right to a trial, placing them in legal limbo, without the right to a lawyer or the right to answer charges and evidence brought against them, even if they are U.S. citizens. Enemy combatants are subject to indefinite detention in a military brig, with the possibility of being brought before a military court at any time. Such drumhead proceedings could result in death sentences, with no right of appeal. U.S. citizens labeled as enemy combatants in the wake of the attacks of September 11, 2001, are challenging in federal courts the authority of the president to issue such orders. They allege that fundamental constitutional rights are denied to them. The Bush administration claims that the law of war and Supreme Court precedent support the president's authority to detain U.S. citizens incommunicado and without filing a criminal charge if they are regarded as enemy combatants. The administration views this power as inherent in the president's commander-in-chief authority and believes that congressional authorization, while unnecessary, is implied in statute.

Executive Order   Executive orders are official documents, numbered consecutively, through which the President of the United States manages the operations of the Federal Government. The text of Executive orders appears in the daily Federal Register as each Executive order is signed by the President and received by the Office of the Federal Register. The text of Executive orders beginning with Executive Order 7316 of March 13, 1936, also appears in the sequential editions of Title 3 of the Code of Federal Regulations (CFR). Generally, executive orders are used by a president to exercise executive authority. For example, E.O. 12370 was issued to create an emergency board to investigate a railroad dispute. Proclamations are often used to announce something ceremonial in nature, such as National Medal of Honor Day (Proclamation 6263).The first executive order was issued in 1789 but none was numbered or issued uniformly until 1907. At that time, the State Department began a numbering system and designated an 1862 order as executive order #1. Orders issued between 1789 and 1862 are unnumbered and are referred to as "unnumbered executive orders."

Ex Parte **Motion**   An application to a court made by one party without any notice to the adverse party. These motions are permitted under the Criminal Justice Act, 18 USC Section 3006 A (e) (1); they are filed with the District Court judge or Magistrate judge assigned to the case rather than in the Clerk's office and are filed under seal. While ex parte motions are not routinely permitted, the Criminal Justice Act authorizes ex parte motions under limited circumstances.

"Fifth Column"   A clandestine group or faction of subversive agents who attempt to undermine a nation's solidarity by any means at their disposal. The term is credited to Emilio Mola Vidal, a Nationalist general during the Spanish Civil War (1936–39). As four of his army columns moved on Madrid, the general referred to his militant supporters within the capital as his "fifth column." It became a well known term during the Second World War because of Nazi Germany's use of groups of secret sympathizers or supporters that engage in espionage or sabotage within defense lines or national borders of Norway and other countries invaded by Nazi Germany.

"Great Satan"   "Americans are the Great Satan, the wounded snake," said Ayatollah Ruhollah Khomeini, (1900–1989), the Iranian religious leader who, in 1979, seized the American Embassy in Teheran and held over 80 Americans captive until 1981. He was the Supreme Leader of Iran, 1979–89 and leader of Shiite Moslems in Iran. Osama Bin Laden, who leads Al Qaeda, and other Islamic fundamentalist leaders have continued to refer to the United States as the "Great Satan."

Habeas Corpus   Originally an extraordinary writ of equity, going back centuries in English law. Its central purpose is to obtain immediate relief from a court from illegal confinement; to free those imprisoned without sufficient cause; and to deliver them from unlawful custody. This extraordinary writ was brought to the American colonies, and, in 1787, enshrined in the Constitution. The Suspension Clause of Section 9, Clause 2 of Article I of the Constitution provides that "[t]he Privilege of the Writ of Habeas Corpus shall not be suspended [by the Congress] unless when in Cases of Rebellion or Invasion the public Safety may require it." It has since been codified as part of the federal criminal code as well as a basic protection found in the constitutions and criminal codes of all fifty American states. For example, 28 U.S.C. § 2241 provides for the issuance of the writ of habeas corpus if a prisoner is "in custody in violation of the Constitution or laws or treaties of the United States." 28 U.S.C. § 2243 authorizes habeas corpus petitioners to "deny any of the facts set forth in the return or allege any other material facts," and provides that courts "shall summarily hear and determine the facts, and dispose of the matter as law and justice require." The habeas corpus remedy has been available to federal prisoners in this country since the Judiciary Act of 1789. Habeas corpus commands the government to "bring the body" that is under custody before the court, and establish to a neutral and detached legal tribunal that the prisoner's sentence or incarceration is lawful.

Haymarket Square, Chicago bombing, 1886   Early in 1886 labor unions were beginning a movement for an eight-hour day. Serious trouble was anticipated and on May 1 many workers struck for shorter hours. An active group of radicals and anarchists became involved in the campaign. Two days later shooting and one death occurred during a riot at the McCormick Harvester plant when police tangled with the rioters. On May 4 events reached a tragic climax at Haymarket Square where a protest meeting was called to denounce the events of the preceding day. At this meeting, while police were undertaking to disperse the crowd, a bomb was exploded. Policeman Mathias J. Degan died almost instantly and seven other officers died later. Eight men were finally brought to trial and Judge Joseph E. Gary imposed the death sentence on seven of them and the eighth was given fifteen years in prison. Four were hanged, one committed suicide and the sentences of two were commuted from death to imprisonment for life. On June 26, 1893, Governor John P. Altgeld pardoned the three who were in the penitentiary.

Intifada The first intifada, or *uprising*, was sparked on December 9, 1987 in Gaza when an Israeli jeep ran into and killed four Palestinians. It spread into all areas of the West Bank and the Gaza Strip and lasted until 1993. It came as a complete surprise to both the Israeli government and Yasser Arafat's Palestinian Liberation Organization (at the time in exile in Tunisia). Much of the resistance, or uprising, was nonviolent; the protesters were not armed with guns. The current (2000-) Intifada in the Palestinian territories and Israel is widely referred to as the "Al Aqsa Intifada." There are clear differences between the late 1980s and the current uprising. There is an extremely high level of violence in the area, with suicide bombers responsible for the deaths of hundreds of Israeli civilians. Also, unlike the 1980s, Arafat's Palestinian Authority is the putative government of the Palestinian territories and is responsible for prevention of Intifada violence.

Islamic Fundamentalism Islamic fundamentalism refers to the belief by Muslims that the Quran was dictated by Allah through the Archangel Jabril to the prophet Muhammed, that the current text of the Quran is identical to what was said by Muhammed to be the Quran, and that the correct interpretation of the Quran must rely solely on the Quran and prophetic Hadith (oral accounts of Muhammed's teaching and practices), and nothing else. Islamic fundamentalism holds that the problems of the world stem from modern influences, and that the path to salvation lies in a return to the original message of the faith, combined with a total rejection of all innovation and outside traditions. Reading the Quran in reference to the practices of Muhammed allows one to unambiguously determine how Muslims should behave. Islamic fundamentalism is not only a religious movement; it is also a political movement. Muslim fundamentalists seek to change the laws of their nation to conform strictly to their interpretations of the Quran and Hadith. Islamic fundamentalists assert their views through violence or oppression, rather than persuasion. Examples of Islamic fundamentalist groups include Al Qaeda, Hamas, and the Taliban regime of Afghanistan, ousted in late 2001 by a coalition of forces led by the United States.

"Jihad," Holy War The following is from the article "JIHAD (The Holy War of Islam and Its Legitimacy in the Quran)," by Ayatullah Morteza Mutahhari, 1985.

> *And Fight those who have not faith in God, nor in the Hereafter, and (who) forbid not what God and His Prophet have forbidden and (who) are not committed to the religion of truth, of those who have been brought the Book, until they pay tribute by hand, and they are the low. (9:29)*

This Quranic verse concerns the People of the Book, meaning those non-Muslims followers of one of the holy books, namely the Jews, Christians, and perhaps the Zoroastrians. The verse is one of war with the People of the Book, but at the same time, it does not tell us to fight them; it tells us to fight only those of them who have no faith in God, in the Hereafter, and who do not abide by the rule of God, allowing what He has forbidden—and who are not religious according to the religion of truth. It is these People of the Book whom we are to fight until they pay the Jezyah (tribute). That is, when they are ready to pay the Jezyah and are humble before us, we are to fight them no more. This verse gives rise to many questions which remain to be answered through a study of those Quranic verses pertaining to jihad, which we will set apart and review. The first question that arises is what exactly is meant by the words, *«Fight those who have not faith in God»*. Do they mean that we are to drop everything and start fighting or is it meant that we must fight them the moment they go beyond their territory and violate ours? In the terms of the learned of Islam, the ulema, this is an unconditional verse that, if there are similar verses that are conditional, must be interpreted as being conditional.

Judicial Review—(*Marbury v. Madison,* 1803)   Under the administrations of Washington and his successor, John Adams, only members of the ruling Federalist Party were appointed to the bench, and under the terms of the Constitution, they held office for life during "good behavior." Thus, when the opposing Republicans won the election of 1800, the Jeffersonians found that while they controlled the presidency and Congress, the Federalists still dominated the judiciary. One of the first acts of the new administration was to repeal the Judiciary Act of 1800, which had created a number of new judgeships. Although President Adams had attempted to fill the vacancies prior to the end of his term, a number of commissions had not been delivered, and one of the appointees, William Marbury, sued Secretary of State James Madison to force him to deliver his commission as a justice of the peace. The new chief justice, John Marshall, understood that if the Court awarded Marbury a writ of mandamus (an order to force Madison to deliver the commission) the Jefferson administration would ignore it, and thus significantly weaken the authority of the courts. On the other hand, if the Court denied the writ, it might well appear that the justices had acted out of fear. Either case would be a denial of the basic principle of the supremacy of the law. Marshall's decision in this case has been hailed as a judicial tour de force. In essence, he declared that Madison should have delivered the commission to Marbury, but then held that the section of the Judiciary Act of 1789 that gave the Supreme Court the power to issue writs of mandamus exceeded the authority allotted the Court under Article III of the Constitution, and was therefore null and void. Thus he was able to chastise the Jeffersonians and yet not create a situation in which a court order would be flouted.

The critical importance of Marbury is the assumption of several powers by the Supreme Court. One was the authority to declare acts of Congress, and by implication acts of the president, unconstitutional if they exceeded the powers granted by the Constitution. But even more important, the Court became the arbiter of the Constitution, the final authority on what the document meant. As such, the Supreme Court became in fact as well as in theory an equal partner in government, played that role ever since. The Court would not declare another act of Congress unconstitutional until 1857, and it has used that power sparingly. But through its role as arbiter of the Constitution, it has, especially in the twentieth century, been the chief agency for the expansion of individual rights.

Ku Klux Klan   The KKK was two distinct secret terrorist organizations in the United States, one founded immediately after the Civil War and lasting until the 1870s, the other beginning in 1915 and continuing to the present.

"The nineteenth-century Klan was originally organized as a social club by Confederate veterans in Pulaski, Tenn., in 1866. They apparently derived the name from the Greek word kyklos, from which comes the English "circle"; "Klan" was added for the sake of alliteration and Ku Klux Klan emerged. The organization quickly became a vehicle for Southern white underground resistance to Radical Reconstruction. Klan members sought the restoration of white supremacy through intimidation and violence aimed at the newly enfranchised black freedmen. A similar organization, the Knights of the White Camelia, began in Louisiana in 1867.

"In the summer of 1867, the Klan was structured into the 'Invisible Empire of the South' at a convention in Nashville, Tenn., attended by delegates from former Confederate states. The group was presided over by a grand wizard (Confederate cavalry general Nathan Bedford Forrest is believed to have been the first grand wizard) and a descending hierarchy of grand dragons, grand titans, and grand cyclopses. Dressed in robes and sheets designed to frighten superstitious blacks and to prevent identification by the occupying federal troops, Klansmen whipped and killed freedmen and their white supporters in nighttime raids.

"The nineteenth-century Klan reached its peak between 1868 and 1870. A potent force, it was largely responsible for the restoration of white rule in North Carolina, Tennessee, and Georgia. But Forrest ordered it disbanded in 1869, largely as a result of the group's excessive violence. Local branches remained active for a time, however, prompting Congress to pass the Force Act in 1870 and the Ku Klux Act in 1871. . . .

"In *United States v. Harris* in 1882, the Supreme Court declared the Ku Klux Act unconstitutional, but by that time the Klan had practically disappeared. . . .

"The 20th-century Klan had its roots more directly in the American nativist tradition. It was organized in 1915 near Atlanta, Ga., by Colonel

William J. Simmons, a preacher and promoter of fraternal orders who had been inspired by Thomas Dixon's book *The Clansman* (1905) and D.W. Griffith's film *The Birth of a Nation* (1915). The new organization remained small until Edward Y. Clarke and Mrs. Elizabeth Tyler brought to it their talents as publicity agents and fund raisers. The revived Klan was fueled partly by patriotism and partly by a romantic nostalgia for the old South, but, more importantly, it expressed the defensive reaction of white Protestants in small-town America who felt threatened by the Bolshevik revolution in Russia and by the large-scale immigration of the previous decades that had changed the ethnic character of American society.

"This second Klan peaked in the 1920s, when its membership exceeded 4,000,000 nationally, and profits rolled in from the sale of its memberships, regalia, costumes, publications, and rituals. A burning cross became the symbol of the new organization, and white-robed Klansmen participated in marches, parades, and nighttime cross burnings all over the country. To the old Klan's hostility toward blacks the new Klan—which was strong in the Midwest as well as in the South—added bias against Roman Catholics, Jews, foreigners, and organized labor. The Klan enjoyed a last spurt of growth in 1928, when Alfred E. Smith, a Catholic, received the Democratic presidential nomination.

"During the Great Depression of the 1930s the Klan's membership dropped drastically, and the last remnants of the organization temporarily disbanded in 1944. For the next 20 years the Klan was quiescent, but it had a resurgence in some Southern states during the 1960s as civil-rights workers attempted to force Southern communities' compliance with the Civil Rights Act of 1964. There were numerous instances of bombings, whippings, and shootings in Southern communities, carried out in secret but apparently the work of Klansmen. President Lyndon B. Johnson publicly denounced the organization in a nationwide television address announcing the arrest of four Klansmen in connection with the slaying of a civil-rights worker, a white woman, in Alabama.

"The Klan was unable to stem the growth of a new racial tolerance in the South in the years that followed. Though the organization continued some of its surreptitious activities into the late twentieth century, cases of Klan violence became more isolated, and its membership had declined to a few thousand. The Klan became a chronically fragmented mélange made up of several separate and competing groups, some of which occasionally entered into alliances with neo-Nazi and other right-wing extremist groups" (search.eb.com/blackhistory/micro/329/99.html).

Military Order Similar to an Executive Order of the President, this order focuses on military policy that the president, as commander-in-chief, establishes. For example, here is President Bush's Military Order titled: *"Detention, Treatment, and Trial of Certain Non-Citizens in the War Against Terrorism:*

"By the authority vested in me as President and as Commander in Chief of the Armed Forces of the United States by the Constitution and the laws of the United States of America, including the Authorization for Use of Military Force Joint Resolution (Public Law 107–40, 115 Stat. 224) and sections 821 and 836 of title 10, United States Code, it is hereby ordered as follows:

Section 1. Findings.

(a) International terrorists, including members of al Qaida, have carried out attacks on United States diplomatic and military personnel and facilities abroad and on citizens and property within the United States on a scale that has created a state of armed conflict that requires the use of the United States Armed Forces. (b) In light of grave acts of terrorism and threats of terrorism, including the terrorist attacks on September 11, 2001, on the headquarters of the United States Department of Defense in the national capital region, on the World Trade Center in New York, and on civilian aircraft such as in Pennsylvania, I proclaimed a national emergency on September 14, 2001 (Proc. 7463, Declaration of National Emergency by Reason of Certain Terrorist Attacks).

(c) Individuals acting alone and in concert involved in international terrorism possess both the capability and the intention to undertake further terrorist attacks against the United States that, if not detected and prevented, will cause mass deaths, mass injuries, and massive destruction of property, and may place at risk the continuity of the operations of the United States Government. (d) The ability of the United States to protect the United States and its citizens, and to help its allies and other cooperating nations protect their nations and their citizens, from such further terrorist attacks depends in significant part upon using the United States Armed Forces to identify terrorists and those who support them, to disrupt their activities, and to eliminate their ability to conduct or support such attacks. (e) To protect the United States and its citizens, and for the effective conduct of military operations and prevention of terrorist attacks, it is necessary for individuals subject to this order pursuant to section 2 hereof to be detained, and, when tried, to be tried for violations of the laws of war and other applicable laws by military tribunals.

(f) Given the danger to the safety of the United States and the nature of international terrorism, and to the extent provided by and under this order, I find consistent with section 836 of title 10, United States Code, that it is not practicable to apply in military commissions under this order the principles of law and the rules of evidence generally recognized in the trial of criminal cases in the United States district courts. (g) Having fully considered the magnitude of the potential deaths, injuries, and property destruction that would result from potential acts of terrorism against the United States, and the probability that such acts will occur, I have determined that an extraordinary emergency exists for national defense purposes, that this emergency constitutes an urgent and compelling government interest, and that issuance of this order is necessary to meet the emergency.

Sec. 2. Definition and Policy.

(a) The term "individual subject to this order" shall mean any individual who is not a United States citizen with respect to whom I determine from time to time in writing that: (1) there is reason to believe that such individual, at the relevant times,

(i) is or was a member of the organization known as al Qaida; (ii) has engaged in, aided or abetted, or conspired to commit, acts of international terrorism, or acts in preparation therefor, that have caused, threaten to cause, or have as their aim to cause, injury to or adverse effects on the United States, its citizens, national security, foreign policy, or economy; or (iii) has knowingly harbored one or more individuals described in subparagraphs (i) or (ii) of subsection 2(a)(1) of this order; and (2) it is in the interest of the United States that such individual be subject to this order. (b) It is the policy of the United States that the Secretary of Defense shall take all necessary measures to ensure that any individual subject to this order is detained in accordance with section 3, and, if the individual is to be tried, that such individual is tried only in accordance with section 4. (c) It is further the policy of the United States that any individual subject to this order who is not already under the control of the Secretary of Defense but who is under the control of any other officer or agent of the United States or any State shall, upon delivery of a copy of such written determination to such officer or agent, forthwith be placed under the control of the Secretary of Defense.

Sec. 3. Detention Authority of the Secretary of Defense. Any individual subject to this order shall be—(a) detained at an appropriate location designated by the Secretary of Defense outside or within the United States; (b) treated humanely, without any adverse distinction based on race, color, religion, gender, birth, wealth, or any similar criteria; (c) afforded adequate food, drinking water, shelter, clothing, and medical treatment; (d) allowed the free exercise of religion consistent with the requirements of such detention; and (e) detained in accordance with such other conditions as the Secretary of Defense may prescribe.

Sec. 4. Authority of the Secretary of Defense Regarding Trials of Individuals Subject to this Order. (a) Any individual subject to this order shall, when tried, be tried by military commission for any and all offenses triable by military commission that such individual is alleged to have committed, and may be punished in accordance with the penalties provided under applicable law, including life imprisonment or death. (b) As a military function and in light of the findings in section 1, including subsection (f) thereof, the Secretary of Defense shall issue such orders and regulations, including orders for the appointment of one or more military commissions, as may be necessary to carry out subsection (a) of this section. (c) Orders and regulations issued under subsection (b) of this section shall include, but not be limited to, rules for the conduct of the proceedings of military commissions, including pretrial, trial, and post-trial procedures, modes of proof, issuance of process, and qualifications of attorneys, which shall at a minimum provide for—

(1) military commissions to sit at any time and any place, consistent with such guidance regarding time and place as the Secretary of Defense may provide; (2) a full and fair trial, with the military commission sitting as the triers of both fact and law; (3) admission of such evidence as would, in the opinion of the presiding officer of the military commission (or instead, if any other member of the commission so requests at the time the presiding officer renders that opinion, the opinion of the commission rendered at that time by a majority of the commission), have probative value to a reasonable person; (4) in a manner consistent with the protection of information classified or classifiable under Executive Order 12958 of April 17, 1995, as amended, or any successor Executive Order, protected by statute or rule from unauthorized disclosure, or otherwise protected by law, (A) the handling of, admission into evidence of, and access to materials and information, and (B) the conduct, closure of, and access to proceedings; (5) conduct of the prosecution by one or more attorneys designated by the Secretary of Defense and conduct of the defense by attorneys for the individual subject to this order; (6) conviction only upon the concurrence of two-thirds of the members of the commission present at the time of the vote, a majority being present; (7) sentencing only upon the concurrence of two-thirds of the members of the commission present at the time of the vote, a majority being present; and (8) submission of the record of the trial, including any conviction or sentence, for review and final decision by me or by the Secretary of Defense if so designated by me for that purpose.

Sec. 5. Obligation of Other Agencies to Assist the Secretary of Defense.

Departments, agencies, entities, and officers of the United States shall, to the maximum extent permitted by law, provide to the Secretary of Defense such assistance as he may request to implement this order.

Sec. 6. Additional Authorities of the Secretary of Defense.

(a) As a military function and in light of the findings in section 1, the Secretary of Defense shall issue such orders and regulations as may be necessary to carry out any of the provisions of this order. (b) The Secretary of Defense may perform any of his functions or duties, and may exercise any of the powers provided to him under this order (other than under section 4(c)(8) hereof) in accordance with section 113(d) of title 10, United States Code.

Sec. 7. Relationship to Other Law and Forums.

(a) Nothing in this order shall be construed to—(1) authorize the disclosure of state secrets to any person not otherwise authorized to have access to them;

(2) limit the authority of the President as Commander in Chief of the Armed Forces or the power of the President to grant reprieves and pardons; or (3) limit the lawful authority of the Secretary of Defense, any military commander, or any other officer or agent of the United States or of any State to detain or try any person who is not an individual subject to this order. (b) With respect to any individual subject to this order—(1) military tribunals shall have exclusive jurisdiction with respect to offenses by the individual; and (2) the individual shall not be privileged to seek any remedy or maintain any proceeding, directly or indirectly, or to have any such remedy or proceeding sought on the individual's behalf, in (i) any court of the United States, or any State thereof, (ii) any court of any foreign nation, or (iii) any international tribunal. (c) This order is not intended to and does not create any right, benefit, or privilege, substantive or procedural, enforceable at law or equity by any party, against the United States, its departments, agencies, or other entities, its officers or employees, or any other person. (d) For purposes of this order, the term "State" includes any State, district, territory, or possession of the United States.

(e) I reserve the authority to direct the Secretary of Defense, at any time hereafter, to transfer to a governmental authority control of any individual subject to this order. Nothing in this order shall be construed to limit the authority of any such governmental authority to prosecute any individual for whom control is transferred.

Sec. 8. Publication.

This order shall be published in the Federal Register.

GEORGE W. BUSH

THE WHITE HOUSE,

November 13, 2001.

Operation Desert Storm "Soldiers, sailors, airmen and Marines of the United States Central Command, this morning at 0300, we launched Operation DESERT STORM, an offensive campaign that will enforce the United Nation's resolutions that Iraq must cease its rape and pillage of its weaker neighbor and withdraw its forces from Kuwait. My confidence in you is total. Our cause is just! Now you must be the thunder and lightning of Desert Storm. May God be with you, your loved ones at home, and our Country."—General H. Norman Schwarzkopf, USA Commander-in-Chief U.S. Central Command, in a message to the command, 16 January 1991

On 17 January, 1991, DESERT STORM began with a coordinated attack, which included Tomahawk land attack missiles (TLAMs) launched from cruisers, destroyers and battleships in the Persian Gulf and Red Sea. The TLAM launches opened a carefully crafted joint strategic air campaign. The initial barrage of over 100 TLAMs took out heavily defended targets in the vicinity of Baghdad and made a critical contribution to eliminating Iraqi air defenses and command and control capabilities. In all, 288 TLAMs were launched as part of the integrated air campaign. Launches were conducted from both the Red Sea and the Persian Gulf from nine cruisers, five destroyers, two battleships and two nuclear powered attack submarines. The TLAM and other precision-guided and high-tech munitions used by the Army, Navy, Marine Corps and Air Force clearly produced a revolution in the art of warfare. The joint air campaign was successful beyond the most optimistic expectations. As full partners in that campaign, Navy and Marine Corps aviators flew from carriers and amphibious ships in the Red Sea and Persian Gulf, and from bases ashore, from the day hostilities began until the cease-fire was ordered. Navy aircraft struck targets up to 700 miles distant, with Red Sea sorties averaging 3.7 hours in length, and Persian Gulf sorties averaging 2.5 hours. As was also the case for their ground-based Air Force counterparts, many flights lasted as long as five hours, and virtually every flight required airborne refueling at both ends of the journey.

Pen Register A device that monitors numbers dialed *from* a telephone line—without obtaining a warrant based on probable cause. A "reasonable suspicion" is sufficient for pen register surveillance to be initiated. Most pen registers include a regular wiretapping feature to supplement the number recording feature.

Presidential Directives From the founding of this nation, Presidents have developed and used various types of presidential or executive "directives." The best known of these are Executive Orders and Presidential Proclamations, but many other documents have a similar function and effect. The presidential directive is a written set of instructions issued by the National Security Council under the name of the president. Most are classified as "Secret" or "Top-Secret." They have been given names by different presidential administrations: National Security Action Memoranda (NSAM's)—Kennedy and Johnson; National Security Decision Memoranda (NSDM's)-Nixon and Ford; Presidential Directives (PD)- Carter; National Security Decision Directives (NSDD's)-Reagan; National Security Directives (NSD's)-Bush; Presidential Decision Directives (PDD's)-Clinton; National Security Presidential Directives (NSPD's)- George W. Bush.

Preventive Justice Because preventing the next attack is the nation's primary concern, criminal law cannot be the sole legal vehicle for dealing with those terrorists who have declared *Jihad* against the United States. Their threats must be viewed through a different and new legal paradigm. This new process is a preventative one for dealing with suspected terrorists who are detained by the government and with the vital need to collect up-to-date information about terrorist plans. Preventive justice was used during World War II when the courts upheld trial and execution by military commission, detaining until the end of the war an American citizen captured fighting for the enemy, and the preventive detention of over 120,000 persons and citizens of Japanese ancestry until the end of the war. Given the unique nature of America's war on terrorism, foiling the enemy's plans is the central factor whenever the government has evidence of a person's suspected involvement in terror and is deciding issues such as whether to charge a detainee criminally and whether to keep secret information about detainees.

Search Warrant   A written order, issued and signed by a neutral magistrate in the name of the people, directing a law enforcement officer to search for personal property to discover stolen goods, contraband, or some evidence of guilt to be used in the prosecution of a criminal action. The Fourth Amendment commands that the law enforcement officer show "probable cause" for the issuance of the search warrant.

Sneak-and-Peek Search Warrant   This warrant (also called a covert entry or a surreptitious entry search warrant) authorizes law enforcement officers executing it to effect physical entry into private premises without the occupant's permission or knowledge and to clandestinely search the premises; usually, such entry requires a stealth-like breaking and entering. Section 213 of the USA Patriot ACT of 2001 is the first express statutory authorization for the issuance of sneak and peek search warrants in American history. In part, it states: Any notice required "may be delayed if the court finds 'reasonable cause' to believe that providing immediate notification of the execution of the warrant may have an adverse result." Notification may be delayed indefinitely by the Court "for good cause shown." Section 213 is not restricted to terrorists or suspected terrorists; it may be used in connection with any federal crimes, including misdemeanors. The section is not covered by a "sunset" provision.

Sunset Provisions   "Sunlight" and "Transparency" are two hallmarks of lawmaking in a democracy. "Sunset" is another democratic marker; it means that it is time for the sun to set on the law. When a statute contains such a provision, it means that, after a certain number of years (2, 4, 5, and 10 years are commonly used), the statute or a specific segment of the statute "expires" unless the Congress chooses to renew the law.

Terrorism   There are over 100 definitions of terrorism. There are, however, common and recurring themes in all of them: violence/force (84 percent); political (65 percent); fear/terror (51 percent); threats (47 percent); innocent victims (38 percent); intentional, systematic action (32 percent); and methods of combat, strategy, and tactics (31%). The USA Patriot Act defines terrorism as "acts dangerous to human life that are a violation of the criminal laws" and are intended "to influence the policy of a government."

"Trap-and-Trace" Device This device, as noted in Section 216 of the USA Patriot ACT of 2001, is "a device or process which captures the incoming electronic or other dialing, routing, addressing, and signaling information reasonably likely to identify the source of a wire or electronic communication; provided, however, that such information shall not include the contents of any communication.

Index

About the Author

Howard Ball grew up in New York City, attending Taft High School and Hunter Colege–CUNY. He went to Rutgers University, where he received his M.A. and Ph.D. degrees in Political Science in 1970. He has taught at Hofstra University, Mississippi State University, the University of Utah, and the University of Vermont. He was a sergeant in the U.S. Air Force, serving in Germany when the Berlin Wall went up in 1961.

Ball's areas of teaching and research competence are judicial politics, the U.S. Supreme Court, civil rights, civil liberties, international law, and war crimes and justice. Ball has authored more than three dozen articles in refereed political science, public administration, and law journals and more than two dozen books, including a biography of Thurgood Marshall (A Defiant Life), and biographies of Hugo Black and William O. Douglas. He has written texts for students of the U.S. Supreme Court as well as books touching upon the international laws of war and the new (2002) international criminal court. His most recent publications are *War Crimes and Justice* (ABC CLIO, 2002); *The Supreme Court in the Intimate Lives of Americans* (NYU Press, 2d ed., 2004), and *Murder in Mississippi* (University Press of Kansas, 2004). He is presently working on a book for ABC-CLIO on homeland security as well as another book for NYU Press that looks at one of the gruesome consequences of genocide and war crimes: finding and identifying the bodies of the disappeared.

Ball lives in Richmond, Vermont, with his wife of forty-one years, Carol. They are surrounded by their three Chessies—Maggie, Charlie, and Sam—and their three horses—Stormin' Norman, Smokey, and Dirty Harry. They have three grown daughters, Sue the actor, Melissa the teacher, and Sheryl the occupational therapist. They are blessed with two grandchildren, Lila and Nate, and another on the way. The daughters visit, two with their husbands and children, occasionally.